LIBRARY OF HEBREW BIBLE/
OLD TESTAMENT STUDIES

438

Formerly Journal for the Study of the Old Testament Supplement Series

WRITING THE HISTORY OF ISRAEL

Diane Banks

t&t clark

NEW YORK • LONDON

T & T Clark International, 80 Maiden Lane, New York, NY 10038

T & T Clark International, The Tower Building, 11 York Road, London SE1 7NX

T & T Clark International is a Continuum imprint.

Library of Congress Cataloging-in-Publication Data
Banks, Diane, 1942-
    Writing the history of Israel / Diane Banks.
        p. cm. -- (Library of Hebrew Bible/Old Testament studies ; 438)
    Includes bibliographical references (p.   ) and index.
    ISBN 0-567-02662-0 (hardcover)
    1. Jews--History--To 70 A.D.--Historiography. 2. Old Testament scholars--History.
    3. Bible. O.T.--Historiography. 4. Palestine--History--To 70 A.D.--
    Historiography. I. Title. II. Series.
     DS115.5.B33 2006
     221.9'50072022--dc22
                                    2006007721

Printed in the United States of America

06 07 08 09 10   10 9 8 7 6 5 4 3 2 1

Gaia, Amanda, Carrie, Hosanna, and Clare

CONTENTS

Acknowledgments   xiii

Chapter 1
INTRODUCTION   1
  1. The Argument   1
  2. The Scope of the Study   3
  3. Philosophical Issues and Assumptions
    in the Practice of History   8
    a. The Characteristics of Historical Knowledge 8
      (1) The Choice of Subject   8
      (2) The Historian's Location   9
      (3) Historical Variety   10
      (4) Moral Relativism   10
      (5) The Usefulness of History   11
      (6) Scientific History   12
    b. The Meaning of History   13
  4. Writer's Assumptions   15

Chapter 2
HISTORIOGRAPHY IN NINETEENTH-CENTURY GERMANY   16
  1. Historicism   17
  2. The Character of the Historical Tradition   19
    a. Historicism's Foundation in Vico   21
    b. Herder's Contribution   25
    c. The Influence of Humboldt   27
    d. Ranke's Historical Principles   31
      (1) History Distinguished from Philosophy
        and Natural Science   34
      (2) The Idealistic Theory of the State 34
      (3) The Practice of Writing History   37
  3. The Generation of Liberal Historians   38
  4. Historiography Distinct from Philosophy and Natural Science 40
    a. The Positivist Challenge   41
    b. Understanding and Explanation   42
    c. The Ethical Role of the Historian   42
  5. The Ethical Nature of the State   44

6. The Last of the Literary Historians   45
7. The Move to Specialization   46
8. Conclusion   47

Chapter 3
JULIUS WELLHAUSEN AND THE *PROLEGOMENA TO THE HISTORY OF ISRAEL*   50
1. Wellhausen the Man   52
2. Wellhausen the Historian   52
3. Influences and Assumptions   54
    a. Empiricism and Idealism   55
    b. Historicism   56
    c. Romanticism, Culture, and Nation   57
    d. The "Total View"   58
4. Persistent Criticisms   59
    a. Wellhausen and Hegel   59
    b. Wellhausen and Darwin   61
    c. Anti-Semitism   63
        (1) Judgment of the Past   63
        (2) Wellhausen's Anti-Institutional Bias   64
5. Wellhausen's Liberalism   65
6. The Idea of the Nation   66
7. The Search for Historical Truth   67
8. Method   68
    a. Sources   69
    b. Style and Language   70
    c. Tradition and Culture   71
9. Conclusion   74

Chapter 4
HISTORIOGRAPHY IN GERMANY AND THE UNITED STATES
TO WORLD WAR II   76
1. Part One: Germany   76
2. Karl Lamprecht and the Challenge to Tradition   78
3. History as a Scientific Discipline   80
    a. Empirical Reality and Subjective Understanding   81
4. The Conflict of Values   82
    a. Rational Human Behavior   82
    b. Science and Culture   83
    c. The Crisis of Historicism   84
5. Troeltsch and Religious Relativism   85
    a. The History of Religions   85
    b. The Effects of World War I   86
6. The Failed Political System and the Diversity of Interests   87
    a. The Conflict with the German Spirit   88
7. The Challenges to Classical Historicism   89

8. Part Two: The United States   91
9. The German University as Model   91
    a. The Problem of Scientific Objectivity   92
    b. Ranke in the United States   94
    c. Science, Facts, and Impartial Observation   95
10. Professionalization of the Discipline   96
    a. Authority and High Culture   97
    b. A New Audience   99
    c. Professional Standards and the Pressure for Orthodoxy   100
    d. National Unity   101
11. The Advent of Social History   102
    a. Material Interests   103
12. The New History, Reform, and Progress   104
    a. Conflict and Discontinuity   105
    b. The Problem of Presentism   106
    c. Relativism and Progress   107
13. The Challenges of World War I   107
    a. Objectivity, Knowledge, and Relativism   109
    b. Everyman as Historian   110
14. The Passing of "Scientific" History   111
15. The Noble Dream   112
16. Conservatives and Relativists   114
17. Conclusion   115

Chapter 5

BIBLICAL HISTORY AT MID-CENTURY:
JOHN BRIGHT AND MARTIN NOTH

JOHN BRIGHT AND MARTIN NOTH   118
1. Three Approaches to the Bible as a Historical Source   120
2. Part One: Martin Noth   122
3. Assumptions and Approach   124
    a. The Limitations of Sources   124
    b. The Subject of History   125
    c. Israel's Identity Found in History   126
    d. The Traditions   127
    e. The Value of Artifacts   128
    f. Standards for Using the Biblical Traditions   129
    g. The Period for Study   130
4. The Traditio-Historical Approach   131
    a. Cultic Themes Shaping the Form of the Pentateuch   132
    b. The Contributions of Form Criticism   133
    c. Scholarly Influences on Noth   134
5. The Historical Compositions   135
6. Traditio-Historical Criticism of the Pentateuch   137
    a. Tales of the Pentateuch   138
7. Reliability   140

8.	Conclusion	141
9.	Part Two: John Bright	143
10.	Assumptions	144
	a. Israel Unique in History	145
11.	Sources	145
	a. Israel's Traditions	145
	b. Regional Culture	146
	c. Scope of Study	146
	d. The Use of Archaeology	148
	e. Reaction to Liberal Theology	148
12.	Method	149
13.	Theology Based in History	150
	a. Material Culture	151
	b. Evaluation of the Text	151
	c. Use of Evidence	152
14.	Criticism of Alt and Noth	153
15.	Conclusion	155

Chapter 6
HISTORIOGRAPHY AND CONTROVERSY IN THE RECENT PAST | 158

1.	The New Scientific History	161
	a. Marxist History	162
	b. The *Annales*	162
	c. American Historians at the Close of World War II	164
	d. History as Social Science	166
	e. American Cliometricians	167
2.	Critical History in Germany	168
3.	Decline of Social Science	169
4.	Universalism or Particularism	171
5.	Professionalism and Public History	172
6.	The Postmodern Challenge	174
7.	The Linguistic Turn: The Historian as Rhetorician	175
8.	The Modes of Historiography	177
9.	Relativism and Objectivity Again	179
10.	The Task of the Historian	180
11.	Conclusion	181

Chapter 7
WRITING ISRAEL'S HISTORY TODAY | 184

1.	The Argument	187
2.	Historiography of Ancient Israel	188
3.	The Challenge to Genesis	189
	a. Historicity of the Patriarchal Narratives	189
	b. The Abraham Tradition	193
	c. The Use of Traditions	195
	d. The Origins of Ancient Israel	196

4.	New Methodology	198
5.	The New Archaeology	199
	a. The Present Situation	201
	b. The Search for Ancient Israel	202
6.	"Maximalism" and "Minimalism"	205
	a. The Debate	206
	b. The Development of the Debate	208
	c. Escalation of the Debate: The Inscription from Tel Dan	209
	d. Charges of Ideology	211
	e. "Maximalists" and "Minimalists" Face to Face	213
	f. "Minimalism," Ideology, and Anti-Semitism	215
7.	Academic Historiography	218
	a. Scientific History	218
	b. Dissent from the Scientific Model	220
8.	Biblical History and History	222
9.	Conclusion	224

Chapter 8
CONCLUSION 225
1.	Wellhausen	227
2.	Mid-Century	228
3.	History in the Present	230
4.	The History of Ancient Israel	231
5.	The Scope of This Study and Future Research	232

Bibliography 235
Index of Authors 246

ACKNOWLEDGMENTS

The support of Vanderbilt University has been significant for the writing of this book. I am grateful for the opportunities to teach, for other employment in the university, and for a grant that allowed me to travel to Göttingen in 2000. Eileen Crawford, Ann Ercelawn, and Amy Limpitlaw in the Divinity Library have kindly assisted me in locating obscure journals and helped me in numerous other ways. To them I am forever indebted. Professor Douglas Knight, Chair of the Graduate Department of Religion, has been a friend and mentor to me. His wisdom and insight aided me in shaping the concept of this book. Professor Rudolf Smend kindly received me in Göttingen and shared his knowledge of Julius Wellhausen. I thank Professor Kassian Kovalcheck who read successive drafts and offered his helpful comments. I thank Gaia Banks and Nikolaij Schibura for help with German texts, Amanda Banks for research assistance, and Duncan Burns for copyediting the final draft. I am grateful to my parents Marjorie and Douglas Nunn for their abiding confidence and thankful beyond recounting for the support, encouragement, and stimulation of my excellent daughters and their families.

Chapter 1

INTRODUCTION

It is a fact worthy of remark that no biblical historian is included in the standard dictionaries of historians. A search of the indices will show Herbert Butterfield, famous for his *Whig Interpretation of History*, has written on the subject of biblical history.[1] No one trained in departments of religion or in Semitic languages, however, has an entry. Specifically, historians of ancient Israel, well known to generations of students—such as Kittel, Eissfeldt, Oesterley, Lods, and Olmstead—find no place in these dictionaries. Some few archaeologists of the ancient world—such as Flinders Petrie and Leonard Woolley—are mentioned, though scholars of the stature of William Foxwell Albright, Kathleen Kenyon, and Yigal Yadin, or indeed any scholars working in the area of ancient Israel, are excluded. The disciplinary boundaries appear to be firmly set. Yet there are connections to be discovered. This study will examine these boundaries as well as the links that do exist between history writing in biblical studies and the practice of history in professional departments of history within the university.

1. *The Argument*

The rhetorical demands of the Reformation promoted the study of history as a means to discover evidence for those who wished to legitimate various social or religious claims, or to buttress arguments for a particular telos. With professionalization of the discipline of history in the nineteenth century, a new standard for objectivity was advanced, which disallowed polemical or apologetic history. Confidence in the notion of objectivity was quickly undermined, however, by the understanding that every writer has individual interests and biases and, perhaps even more

1. Herbert Butterfield, *The Origins of History* (ed. Adam Watson; New York: Basic Books, 1981). The six chapters in Section 3 are devoted to the history of Israel.

important, that the past that can be recovered is always only fragmentary. Coming to grips with the epistemological limits of our understanding of the past makes it impossible to ignore our often unstated purposes in writing history and the calculated uses we make of the past. What influence the present has on the historian, what authority the historian has to make moral judgments on the past, and, possibly the most disputed question, under what category historical investigation should be located, continue to be pressing issues. Can history be a scientific endeavor with the critical procedures and standards of objectivity customary to its search for truth? Or should history be conceived as a literary genre, striving to engage the reader in an empathic comprehension of the past? These notions may be traced in the work of historians and philosophers who have reflected on these matters throughout the last century and a half. Anyone who undertakes to write the history of Israel is affected by these issues at some level, conscious or unconscious, but biblical scholars have seldom commented publicly on their understanding of the problems of historical knowledge, theories of history, or their own assumptions or worldviews derived from their social perspective, religious beliefs, class, race, sex, national allegiance, ethnic or social affiliations, or economic position. Despite these omissions, biblical scholarship is closely linked to currents in historiography throughout the entire period since the professionalization of the discipline of history in the nineteenth century.

In this study, I shall argue that, while the influence of professional history on the work of history writing in biblical studies is clearly apparent in each of the historical periods chosen as examples, there are strong countervailing influences related to audience. The traits of the historiographical traditions in Germany and the United States in the late nineteenth century, the mid-twentieth century, and the last quarter century, and their mark on the practice of history in biblical studies, will be the subject of investigation, while the constraints on historians exerted by their audiences will also require analysis. The interplay of these two powerful influences will be a continuing theme in the following chapters. The presupposition that the Bible is a book of history or, at the very least, contains the historical record of the people of Israel to a greater or lesser degree, conditions the outcome of historical research in biblical studies. Julius Wellhausen notes this sharply: "the arguments which were brought into play as a rule derived all their force from a moral conviction..."[2] In the nineteenth century and again in the present, alternative

---

2. Julius Wellhausen, *Prolegomena to the History of Israel* (Atlanta: Scholars Press, 1994); repr. of *Prolegomena to the History of Israel* (trans. J. Sutherland Black and Allan Enzies, with preface by W. Robertson Smith and foreword by

views of the character of the Bible have been proposed.[3] The prospects of
a history of Israel, written as histories of other entities are written, in this
case independent of the authority of the Bible, will be another theme of
this study. I shall argue that Julius Wellhausen's history of Israel set in
motion the general tendency toward ever greater congruence between
historiography in biblical studies and in academic departments of history;
that the initial tension caused by Wellhausen's work produced a reaction
which effectively stalled the movement toward accommodation between
secular, academic history and biblical studies; and that a new generation
of scholars applying the methods used by secular historians has revived
and continued the tendency to promote the practice of secular, academic
historiography in biblical studies.

2. *The Scope of the Study*

The complete history of the historiography of the Hebrew Bible cannot
be undertaken here; neither can the history of the professionalization of
the field of history. Instead, I have chosen three representative periods
and will inquire thoroughly into the academic context of biblical studies
in these periods. James Barr notes that biblical scholarship may be
understood and evaluated either philosophically, pragmatically, or bio-
graphically, "through an investigation of what particular biblical critics
actually think or thought, what their loyalties and values are or were."[4]

Julius Wellhausen, Martin Noth, John Bright, and Thomas Thompson
will be principal the subjects of this study. The first step is a detailed
overview of historical thought in the mid- to late nineteenth century.
Wellhausen's scholarship will be examined in relation to this body of
tradition in terms of his philosophy, his presuppositions, and his historical theory and method. The choice of Wellhausen will allow me to look
into the controversies surrounding the historico-critical approach to biblical study in the mid- to late nineteenth century. The work for which
Wellhausen is justly remembered is his synthesis of the so-called documentary hypothesis. His *Prolegomena to the History of Israel* provides

Douglas A. Knight; Edinburgh: A. & C. Black, 1885); trans. of *Prolegomena zur
Geschichte Israels* (2d ed.; Berlin: G. Reimer, 1883), 11–12.

3. Rudolf Smend reports that de W. M. L. de Wette found the Old Testament
"inadequate as an historical source" and believes it "belongs in the category of
myth" ("Tradition and History: A Complex Relation," in *Tradition and Theology
in the Old Testament* [ed. Douglas A. Knight; Philadelphia: Fortress, 1977], 49–68
[54]).

4. James Barr, "Allegory and Historicism," *JSOT* 69 (1996): 105–20 (108–9).

compelling arguments for the characteristics and chronology of the four major source documents of the Pentateuch. The development of the modern German university and the place of historical study within that system are important for the work of Wellhausen. The themes of Romanticism and the enthusiasm for scientific investigation are also aspects of scholarly inquiry which must be accounted for in relation to his work.

The twentieth century brought remarkable changes to the practice of history writing. Alongside these innovations, however, the influence of Leopold von Ranke remained strong. His famous dictum that the historian should write history *wie es eigentlich gewesen ist* ("as it actually happened") is unquestionably the most often-quoted phrase in the field of historiography to this day. On the other hand, the conclusions of Wilhelm Dilthey had enormous impact in Germany, and only much later did he become widely read in the United States. Here, economic and social histories began to displace those written from the standpoint of singular men, particularly those involved in political and military history. In addition to the shifts in emphasis that were occurring in the field of history, important new information became available to biblical historians through the discovery and interpretation of a series of documents and correspondence from sites in the ancient world. Against this background I will compare the work of Martin Noth and John Bright.

Noth, beginning from the position established by Albrecht Alt in regard to the settlement of Israelite tribes, examined the books of the Pentateuch and proposed a novel means by which to account for the aggregation of ancient traditions in Israel, for which he is famous. He hypothesized the existence of a religious confederation on the analogy of the Greek amphictyonies where the traditions of the member tribes were recounted and ultimately became the collective memory of the nation. Noth's study of the Pentateuch led him to postulate the existence of an independent work of history beginning in the book of Deuteronomy and extending through Judges, 1–2 Samuel and 1–2 Kings. His work on this collection of texts is a source for some of his notions on what constitutes historiography.

Bright's *History of Israel* has been a standard work for many years, passing through three editions. He stayed close to the biblical text as he understood it and turned to archaeology for support of the events and locations mentioned by the biblical writers. He used an interesting phrase to describe his approach to evaluating the text. He claimed to seek a *balance of probability*. By this Bright presumably meant that, in instances where the credibility of the biblical account cannot be established, one will assume the authority of the text. In the absence of countervailing evidence, the biblical text should be accepted as sufficient witness to the events of the past. This principle must be compared to Noth's imaginative speculation on the basis of clues which he derives from the text, and both these procedures in turn related to the precepts of standard historical method. These two scholars also offer an opportunity to compare scholarship in Germany and America in terms of presuppositions, procedures, and values during the years preceding, during, and immediately after World War II.

Since the 1960s, while the broader field of history has struggled with difficult philosophical questions concerning truth and objectivity, language and meaning, readers and texts, narrative and history, there has been little impetus in biblical studies to make direct forays into the theoretical battles over the possibilities of history writing. The concrete issues of the reliability of ancient texts for reconstructing history and their relationship to artifacts recovered by archaeology have required sustained attention. Within the last several years, however, biblical scholars have begun to take note of concepts current in the discipline of history.

Hans Barstad opens a recent article, which seeks to understand "what it is that is going on in biblical studies,"[5] with a critique of the scientific model of history writing. In pointing out that the historicist methods and views of text and truth prevailing in biblical studies are in conflict with the methods and perspectives now dominant in the larger field of history, Barstad argues that many biblical scholars appear to be unaware of any discussion "about the nature of history and the possibilities of history writing in general." Barstad uses this critique to move to his thesis that narrative history is the way out of the impasse brought about by the "maximalist–minimalist" conflict. The 1996 study by Keith Whitelam, *The Invention of Ancient Israel: The Silencing of Palestinian History*,[6] examines several reconstructions of "Israel's" history through the lens of theory. He employs Edward Said's well-known concept of Orientalism to argue that the national destiny of biblical Israel has been clearly drawn in terms of Western imperial consciousness over against the image of Canaan/Palestine as debased and ripe for dispossession.

Jack Sasson, in his suggestive article which appeared in 1981, argues that cultural themes constrain the interpretation of history.[7] Sasson

---

5. Hans Barstad, "History and the Hebrew Bible," in *Can a History of Israel be Written?* (ed. Lester Grabbe; Sheffield: JSOT Press, 1997), 37–64 (39).

6. Keith Whitelam, *The Invention of Ancient Israel: The Silencing of Palestinian History* (London: Routledge, 1995).

7. Jack Sasson, "On Choosing Models for Recreating Israelite Pre-Monarchic History," *JSOT* 21 (1981): 3–24.

demonstrates the presence of motifs of national identity, immigrant struggle, social conflict, and the promised land in twentieth-century constructions of Israel's history.

For the purposes of this study, Thomas Thompson will represent current scholarship in the history of Israel. Beginning with his *Historicity of the Patriarchal Narratives* published in 1974, Thompson established himself as a controversial figure in historical research. While he has not written a traditional history of Israel, treating even such a continuous period as the monarchy to the exile, Thompson has been deeply engaged in the issues surrounding history writing in biblical studies. In his *Early History*,[8] he discusses historiography, methodology, the Bible as a source for history, and contemporary scholarship. While other contemporary scholars might be studied profitably, Thompson, in addition to his command of issues pertaining to the practice of history, provides continuity in academic background with other figures under consideration here. His training includes work at both American and German institutions. While Thompson himself suggests that "the geographical center of our field also has shifted decisively...from Germany...to the periphery," to Sheffield, Geneva, and Copenhagen,[9] it seems unwise to introduce a third national tradition of history writing into this study. Thompson's penetrating analysis of the issues under debate for a quarter of a century, along with his association with German and American traditions in history writing, make him an attractive subject.

Centering this study on these four scholars offers the benefit of an intensive look into several perspectives on writing history. Others could have been chosen, but these scholars are universally acclaimed as important in the field. Their particular theories are disputed, often subject to modification, even outright rejection, but unquestionably their work has served as seminal scholarship, and these figures stand as representatives of their time. To offer a perspective on particular time periods is an especially useful aspect of each of these scholars' work and, coupled with the fact that German academic and cultural views may be compared with those of the United States, makes them appealing on a level beyond that of their particular views.

Limiting the study to four major writers of Israel's history, however, also has certain drawbacks. Many positions are excluded from study. Especially notable in this regard is the investigation into folk literature

---

8. Thomas L. Thompson, *Early History of the Israelite People: From the Written and Archaeological Sources* (Leiden: Brill, 1992).

9. Thomas L. Thompson, "Offing the Establishment," *Biblische Notizen* 79 (1995): 71–87 (74).

conducted early in the twentieth century by scholars such as Hermann Gunkel. The results of archaeological research are represented in the work of Noth, especially Bright, and certainly Thompson, though none is recognized as a practicing archaeologist. Thompson employs data from other areas of social scientific investigation, including demographics, information on climate and geography, analyses of pottery types and distribution, building design, and sociological research on pastoral societies and urban centers. Though some attention is given to the long-standing economic patterns of the region, true social history is not represented in the work of these scholars.

The continuous development of historical research in biblical studies is also outside the scope of this study. Biblical scholarship of the early twentieth century to that of Albrecht Alt, as well as work done between the 1960s and 1970s, present gaps. Both eras are remarkable for innovation in the broader field of historiography. The views which were advocated in these two periods in departments of history will, nevertheless, provide background for the biblical history writers. The times typified by the four scholars are important periods in biblical studies. Wellhausen's work is the culmination of decades of study on the Pentateuch and its possible sources or source documents. Bright and Noth worked in the difficult years surrounding World War II and its aftermath. This epoch produced solid advances in text criticism and synthesis of interdisciplinary work on the transmission of traditional material, and the establishment of pottery chronologies and relative dating of excavated strata. Thompson and those who presently undertake to write the history of Israel are working in a unique time in biblical studies. Israel is now more often seen as part of the history of a larger geographic area, and frequently the nation itself as subject of inquiry is questioned. Where these developments may lead historians of Israel remains to be seen.

The century and a quarter covered by the working life of these four historians of Israel has seen biblical studies first overcome objections to the critical scrutiny turned on the sacred text by scientific scholarship and more recently give voice to some uncertainty regarding the value of the accomplishments. A call is raised in some quarters to seek "meaning" in the texts, rather than history. Implicit in this view is a radical shift from the theology which taught that meaning was to be found *in* history; that we, no less than the Israelites, were to recognize God's activity in the concrete events of history. Though presently biblical studies appears to be appropriating many techniques of reading and text criticism initiated in departments of English or literature, this study will be concerned to establish the coincidences between the historiography in biblical studies and departments of history.

3. *Philosophical Issues and Assumptions in the Practice of History*

The practice of writing history is not obviously dependent on philosophy or theory. Historians can research and study the past and record their findings without directly confronting philosophical questions about the nature of history. They can go about their work never discussing theories of history. Yet assumptions about the process of history will be implicit in their writing, and to the degree that they fail to consider those assumptions and such questions as context and objectivity, critics will call them to their attention. Many centuries ago, Herodotus proclaimed that, unlike his predecessors, he would base his history on reliable sources. His remark was based on an awareness of the inadequacy of certain approaches to producing history. History writing is judged by its trustworthiness, its credible recounting of past events. Reflections on standards of conscientious reconstruction, on the possibility of constructing such standards, as well as on the meaning of history itself are the province of the philosophy of history. It is well to have in mind the issues which shape the historian's craft, and to this end, a brief outline of questions which condition the practice of history follows.

Reflections on history fall into two modes. In the first mode, reflection takes the form of metaphysical speculation which, in the words of W. H. Walsh, aims

> to attain an understanding of the course of history as a whole; to show that, despite the many apparent anomalies and inconsequences it presented, history could be regarded as forming a unity embodying an overall plan, a plan which, if once we grasped it, would both illuminate the detailed course of events and enable us to view the historical process as, in a special sense, satisfactory to reason.[10]

The second mode is analytical and deals with the characteristics of historical knowledge itself. Roughly grouped, questions about the characteristics of historical knowledge concern the definition of the subject of history, the context of the historian, the moral judgment of history, the usefulness of history, and the extent to which history can be seen as an empirical endeavor, like or unlike other fields of study.

a. *The Characteristics of Historical Knowledge*
(1) *The Choice of Subject.* The subject or unit of history to be investigated varies considerably according to the preference or interest of

_____

10. W. H. Walsh, *Philosophy of History: An Introduction* (Rev. ed.; New York: Harper & Row, 1967), 12.

individual historians. For Ranke, the appropriate unit of study was the state; for Fernand Braudel it was the development of forms of social life taking place over centuries. Biblical historians often began their histories with the creation or the migration of Abraham, or more recently with the settlement or the monarchy. The choice and delineation of topic exhibits both subjective elements and the influences of contemporary concerns. The effects of such choices are considered in the analytic reflection on historical knowledge. Arnold Toynbee argues that historical knowledge must include all possible influences on a given subject of study. Serious distortion occurs when a narrow topic is viewed in isolation.[11] Whether or not this goal may realistically be approached in practice is a problem for the philosopher of history.

The inevitable distortion brought about by the choice and limitation of subject is mirrored by the distortion inherent in the historian's own context. The time, the social location, as well as the prevailing cultural assumptions have a subtle and not-so-subtle impact on historians. We have become sensitive to the imprint of class, religion, political ideology, race, and sex on academic work, but there are other views which provide historians with frameworks for their historical reconstructions. A commitment to any form of determinism directs the historian to locate and record social, economic, legal, or physical forces at play in the concrete historical situation under review. This attention to external forces comes at the expense of a focus on personal agency and individual responsibility. Each of these positions has been ascendant in different periods.

(2) *The Historian's Location.* It was common in times past to take little note of a historian's religion, politics, or class. Unless the historian wrote with clear bias or was given to outright polemical composition, the assumption was that one could strive to recognize one's own interests and avoid any appearance of partiality. Some philosophers of history maintain that, as we have become more convinced that the factors which form a historian's view cannot be transcended, we must conclude that objectivity is an impossibility. Others "argue that past failure of historians to reach objective truth is no evidence that it will always elude them" and that it may be possible ultimately to "develop a common historical consciousness."[12]

---

11. Arnold J. Toynbee, "The Unit of Historical Study," in *The Philosophy of History in Our Time* (ed. Hans Meyerhoff; Garden City, N.Y.: Doubleday, 1959), 101–14.

12. Walsh, *Philosophy*, 23.

(3) *Historical Variety.* It is necessary here to say something about historicism. Historicism is a feature of the romantic reaction to the rationalism of the Enlightenment. Hans Meyerhoff describes historicism as the investigation of "human life in its totality and multiplicity."[13] The emphasis is on the "unsystematic variety" and the "process of continuous growth and transformation," and finally the inadequacy of philosophical concepts for rendering the human experience, the "concrete realities of history." Historicism has become linked in contemporary consciousness with the scientific approach associated with the school of Ranke and with certain misinterpretations of this approach. Indeed, Karl Popper's famous indictment of historicism attacks the notion that scientific method can be applied to the study of history. Popper's thesis holds that "belief in historical destiny is sheer superstition and that there can be no prediction of the course of human history by scientific or any other rational methods."[14] Popper's criticism does not apply to German historicism of the nineteenth century, which neither suggests that forecasts of the future may be attempted on the basis of history, nor understands "scientific" in the sense of the English Lockean tradition. The classic definition of historicism written by Friedrich Meinecke describes historicism as nothing less than a spiritual revolution, a rejection of philosophical systems or metaphysical approaches to history.[15] Historicism repudiates views of history dependent on the process of reason or providence, on phases of history moving toward some predictable goal, on all rational structures of history or laws of history. Determinism is not compatible with historicism. Johann Gottfried Herder's enthusiasm for the variety of human expression, the wealth of historical possibility, is in direct opposition to every attempt to force history into rational schemes. It is clear that historicism, as it developed in the nineteenth century, lays no claim to prediction and offers no sense of destiny. It is rather the emphasis on the unique and various that characterizes historicism and is celebrated by romanticism.

(4) *Moral Relativism.* One of the effects of historicism and its understanding of the particularity of historical forms is a new awareness of relativism. "All stand under the influence of time and space," Wilhelm Dilthey tells us. "Every world-view is conditioned historically and

13. Hans Meyerhoff, "Introduction," in Meyerhoff, ed., *The Philosophy of History in Our Time*, 1–25 (10).
14. Karl R. Popper, *The Poverty of Historicism* (New York: Harper & Row, 1964), v.
15. Friedrich Meinecke, *Historism: The Rise of a New Historical Outlook* (trans. J. E. Anderson; trans. rev. H. D. Schmidt; London: Routledge & Kegan Paul, 1972).

therefore limited and relative."[16] From this vantage, the actions of the past may be recorded and investigated in terms of causes and consequences, but moral judgment cannot be rendered. Not only are we in no position to apply the customs, beliefs, and legal sentiments of our own world to historical situations, but also we cannot fully understand the motives and intentions of actors in the past and so must not play the judge. This position is countered by some who argue that we must not let our historical consciousness lead us to excuse too much, that broad principles of honor, truthfulness, justice, and mercy are, after all, timeless.[17] They insist we claim some ground on which to condemn men like Hitler and Stalin, that we be able to distinguish between natural disasters and the rational evil of the Holocaust. At what point does disinterested scholarship become banal in its effort to achieve objectivity? What is the boundary between history and polemics? These questions, while yielding no final answer, lead us to the problem of the usefulness of history.

(5) *The Usefulness of History.* We are often exhorted to learn the lessons of history without any very clear guidelines for developing analogies between situations of past and present. To attempt to identify the pertinent elements of a situation in order to understand an event or an occurrence in the past, reminds us again that our best efforts will only produce the thinnest slice of a historical reality. We will inevitably disregard aspects of the particular moment in the past and the historical period we are investigating. This disregard is due both to our individual biases and to our ignorance. Moreover, significant elements of the past are overlooked because there is no material trace available. The historical record is subject to chance at every turn. What was considered worthwhile to save, what was stored and forgotten, what was destroyed by fire or flood, leaves a haphazard record for historians, who then choose only such items as fit their interest. The partial character of our understanding of any event or moment in the past is indisputable.

Similar problems occur for our present understanding. Most would agree that some time must elapse before a reasonable judgment can be made about an event or situation. Factors which first appeared important recede in favor of some little-noticed considerations. Elements are discovered which add clarity. A suggestion that we derive instruction for the present from our study of the past would require a one-to-one correspondence of all elements of the situations to be compared. Our

16. William Kluback, *Wilhelm Dilthey's Philosophy of History* (New York: Columbia University Press, 1956), 103–9.

17. Meyerhoff outlines this argument in his *Philosophy*, 225–28.

incomplete grasp of the past and insubstantial view of the present will not allow this neat congruence.

The value of history, nevertheless, must always lie in the interests of its present audience. In the often-quoted statement of J. Huizinga, "History is the intellectual form in which a civilization renders account to itself of its past,"[18] judgment is the province or privilege of the present. This view is amplified by John Dewey who points out that "historical inquiry is controlled by the dominant problems and conceptions of the culture of the period in which it was written."[19] If not to find lessons in the past for present behavior, then the usefulness of history for the present lies in "a desire to 'understand' the present, or some present, by ascertaining its antecedents."[20] Arthur Lovejoy points out that we will not derive insight into the problems of contemporary urban life by study of earlier societies nor will such topics as Aristotle's science be useful to us today, but that it is "of value to us to understand interests and valuations not our own."[21] The historian should seek to discover the variety of human responses to the exigencies of living, to become acquainted with the great repertoire of human actions. It is with this understanding of the past that we inform the future.

(6) *Scientific History.* Perhaps the question regarding historical knowledge most contested today is that of the scientific character of history writing and research. This question addresses the possibility of verifying evidence, of producing reliable reconstructions of the past, and discovering laws for human behavior. The issues previously discussed (the interests of the historian, the choice of subject, the assumptions, preferences, and concerns of the time, and the right to offer moral judgment) all compromise the objectivity of the historian. Some theorists go so far as to argue that all historical narratives are necessarily fictions, representing the interests, ideas, views, and perspectives of their authors. Without denying that events, situations, and individuals existed in the past, the idiosyncratic nature of history writing places any attempt at reconstructing the past within the realm of fictional literature. Other, less extreme,

18. Jan Huizinga, "A Definition of the Concept of History," in *Philosophy and History: Essays presented to Ernst Cassirer* (ed. R. Klibansky and H. J. Paton; New York: Harper Torchbooks, 1963), 1–10 (9).

19. John Dewey, *Logic: The Theory of Inquiry* (New York: Henry Holt, 1938), 236.

20. Arthur O. Lovejoy, "Present Standpoints and Past History," *Journal of Philosophy* 26 (1939): 477–89 (480).

21. Ibid., "Present," 483.

positions acknowledge the problematic nature of objectivity and join in the project to dethrone the scientific model of history. The difficulties inherent in gathering empirical data and in fixing that information in narrative have been noticed and debated since ancient times. It is probable that there is some misunderstanding at the root of the attack on scientific history writing. The current flurry of energy devoted to exposing the inadequacies and arrogance of science may, at least in part, be due to the conception in English-speaking countries of science as a well-defined procedure beginning with a hypothesis to be tested by observation. The evidence gathered in the process of observation becomes the basis for the conclusion and must be such that it can yield the same results again and again, regardless of the identity of the investigator. The notion of scientific investigation in Germany, on the other hand, can include disciplined research following an accepted method. For Ranke and his followers, "scientific" indicates careful research and the critical use of evidence. To choose the strict program of the natural sciences as a model for doing history supposes that the past can be mined for generalizations about human behavior. In the German tradition, instead, historians are most interested, most concerned to reconstruct the unique, particular, concrete, individual events of the past. Scientific study also pays close attention to cause and effect, but in events and episodes of the past, cause and effect are matters of interpretation. Historians are not dealing with forces that can be isolated and expected to produce an identical outcome time after time. History thus cannot be said to be scientific in the sense of the natural sciences, but can it be considered scientific if it employs objective methodology, if it simply reports the "facts"? Presently there can be no agreement on the definition of facts. Every presentation of history is interrogated to discover whose history is being told, whose interests are served by the particular interpretation. Joyce Hunt, Lynn Appleby, and Margaret Jacobs claim, "Since no one can be certain that his or her explanations are definitively right, everyone must listen to other voices. All histories are provisional; none will have the last word."[22] The scientific character of history is severely undermined by the inability to establish universally agreed facts.

b. *The Meaning of History*

Here we leave the analytical arguments pertaining to the nature of historical knowledge and the possibility of discovering and reconstructing the past. We turn to metaphysical or speculative inquiry into the meaning

---

22. Joyce Appleby, Lynn Hunt, and Margaret Jacobs, *Telling the Truth About History* (New York: Norton, 1994), 11.

of history. If not unique, certainly important in the tradition of history writing pertinent to this study is the biblical view of the religious significance of history. For Israel, the events of history offered evidence of God at work in the world. In *The City of God*, Augustine articulated a view of history as theodicy, that God's providential design will ultimately redeem the events of the world. This model, whose meaning and conclusion lay beyond history, prevailed until the modern period, when rational concepts for the movement of history replaced the religious. Secular, temporal forces were called upon to explain historical events. The idea of progress, the notion that every age builds on the experience of the past, moving history along a trajectory of advancement, became a prominent tool for the interpretation of history. This notion, however, implied a historical inevitability not demonstrable in the study of the past. In one modification responding to the question of inevitability, evolution replaced the idea of progress. Here, events evolved from their historical antecedents, but might represent decline as well as gain.

The search for meaning in history supposes that some law, divine or rational, is at work in the succession of human events. These "laws" might be ascribed to Divine Providence or, as Hans Meyerhoff observes,

> according to the secular philosophies of history, they might be the laws of dialectics; or they might reflect the sad spectacle of the eternal return of the same, the inevitable succession of rise and fall...or they might be more gentle and vague as in the application of a progressive, evolutionary law to history.

But whether imposed or immanent, both views assumed that some kind of metaphysical determinism provided a clue to the meaning of history.[23]

We have mentioned historicism previously in terms of the heightened awareness of the multiplicity of human action and experience and the resulting appreciation of relativism in regard to the evaluation of the past. The emphasis on the particularity and variety of human expression in institutions, customs, goals, and production led away from the notion of systematic or philosophical organization in the conception of history. Furthermore, the demands that the historian put aside bias and personal preference, transcend the interests of moment, and simply record the facts of history, produced a dilemma for historians keenly aware that their own peculiar context made true objectivity impossible. Confronted with the clear limitations on the possibilities for reconstructing history, the focus of inquiry about history writing turned, not surprisingly, to the problems of methodology. For much of the twentieth century, questions

---

23. Meyerhoff, *Philosophy*, 7.

about how to write history, the appropriate subject and approach, replaced in importance questions about the nature of history and status of historical knowledge.

4. *Writer's Assumptions*

In the following chapters, I will discuss the historical contexts of three periods—the second half of the nineteenth century, the mid-twentieth century, and the present—attending to the problems, issues, and status of professional history writing, and those of history writing in biblical studies in these same periods. The interests of each period are reflected in unique ways in histories devoted to secular topics and those whose focus is Israel. The composition of the audience for historical work constitutes an important constraint on the writer. The question of history's relation to empirical science shapes the discipline throughout all three periods. The role of subjectivity varies sharply from the nineteenth-century view that it offered intimate access to the past to becoming an insurmountable obstacle to writing history in the present. I shall begin with the assumption that history is a continuous process, which exhibits coherence and causality, while being neither progressive nor evolutionary. History has individualized aspects, instances of the particular and unrepeatable, as well as aspects which lend themselves to generalizations. Generalizations may take the form of propositions familiar in the social sciences. Statistics are useful in conveying information and providing support for historical arguments, but do not in themselves represent science as an approach to history. An adequate approach today must include more than a rigorous method, a striving for objectivity. It must begin with theory, that is, a question must be posed to the past. Accumulated knowledge from many sources, for example information on demographics, climate, geography, and technology give the historian material with which to approach the past, but it is important here to distinguish between the data produced by various methods—literary, social scientific, psychological, and so forth—and the theoretical question put to history. For example, literary theory or a sociological theory may provide a method by which to carry out analysis, while a theoretical question frames the approach to investigation. With this in mind, it is time to begin the next chapter, where I will chart the development of the German historiographical tradition in preparation for the investigation of Wellhausen's historical scholarship.

Chapter 2

HISTORIOGRAPHY IN NINETEENTH-CENTURY GERMANY

The historian is potentially interested in all that has happened, everything that experiences change, in particular the acts of human beings and the consequences of their acts. The task of the historian begins with the recovery of events and the facts surrounding them. It includes the presentation and explanation of these experiences and events. Some confusion has attached to the vocabulary describing this endeavor. The term "history," for example, once designated any narrative, whether fanciful or founded in actual events. Since the eighteenth century, history has been limited to the recitation of real experiences, "things as they are."[1] By 1910, the *Encyclopedia Britannica* notes the dual meaning of history as both the series of happenings in time and the recounting of these events.[2] The word "historicity" denotes the *real* quality of an event or experience, a judgment that an occurrence or a character is neither fictitious, nor legendary. Historicism is perhaps the most problematical term. It refers to the view that cultural phenomena are historically determined and thus all truths and values, including those of the historian, are relative and may only be understood within their historical context.[3]

1. The *Encyclopaedia Britannica* of 1771 defines history as: "a description or recital of things as they are or have been, in a continued orderly narration of the principal facts and circumstances thereof. History, with regard to its subject, is divided into the history of Nature and the history of Actions. The history of Actions is a continued relation of a series of memorable events" (*Encyclopaedia Britannica* [3 vols.; Edinburgh, 1771], 2:788).
2. The definition given in the 1910 *Encyclopaedia Britannica* includes the following statements: "The word 'history' is used in two senses. It may mean either the record of events, or events themselves. Originally limited to inquiry and statement, it was only in comparatively modern times that the meaning of the word was extended to include the phenomena which form or might form their subject" (*Encyclopaedia Britannica* [29 vols.; 11th ed.; Cambridge, 1910], 13:527).
3. The *Oxford English Dictionary Online* (2d ed.; Oxford: Oxford University Press, 2000), gives the following definition: "The attempt, found especially among

Historicism is founded on the principle that human experience is unique and unrepeatable and must, therefore, be investigated through methods quite different from those employed by natural science. Historicism, however, has also been used to describe a belief that there are laws which govern historical change, making it possible to predict events, and further that the social sciences are chiefly concerned with historical prediction.[4] Georg Iggers notes the significant difficulty of fixing a meaning for the concept of historicism. He reminds us that

> the term "historicism" is of such recent usage in the United States that it was not yet included in any of the standard dictionaries of the 1950s.[5] Since then, it has been so rapidly adopted and has acquired so many often contradictory meanings that it defies definition.[6]

The term "historism" preceded "historicism" in English.[7] The translation made in England of Friedrich Meinecke's book on the rise of historicism is *Historism*.[8]

1. *Historicism*

Generally speaking, most writers accept that all socio-cultural phenomena are historically determined and that cognition of historical phenomena is also conditioned by time and situation. Thus, historicism has represented the view that no values are absolute, no judgments may be made on the experiences of times and places other than our own, and that methods used to investigate natural phenomena are not appropriate for the study of the experiences of human beings. This study will use the term historicism, the German *Historismus*, in this sense to identify the

German historians since about 1850, to view all social and cultural phenomena, all categories, truths, and values, as relative and historically determined, and in consequence to be understood only by examining their historical context, in complete detachment from present-day attitudes."

4. Popper, *The Poverty of Historicism*, 3.

5. Friedrich Meinecke (*Die Entstehung des Historismus* [Munich: Oldenbourg, 1959], 1) locates the first use of the term "historicism" in an 1879 book on Vico written by Karl Werner. Ernst Troeltsch's volume, *Der Historismus und seine Probleme* (Tübingen: Mohr, 1922), brought the term into broader consciousness.

6. Georg Iggers, *The German Conception of History* (Middletown, Conn.: Wesleyan University Press, 1968), 287. Iggers discusses the usage of the term historism on p. 288.

7. Historicism and historism are both given as definitions of Historismus in *Langenscheidts Enzyklopädisches Wörterbuch, Deutsch–English* (1 Band A–K; Berlin: Langenscheidt, 1996), 802.

8. Meinecke, *Historism*.

new movement in German historical thought. This chapter will establish
the characteristics of this historiographic tradition, the particular understanding of the process of history and its meaning, that prevailed in
Germany until well into the twentieth century. I will argue that German
historicism has roots in Romanticism and is deeply influenced by Idealism, that its political manifestations encourage a view of the state as an
ethical individuality whose inherent destiny unfolds through history, and
that in the historicist view meaning can only be discovered in history.
Challenges to historicism take the form of controversies over history's
unrepeatable nature and the possibility of establishing laws of causality,
and the problem of the relative character of human behavior in regard to
particular judgments and its implications for establishing meaning. The
question of audience and the role of subjectivity are important to the
development of historicism. The examination of the theory and practice
of history in nineteenth-century Germany will provide the basis for
evaluating the historical work of Julius Wellhausen.

The works of three major scholars in particular inform this chapter,
Friedrich Meinecke, Georg Iggers, and Isiah Berlin. Meinecke's study of
the German movement called historicism is described by Isaiah Berlin as
a "story told by a participant, not by a mere observer." He notes that
"Meinecke gives us vividly the founders of the school of which he was,
and probably knew himself to be, the last authentic master."[9] Meinecke
has three works bearing directly on the development of historicism, *Welt-
burgertum und Nationalstaat* (1907), *Die Idee der Staatsräson* (1924),
and *Die Entstehung des Historismus* (1936). Georg Iggers, in his comprehensive study *The German Conception of History*, has produced an
authoritative work on German historicism. Finally, Berlin himself has
written on the background of the new historical thought in Vico and
Herder, and the closely related movement, Romanticism.

Meinecke tells us immediately, in his preliminary remarks to *Die
Entstehung des Historismus*, that

> historism[10] is nothing else but the application to the historical world of the
> new life-governing principles achieved by the great German movement
> extending from Leibniz to the death of Goethe. This movement is the
> continuation of a general Western movement, but its culmination is to be
> sought in the great German thinkers. This was their second great achieve-
> ment, to be ranked along with their first, the Reformation.

9.   Isaiah Berlin, foreword to Meinecke, *Historism*, xv–xvi.
10. The German *Historismus* is translated into English as *historism* in the
English translation of Meinecke's work.

He continues, "The essence of historism is the substitution of a process of individualising observation for a generalising view of human forces in history."[11] The development of this intellectual revolution and its profound implications for history writing may be presented largely through the work of particular historians and their approaches to the philosophical or ideological problems of history. For this reason, this study will introduce the work of several seminal thinkers and notable practitioners of German historicism.

The foundations of historicism are found in the writings of Vico and Herder. Vico was the first to give expression to the notions which were taken up into historicism later in the century, while Herder and his circle brought these notions into the intellectual and political life of nineteenth-century Germany. Wilhelm von Humboldt was a member of this circle, a friend of Goethe and Schiller, influential in the political developments of the Congress of Vienna in the aftermath of the Napoleonic Wars. Humboldt reformed the Prussian educational system and established the University of Berlin. The name of Leopold von Ranke is firmly connected with the development of the academic discipline of history in German universities and with the critical use of documentary evidence. Johann Gustav Droysen founded the so-called Prussian School of historians. Droysen and his fellows represent the high point of historical optimism. Theodor Mommsen, much admired by Wellhausen, was an active political liberal who won the Nobel Prize for Literature for his Roman history.

2. The Character of the Historical Tradition

The importance of primary documents for writing history, most vividly associated with Ranke, had been already well established by previous generations of historians, biblical scholars, classicists, and philologists. Meinecke mentions J. D. Michaelis, J. S. Semmler, and C. G. Heyne.[12] Iggers argues that the critical analysis of documents and attention to factual accuracy were not the defining characteristics of the German historiographic tradition. These critical methods were quite easily exported and were equally useful to historians "in other countries who wrote under the impact of very different outlooks." Rather, the distinguishing features of the main tradition of German historiography were "the theoretical convictions in regard to the nature of history and the character of political power."[13] Iggers singles out three sets of ideas which he believes

11. Meinecke, *Historism*, lv.
12. Ibid., 236.
13. Iggers, *German Conception*, 3–4.

characterize the German historiographical tradition. First, the state is held be an end in itself. As in France and Great Britain, German historicism viewed the state as a product of historical forces, but the notion common to other Western cultures that the state exists to serve the interests of the populace is absent in German thought. Here is "the idealistic concept of the state as an 'individual,' an end in itself, governed by its own principles of life."[14] The state is much more than an empirical entity, it is rather, in Ranke's words, "an idea of God... It would be foolish to consider them [states] as so many institutions existing for the protection of individuals who have joined together, let us say, to safeguard their property."[15] This view is also expressed by Wellhausen. Though he shows attachment to the individual person in religious expression, his history is organized around the principle that Israel was a cultural unity and developed according to its own unique pattern.

The second idea identified by Iggers deals with values. Historicism argues that all values are formed in a concrete historical setting, that all values are relative, and, further, that no rational standards can be used to form judgments on individuals, activities, or institutions. Therefore, "all cultural phenomena are emanations of divine will and represent true values. In the realm of political values, the foundations are thus laid for an ethical theory of the doctrine of the state."[16] The state as an individual and end in itself has as its uppermost task, as Ranke observes, "to achieve the greatest independence and strength among competing powers. To this end individual rights and domestic concerns must be subordinate."[17] A strong state is the only guarantee of freedom or creativity. This notion of the power of the state protecting culture, law, and freedom is not limited to Germany, however; in other nations of the West, national aspirations are identified with universal human values. Within Germany, the notion of nationalism is more historically oriented, based on its own particular traditions, having little or nothing to learn from other nations' traditions. Nevertheless, each and every state expresses its own unique values and ethics and exists as a particular and inimitable spirit. We will see that Wellhausen follows the notion that values are developed in actual concrete situations and that Israel exhibits a spirit unique to itself.

14. Ibid., 8.
15. Leopold von Ranke, "A Dialogue on Politics," in his *The Theory and Practice of History* (ed. Georg Iggers and Konrad von Moltke; New York: Bobbs-Merrill, 1973), 102–30 (118).
16. Iggers, *German Conception*, 9.
17. Leopold von Ranke, "A Dialogue on Politics," in his *The Theory and Practice of History*, 102–30.

The third idea characteristic of the German historiographic tradition is rejection of conceptualized, and especially abstract, thinking. The notion that history is the record of unique individualities and, as such, is beyond the scope of the rational methods of natural science, makes impossible the use of categories, generalizations, or concepts in the study of history. Concepts drain the vital quality from historical reality, the spontaneity and dynamism of life resist reduction to a common denominator. Wellhausen is attracted to the spontaneous and dynamic qualities of Israel's life and takes care not to introduce generalizations into his history. This rejection of abstraction in historiography does not extend to all rationality in scientific inquiry. "Historicism," Iggers reminds us, is

> predominantly a scholarly movement which seeks rational understanding of human reality. Recognizing the emotional qualities of all human behavior, it seeks to develop a logic that takes into account the irrational aspects of human life. The same deep faith in the ultimate unity of life in God, which marks the political and ethical thought of historicism, also marks its theory of knowledge. From Humboldt to Meinecke, German historians are aware that all historical study takes place in an historical framework, but they are also confident that scholarly study leads to objective knowledge of historical reality.[18]

Iggers' three ideas characteristic of German historicism portray the theoretical foundation of the German historiographic tradition of the nineteenth century. This study now turns to the development of historicism in Germany with its roots in the thought of Vico, Herder, and Humboldt and the political pressures of the Napoleonic period.

a. *Historicism's Foundation in Vico*

Vico's *New Science*, first published in 1725, offers the remarkable perception that the new critical method and its criterion of truth exclude most of our common experience.[19] Isaiah Berlin illustrates it this way: Descartes holds that judgments claiming to be true must consist of clear and distinct "ideas," indivisible elements allowing no further analysis. The necessary logical links connecting these elements then produce systems whose structures and movements may be mathematically, or logically, described. It is clear that this procedure is not applicable to humane studies for, as Berlin asks:

---

18. Iggers, *German Conception*, 10.

19. Giambattista Vico first introduced this notion in his seventh inaugural address in 1708. See "On Method in Contemporary fields of Study," in *Vico, Selected Writings* (ed. and trans. Leon Pompa; Cambridge: Cambridge University Press, 1982), 37–45.

> Where in history, or in classical scholarship, or in literature, can we find
> strict definitions, rigorous proofs, concepts exhaustively analysed into their
> ultimate atomic constituents, demonstrated theorems, luminous and self-
> evident premises leading with inexorable logic to unalterable conclusions?

Descartes himself was aware that human activity, production, and expression were not amenable to quantification. His conclusion was simple. Inquiries into such areas might be harmless, but certainly were "not a branch of knowledge in which what had once been established did not need to be proved again, that is to say, in which scientific progress...was possible."[20] Whatever cannot be stated in mathematical terms, most particularly the perceptions of the senses, feelings, memories, and motives, is clearly outside the realm of scientific study.

Vico attacked this view after becoming convinced that the clarity and irrefutable quality of mathematics was simply the result of its having been wholly constructed by the human mind; thus, mathematical propositions are true only because we ourselves have made them.[21] Vico separated knowledge into two categories, that which we know because we create it and that which we can know only through observation. Nature can only be known in this sense, from the outside. Knowledge of nature is based on observation, measurement, calculation of movement, analysis of substances and component parts. This information can be accumulated, and laws regarding the behavior of material objects, plants, and animals can then be established. Thus, it is possible to describe such objects and organisms, to recognize a table, a bird, a tree, but we cannot know what it is to *be* a tree. Human beings are likewise part of the material world, acted on by natural forces, but they also have an existence filled with thought, choice, wishes, desires, fears, and goals. It is this inner life that sets us apart from the strictly natural world. Language and society would be meaningless notions, were it not for our confidence that we share these characteristics with other humans.[22] Vico argued that it would be foolish to ignore these human attributes and to insist that human beings be investigated only at the level of non-human entities.

It is deeply significant that the most important categories of human life and behavior are of a different order than those used in the scientific study of plants, animals, and material objects. This distinction drawn by

20. Isaiah Berlin, *Vico and Herder: Two Studies in the History of Ideas* (New York: Viking, 1976), 10.

21. Giambattista Vico, *New Science* (rev. trans. Goddard Bergin and Max Harris Fisch of 3d ed.; Ithaca, N.Y.: Cornell University Press, 1968 [1744]), 104 para. 349. This edition was Vico's final draft, on which he was working at the time of his death.

22. Vico, *New Science*, 67 para. 162.

Vico underlies the different methods and goals of natural science and humane studies. This becomes plain in his division of knowledge into the category of things which may be observed and analyzed in the natural world and the category of things which includes what human beings can know about other human beings because of their common mental activities and creations.[23] The importance of Vico's perception for historical studies lies in this human capacity to understand what others have made.

Vico's second insight important for historical investigations is that institutions are neither fixed nor immutable. This is a reaction to the Natural Law principle, which states that the existence of an unchanging human nature allows us to deduce a universal and permanent set of laws, rights, and obligations derived from the universal and identical goals of all people. Vico argues to the contrary that cultures develop from one phase to another, neither haphazardly, nor according to rigid rules of cause and effect, but as human beings, guided by providence, become more progressively aware of themselves and their world. Each culture has its own peculiar variations, its own unconscious characteristics. Most revolutionary is Vico's insight that the elements of a culture are intimately connected and change only and always within their own relationships. Thus, technology, law, politics, and customs are all related in a complicated web and change together according to altered needs and circumstances, the developing purposes, and perceived ends of the culture.[24]

There was never a time when humans lived without culture, Vico assures us.[25] Once our primitive ancestors began to communicate they were developing human society and the orderly progression of history. The means for understanding the early stages of human development are to be found in human institutions, in language, myths, especially in poetry, in magical rites, religion, and legal structures.[26] Vico proclaims that the study of cultures demonstrates the unfolding of a process, a succession of phases, indeed, a recurring pattern. Within all the dizzying array of cultural particularities this pattern is revealed: "the rise, progress, maturity, decay and fall."[27] Vico argues that each activity within a culture and each phase of a particular culture is an indispensable part of

23. Vico (*New Science*, 96 para. 331) says, "Whoever reflects on this cannot but marvel that the philosophers should have bent all their energies to the study of nature, which, since God made it, he alone knows; and that they should have neglected the study of the world of nations, or civil world, which, since men had made it, men could come to know."
24. Leon Pompa, Introduction to *Vico, Selected Writings*, 15.
25. Vico, *New Science*, 62 para. 135.
26. Ibid., 65 para. 152, 103–4 paras. 346–47.
27. Ibid., 104 para. 349.

the development of that culture. Each culture develops according to its inner logic, but the pattern of organic development from birth, through maturity to death is common to all. Indeed, one culture follows another passing through this self-same sequence.

Vico begins from the proposition that humans can truly know only what they make—their ideas, their inner life, their cultures. Human nature is not static, but intimately enmeshed in the institutions, social relations, and physical conditions of culture. At the same time, humans make their own lives, both consciously and unconsciously, with respect to their surroundings. It is because humans make their history that it is possible to understand the situations, activities, and events of the past, but it is Vico's insight that because of the changing qualities of human nature in response to altered physical and social needs a process of history may be established. This notion of historical perspective orders empirical data of the past through concepts of change and growth, appropriateness and anachronism, and the irreversible process of history. Berlin says, by way of example:

> When…we say that it is wholly impossible for Hamlet, or anything like it, to have been composed in the kind of society which inhabited Outer Mongolia in the third century A.D., and look on any theory which rests on the opposite assumption as too absurd to be worth a moment's notice; these "could nots" and "impossibles" are categories of the historical sense, of the sense of what goes with what, and of what is incompatible with it.[28]

Two important implications for history writing derive from this sense of historical perspective. First, that history must be perceived as a continuous stream of development in which individual actors and events can only be understood in relation to their customs, art, folk beliefs, laws, and language. Second, that the civilizations of the past are at a great remove from our own. That we can understand them at all is due to our common humanity, but whatever understanding we achieve requires enormous imaginative effort.[29] The differences exhibited in other civilizations, their particular structures and models of development, render them useless as authority for our own. Here is the foundation of the notion of culture as the sum of all aspects of art, expression, religion, policy, law, family life, economics, technology, and environment, a certain particular spirit of time and place.[30] In Johann Gottfried Herder these notions are joined to other ideas of the age with significant implications for the study of history.

28. Berlin, *Vico and Herder*, 33.
29. Vico, *New Science*, 100 para. 378.
30. Ibid., 64 paras. 147–48, 104 para. 348.

b. *Herder's Contribution*

Herder lived in a world where already many had argued that the proper object of the study of history is the life of communities rather than the exploits of individuals. Voltaire, Hume, Montesquieu, and certainly Vico had held this view. The belief that poets and artists expressed the nature and experience of their cultures was current in his youth, as was the notion that civilizations in their great variety are, in large part, formed by the forces of climate and geography. A knowledge of cultural differences promoted an awareness that judgments about different or more remote civilizations could not properly be made by means of eternal rules or laws.[31] Furthermore, Berlin points out that the understanding of a society as an organism has a long history going back to Aristotle and was frequently used by medieval writers. Culture as an entity with a unique "spirit" was found in Vico and in several near contemporaries whom Herder read.[32] Included among the intellectual resources available to Herder were important works on ancient Greece and Rome, coupled with studies of early tribes and simpler societies, and the work of Astruc, Lowth, and Michaelis, treating the Bible as a multi-layered composition.

Herder, like Vico, opposed notions of universal laws, final principles, and eternal truths. Again like Vico, Herder insisted that every culture or civilization exhibited a unique character. The effects of the scientific approach, to force the specific, unique instances of human activity into abstract or universal categories, Herder argued, was to overlook just what was interesting, useful, and worthwhile in history. He proposed instead to investigate the elements which make up a particular social group, the intangible factors which constitute culture, the irrational areas of religion and politics. It must be noted that Herder was well acquainted with contemporary science and as Berlin tells us, "He was fascinated and influenced by the findings of the sciences no less than Goethe, and, like him, thought that false general inferences were often drawn from them."[33]

31. Meinecke (*Historism*, 303) emphasizes the influence of Shakespeare on Herder: "Herder acquired an appreciation of Shakespeare which was destined to become more and more influential in all his subsequent historical thinking. He came to realise that such a phenomenon could not possibly be judged by the hitherto accepted standards of the Enlightenment. It could never be assessed according to its details, but only in its full-grown totality."

32. Herder is not known to have read Vico until some twenty years after composing his own philosophy of history. See Berlin, *Vico and Herder*, 147, and idem, *The Roots of Romanticism* (ed. Henry Hardy; Princeton, N.J.: Princeton University Press, 1999), 60.

33. Berlin, *Vico and Herder*, 146.

Meinecke comments on the chief intellectual and spiritual influences —the Enlightenment, pietism, and Platonism—to which Herder was most indebted. He says, "About the middle of the eighteenth century they were often to be found working in parallel in Germany, but in Herder they coincided."[34] From this confluence of sources, Herder produced three notions, which Berlin calls revolutionary.[35] These notions had powerful significance for the developing Romantic movement and each was antagonistic to the moral, aesthetic, and historical principles of the Enlightenment. First is the signal importance of belonging to a group, neither political, nor national, but to a culture group. Building on the notion that artists and poets expressed their cultures in their creations, Herder perceived that it is in one's culture that one's views, one's nature, one's posture, even one's sense perceptions are molded. One's experience of religion, art, politics, myth, language—in fact, all experience— is part of a particular pattern or context which is one's culture. Thus, a member of that culture will "feel" at home among the familiar artifacts of his or her world. In his *Ideen zur Philosophie der Geschichte der Menschenheit*,[36] Herder demonstrates his knowledge of and fascination with the variety of cultures which make up the history of humankind. He extols the characteristics of particular cultures, always regretting the demise of one group at the hands of another. For Herder, every group should flourish in its own unique expression free from the coercion of some neighbor or invader.[37]

This leads to the second original notion of Herder's. Every culture has its own ideal. Not only is it not possible to judge one culture by the ideals of another, but further, whatever ideal one may admire in its cultural context, one cannot seek to replicate it; indeed, ideals from other cultures are incompatible with one another. The splendor of Greece was for the Greeks. The admirable qualities of the German tribes still fresh and heroic are not available to modern people. They cannot be brought together. Because the best of all the previous centuries or different societies cannot be realized in one place, then it becomes clear that there is no final or universal ideal to be sought. There can be no perfect life or

34. Meinecke, *Historism*, 299.
35. Berlin, *Vico and Herder*, 152–53.
36. Johann Gottfried Herder, *Outlines of a Philosophy of the History of Man* (trans. T. Churchill; New York: Bergman, 1966 [first published in London, 1800]); trans. of *Ideen zur Philosophie der Geschichte der Menschenheit* (1784–91).
37. Meinecke (*Historism*, 305) describes Herder's strong feelings for cultures and societies and extreme distaste for states which came into existence through conquest. The "ideal picture of the political state of a primitive and uncomplicated people remained his ideal of the State in general" (p. 352).

character or politics, for if there were, then all other efforts would be wrong or false. In Herder's view, each answer is right for its own time and place and adds to an immeasurably varied and inexhaustible world. This view of the uniqueness of cultures and the incommensurability of cultures comes into historicism from Herder.[38]

The third new doctrine of Herder's also derives from the belief that all human activity, all the works of human beings, are modes of expression. Works of art, texts, or music are not to be treated as objects detached from their authors, but as forms of communication. The character or nature of an individual is contained in the products of that person's activity. The function of human beings is chiefly to express themselves, and obstacles to this human realization of self-expression are the source of this world's disharmony. In a similar way, the character of a society is expressed in its myths, laws, folk songs, its art, and its politics. Herder argues that art, artifacts, laws, or folk dances, being created by individuals or groups in specific societies or cultures, are recognizable as expressions of that particular group. In order to understand a particular facet of a culture, one must by a strenuous act of the imagination place oneself into the world of that culture. The life of the people must be reconstructed, their goals and desires, their food, their customs. Because the world is made by humans, because humans express themselves through their creations, it is possible to make this reconstruction, to accomplish this act of imagination.[39] More than molding its members, culture provides a text to be read by the historian.

c. *The Influence of Humboldt*

The shift from Enlightenment concepts of Natural Law and their influence on history writing to modern notions of historicism can be traced further in the life and writings of Wilhelm von Humboldt. Humboldt had initially expressed enthusiasm for the French Revolution and wrote the classic work of German liberalism,[40] lauding principles accepted since John Locke, that the state is not an end in itself, but exists to protect the rights of individuals through the least intervention possible, and to provide security from threats from outside. From his theoretical concerns

38. Herder, *Outlines of a Philosophy.* Herder discusses the impact of society on human beings in Book VIII (especially Chapters III, IV, and V), Book IX (Chapters I–IV), and Book XII (Chapter VI).

39. Berlin outlines Herder's contributions to romanticism in his *Vico and Herder*, 145–48, and *Roots of Romanticism*, 57–67.

40. Wilhelm von Humboldt, *The Sphere and Duties of Government* (trans. Joseph Coulthard; Bristol: Thoemmes Press, 1996); trans. of *Ideen zu einem Versuch, die Grenzen der Wirksamkeit des Staats zu bestimmen* (1791).

in *Die Grenzen des Staats*, Humboldt shifted to practical activity when he agreed to Baron von Stein's request that he reorganize the Prussian system of education. During this period, he was an envoy to the Congress of Vienna, drafted the Prussian constitution, reformed the school system from the primary grades through the gymnasium, and founded the University of Berlin, with its emphasis on academic freedom in research and teaching, which served as a model for the modern university.[41] In undertaking these tasks, Humboldt acceded to a view of the state which allowed positive functions, a position which he had previously opposed. More than this even, he concluded that the state must increase its strength:

> Germany must be free and strong, not only to be able to defend herself against this or that neighbor, or for that matter, against any enemy, but because only a nation which is also strong toward the outside can preserve the spirit within from which all domestic blessings flow. Germany must be free and strong, even if she is never put to a test, so that she may possess the self-assurance required for her to pursue her development as a nation unhampered...[42]

The relation of the individual to society and the ultimate meaning of history are addressed by Humboldt in his essay on the work of the historian. "The historian's task is to present what actually happened... An event, however, is only partially visible in the world of the senses; the rest has to be added by intuition, inference, and guesswork." This factor, which brings unity to the scattered and isolated aspects of an event, the influences, motives, and forces, "remains removed from direct observation. For observation can perceive circumstances which either accompany or follow one another, but not their inner causal nexus, on which, after all, their inner truth is solely dependent."[43] Humboldt recognizes that language itself presents problems to the narration of history, lacking as it does "expressions which are free from all connotations." For this reason the facts of history are "little more than the results of tradition and scholarship which one has agreed to accept as true, because they— being most highly probable in themselves—also fit best into the context of the whole."[44] Framing an event by "sorting out what has actually happened" is merely a first step and intuition does not fully aid the

41. Iggers, *German Conception*, 52.
42. Wilhelm von Humboldt, "Denkschrift über die deutsche Verfassung," December, 1813, in *Gesammelte Schriften* (18 vols.; Berlin, 1903–36), 11:95–112 (97), quoted in Iggers, *German Conception*, 54.
43. Wilhelm von Humboldt, "On the Historian's Task," in Ranke, *The Theory and Practice of History*, 5–23 (5).
44. Ibid., 6.

historian in perceiving the event in its fullness. The historian "can only reveal the truth of an event by presentation, by filling in and connecting the disjointed fragments of direct observation...like the poet, only through his imagination." He sums up the approach to history saying, "two methods have to be followed simultaneously...the first is the exact, impartial, critical investigation of events; the second is the connecting of the events explored and the intuitive understanding of them which could not be reached by the first means" for "there is also the breath of life in the whole and an inner character which speaks through it which can be neither measured nor merely described."[45] Humboldt stresses the requirement that the total personality must be engaged in the understanding of history. He rejects any theory of rational ethics or objective criteria of knowledge and argues rather that history is the only source of knowledge about humanity. Humans are irrational and historical method must take this into account. Furthermore, there is no meaning to be discovered in history. There may be a kind of coherence in history, but only of an organic sort, the connection of the individual to community, to nation, and finally to the species as a whole. Purpose in history can only be conceived in terms of the intent that all individualities express themselves, from persons, to communities and nations.[46] Efforts to force the irrational character of history into a meaningful pattern or philosophical system, in order to expose some idea of progress, are fruitless in Humboldt's view. History accumulates in fits and starts, a jumble of events and novelties, high points of civilization destroyed by natural disasters or the ravages of invasions. Above the confusion of history, however, Humboldt still believes that somehow all the medley of personalities and events must be gathered up into a harmonious whole. History left to unfold according to the tendencies of each individual part must compose some mysterious good, while disturbing the natural flow of history constitutes evil.

Confronting the methodological difficulties inherent in presenting the "living" quality of history, Humboldt cautions that external description is not sufficient for any real understanding of history. The individual aspects of history, which cannot be examined under controlled conditions as objects of scientific study, must be approached through a combination of rational observation and poetic imagination.[47] What has happened is only in part accessible to the senses. After investigating all aspects related to an event,

45. Ibid., 7.
46. Iggers, *German Conception*, 57.
47. Humboldt, "On the Historian's Task," 6.

the nature and changes of the soil, the variations of climate, the intellectual capacity and character of nations, the even more particular characters of individuals, the influences of the arts and sciences, and the profoundly incisive and widespread influences of social institutions, there still remains an even more powerfully active principle which, though not directly visible, imparts to these forces themselves their impetus and direction: that is ideas which by their very nature lie outside the compass of the finite, and yet pervade and dominate every part of world history.[48]

Thus for a deeper understanding of the past, the historian must "infer" or "divine" the elements which bind the parts together. The historian does not record mere facts, but tries to discover connections. The historian is aware of causality, but also recognizes the irrational quality of human experience. The historian must seek beyond the facts, yet refrain from imposing concepts on actual experience. The historian must undertake "exact, impartial, critical examination of the events" and employ intuition to discover that "which cannot be reached by this means."[49]

Humboldt represents in his own thinking the shift which occurred in the German attitude toward history from an Enlightenment to an historicist perspective. Iggers argues that the impact of political events in the period 1792 to 1815 was an important factor in this development.[50] Educated Germans, on the whole, had been stirred and encouraged by the French Revolution, only to find bitter disappointment in its aftermath. The turn of events in France brought German intellectuals to further question Enlightenment principles of reason and Natural Law. German national feeling was strengthened during the period of Napoleonic domination and all things French became objects of criticism and distaste. Thus, principles of universal moral and political values, questioned before the Revolution, were decisively rejected in Germany and replaced by the view that instead, rights and values were characteristics of national cultures. It was, therefore, neither desirable nor possible for one nation to adopt another's laws or institutions. In this period, German thought had moved from the cosmopolitan views of Herder suggesting that all nations form a human family, to the position that different nations occupied greater and lesser stature in their missions.[51]

48. Ibid., 19.
49. Ibid., 7.
50. Iggers, *German Conception*, 40. Donald R. Kelley takes issue with Iggers' view, stressing instead the continuity of Humboldt's thought based on a version of Enlightenment science, *vitalism*. This appears insufficient to counter a reading of Humboldt's own words. See Kelley, "Mythhistory in the Age of Ranke," in *Leopold von Ranke and the Shaping of the Historical Discipline* (ed. Georg G. Iggers and James M. Powell; Syracuse: Syracuse University Press, 1990), 3–20.
51. Iggers, *German Conception*, 41.

Humboldt argued in his early writing for the limitation of the powers of the state, believing that the functions of society were best effected by the local community or the civil sector. The state's only mission was to assure protection and order. Humboldt, like Herder and Schiller, had argued that the nation was a cultural rather than a political entity, but by 1813 in his *Memorandum on a German Constitution*, he equates the nation, the people, and the state. Iggers concludes that:

> Historicism, in the course of the revolutionary and Napoleonic Wars, had thus not only increased its hold upon the educated public, but also had changed its character. An aesthetic, culturally oriented approach to nationality increasingly gave place to the ideal of the nation state. The concept of individuality, which Goethe and Humboldt still applied to the uniqueness of persons, now primarily referred to collective groups.[52]

The status of the nation as an entity following its own interests according to the call of a higher morality became a guiding assumption for German historicism, along with the notion that history cannot be approached by the generalizing methods of natural science.

d. *Ranke's Historical Principles*

Two years after Humboldt completed his "Memorandum," Leopold von Ranke published *History of the Latin and Teutonic Nations, 1494–1514*.[53] In an appended essay, "In Criticism of Modern Historians," Ranke presented his critical principles, the demand for genuine and original sources for writing history, and the strict admonition that historians maintain impartiality in their work. He is indebted to the classical scholar B. G. Niebuhr for the outline of this critical approach, but it is clear that his own passion for reliable sources and accurate recounting of the past guides this essay.[54] Eighteenth-century philologists and historians in Göttingen had developed the principles for the faithful use of documents, records, diaries, inscriptions, narratives, and correspondence, but it was Ranke who adapted these critical principles for historical study. More than this, however, it was through the seminar that Ranke promoted the professional approach to the use of sources.

Ranke's seminar is a methodological extension of his insistence on the critical approach to sources for it is in the seminar that tests are applied to the use of original documents and historical sources. It is through discussion and debate that questions on the validity of sources and faithful

52. Ibid., 42.
53. Leopold von Ranke, *History of the Latin and Teutonic Nations, 1494–1514* (trans. P. A. Ashworth; London: G. Bell & Sons, 1887).
54. Meinecke, *Historism*, 498.

presentation are resolved. The seminar was fashioned as a working group, almost an extended family. Seminars met in Ranke's home and the participants discussed one another's papers, the work of a particular author, or a topic from the point of view of several authors. The group was limited usually to eight or ten students, occasionally three or five, and, on one occasion, eighteen. Ranke trained generations of historians in this way. While the use of sources was a constant theme, Ranke "never neglected to raise basic theoretical questions of historical science."[55] It was through these seminars that Ranke's approach to history and historical study was promulgated and institutionalized.

By 1825, the year Ranke was called to Berlin, two opposing circles had formed, one gathered around Hegel, and the other a group of jurists and historians, including Niebuhr, Friedrich Karl Savigny, the theologian Friedrich Schleiermacher, the philologists August Böckh, Franz Bopp, and Karl Lachmann, and the founder of the Historical School, Karl Friedrich Eichhorn.[56] Their arguments focused on the diversity to be observed in the phenomenal world. The Hegelian view held that beneath all diversity lay a rational principle and that truth could be discovered only by reducing this variety to rational concepts. As has been demonstrated, the principles of historicism insist that any such reduction violates individuality and the unique, unrepeatable aspects of history, and therefore distorts truth. While these two circles agreed that metaphysical reality exists behind the historical manifestations which we observe, and that the goal of all study was to grasp this reality, the Historical School argued that this reality could only be apprehended through the study of history. Hegel's conception of the universe could not comprehend the unique, irrational, and elusive qualities of real human experience. Ranke found his own views compatible with those of the Historical School.[57]

The historicist position, as has been discussed above, entails the belief that human beings can only be understood through their history. Neither philosophy nor natural science, because of their aim to generalize, is an appropriate means to understand the diversity and uniqueness of human history. History's purview includes motives, values, intentions, and the human will, while natural science and philosophy devote themselves to abstract causal explanation. Ranke tells us:

55. Georg G. Iggers and Konrad von Moltke, introduction to Ranke, *The Theory and Practice of History*, xxxiii.
56. Iggers, *German Conception*, 66.
57. Though Ranke is most remembered as an innovator in method, in the years of his editorship of the *Historisch-Politische Zeitschrift* (1832–36), he published essays systematically outlining historicist principles.

First of all, philosophy always reminds us of the claim of the supreme idea. History, on the other hand, reminds us of the conditions of existence. The former lends weight to the universal interest, the latter to the particular interest. The former considers the development essential and sees every particular only as a part of the whole. History turns sympathetically also to the particular.[58]

While stating his belief that "there is nothing without God, and nothing lives except through God," he insists that historical practice must not search for a religious or divine principle, but realize that "History elevates, gives significance to, and hallows the phenomenal world, in and by itself, because of what it contains."[59] From these principles, Ranke derives demands for historical practice. First, is "the pure love of truth." This necessitates "a documentary, penetrating, profound study…devoted to the phenomenon itself, to its condition, its surrounding." One may be more or less gifted to accomplish this task, "intelligence, courage, and honesty in telling the truth are sufficient."[60] A universal interest is necessary, however, because "aspects of society are never present separately but always together—indeed, determining each other—and since, for instance, the attitudes of science often influence foreign policy and especially domestic politics, equal interest must be devoted to all of these factors."[61] The historian also must attend to the analysis of cause and effect. Ranke despairs that "selfishness and lust for power" are commonly assumed to be the chief motives of all affairs. "I do not deny that selfishness and lust for power can be very powerful motives and have had a great influence, but I deny that they are the only ones," he says and admonishes the historian to observe carefully, to let events speak through the documentary evidence.[62] He makes a plea for impartiality. He acknowledges that the historian has an opinion, a religious point of view, a worldview which is inescapable, but it is not up to the historian to "judge about error and truth… Our task is to penetrate them to the bottom of their existence and to portray them with complete objectivity."[63] Finally, Ranke notes that a single moment or event is not sufficient for understanding history, it is necessary to locate the connections. To write a history of a particular people, "its development, its deeds, its institutions, and its literature" must be explored.[64]

---

58. Leopold von Ranke, "On the Character of Historical Science," in his *The Theory and Practice of History*, 33–46 (37).
59. Ibid., 38–39.
60. Ibid., 39.
61. Ibid., 40.
62. Ibid., 41.
63. Ibid., 42.
64. Ibid., 44.

(1) *History Distinguished from Philosophy and Natural Science.* "History is distinguished from all other sciences in that it is also an art," Ranke informs us. Its scientific character is manifest in the activities of "collecting, finding, penetrating. It is an art because it recreates and portrays that which it has found and recognized. Other sciences are satisfied simply with recording what has been found; history requires the ability to recreate."[65] History is related to philosophy in its scientific guise and to poetry in its artistic mode. Philosophy and poetry both concern themselves with the ideal, however, while "history has to rely on reality." History is distinct from philosophy and poetry by virtue of its subject matter. Thus, history is a third intellectual endeavor, neither philosophy, nor poetry, but combining the two in the task of understanding the real instead of the ideal.[66] Historical investigation begins with the rejection of speculation. Strict empirical observation allows the historian to establish the relevant facts, but it is not sufficient to simply record a list of details. The historian must immerse him or herself in the historical situation. Through intuition or contemplation the reality becomes clear to the historian. The historian must not force preconceived notions on the historical situation, nor analyze it, but sense the connections, be open to impressions and insights. It is Ranke's confidence that there is "something infinite in every existence: in every condition, in every being, something eternal, coming from God," that allows comprehension across historical time and place.[67] The spiritual content of historical individualities, cultures, or institutions may not be immediately apparent, for external facts do not reveal the spiritual; nevertheless, all expressions of individuals, cultures, and nations are permeated by a spiritual character. By immersing oneself in the concrete historical realities, one may begin to understand (*Verstehen*) the essential quality of the particular past. The method of the historian is not inductive, nor deductive, but imaginative.[68] Wellhausen, as an intuitive historian, derives his approach from this method.

(2) *The Idealistic Theory of the State.* The theoretical foundation for Ranke's conception of the state is found in his essays for the *Historisch-Politische Zeitschrift* written between 1832 and 1836. He insists that the history of the world is not a chaotic succession of governments and

---

65. Ibid., 33.
66. Ibid., 34.
67. Ibid., 38.
68. See Rudolf Vierhaus, "Historiography between Science and Art," in Iggers and Powell, eds., *Leopold von Ranke and the Shaping of the Historical Discipline*, 61–69.

peoples. "There are forces and indeed spiritual, life-giving, creative forces, nay life itself, and there are moral energies, whose development we see. They cannot be defined or put in abstract terms, but one can behold them and observe them. One can develop a sympathy for their existence."[69] In his "Dialogue on Politics," Ranke elaborates:

> States are spiritual substances, by necessity and idea different from each other. The forms of the constitution and the different institutions are necessitated by the general conditions of human existence; they are, however, modified by this idea, and develop their fullest reality only through it. Hence they are necessarily divergent... Private life, too, is dependent on the idea which animates the state...these many separate, earthly-spiritual communities called forth by genius and moral energy, growing irresistibly, progressing amidst all turmoil of the world toward the ideal, each in its own way.[70]

Each state, then, is the product of certain spiritual energies embodied in its people, customs, language, and institutions. Each develops according to its own inner tendencies. Meinecke explains that, for Ranke, this spiritual power, which works itself out in the practical activities of a particular state, gives the state the character and the properties of an individual.[71] The state, society, cultures, individual persons, all follow their own vital interests and their own developmental patterns are of necessity good, of equal value to God, who knows as we cannot the ultimate harmony of world history.

Iggers points to the profoundly disturbing problem in this view of history. He says, "But what is almost entirely missing in Ranke, despite his pronounced Christianity, and for that matter is absent in most Romantic thought, is the recognition of an element of evil in man and in human institutions."[72] In this regard, Ranke fails to consider seriously the possible abuses of power by the state. Imbued with a Lutheran respect for authority, Ranke assumes that states must not be judged by universal ethical principles, but rather on the basis of their fidelity to their own particular lines of development. Discerning the proper path of development offers no serious obstacle for Ranke. True politics is concerned with the practical, the necessary, and the possible; its aim is tranquil progress and gradual development. It follows the dominant trends of the time, carefully avoiding revolutionary measures and planned reform, for

69. Leopold von Ranke, "The Great Powers," in his *The Theory and Practice of History*, 65–101 (100).
70. Ranke, "A Dialogue on Politics."
71. Meinecke, *Historism*, 499.
72. Iggers, *German Conception*, 80.

these would circumvent the regular progress of the natural tendencies of the state. Again, a troubling problem with this view becomes apparent. Even if the historian traces the forces at work within a society, and excludes the revolutionary as illegitimate, choosing the forces among the many remaining which represent the true course of development would be arbitrary.

Ranke failed to understand the impossibility of recognizing this innate historical direction. For him, only the dominant trends of society have value. Justice in this view is always with the powerful; indeed, Ranke tells us statesmen throughout history have been aware of "what constituted progress and what decay."[73] Beyond this optimistic view of the orderly inner progress of the life of the state, the state is ultimately in the care of "the guardian spirit which always protects Europe from domination by any one-sided and violent tendency...and has happily preserved the freedom and separate existence of each state."[74] This is Ranke's idealistic theory of the state which he shares with Humboldt and the Historical School. It differs from Hegel in the significant point that for Ranke knowledge of the state must be garnered from the study of history. It is the particular event that reveals the essence of the spirit of a culture, an individual, or a state. Abstract concepts inevitably disfigure historical knowledge. Unlike Hegel, Ranke is convinced that humans cannot discover the plan of the universe, but Ranke has a serene confidence in the inner necessity of the development of the state. While it seems that the forces of development cannot be denied, Ranke knows that history is not predictable, that often enough in the past, the people or culture that appeared the stronger, wiser, or more sophisticated fell victim to a cruel or barbaric conqueror. For Ranke, the answer to this apparent mystery is known only to God.

Against Hegel's reliance on the logic of history as the sole moving force, Ranke argues that individuals have will and exercise choice.[75] Hegel's individuals remain tools of the world spirit. Ranke says, "If this view were correct, the world spirit alone would be truly alive. It would be the sole actor; even the greatest men would be instruments in its hand..." This, he argues, would require that God were developing through history, a notion he rejects in favor of an eternal immutable

---

73. Ibid., 73.

74. Ranke, "The Great Powers," 73.

75. Hajo Holborn ("The History of Ideas," *American Historical Review* 73, no. 3 [1968]: 683–95) describes Hegel's position: "Thus history is dominated by the world mind. Though building the work of the objective mind, man is only a laboring puppet" (p. 686).

God.[76] On the other hand, Meinecke points out that Ranke would not have agreed entirely with Heinrich von Treitschke's claim that history is made by individuals. Ranke addressed the question whether great events were the work of creative personalities or the expression of the needs and tendencies of human communities, by recognizing the claims of both the individual and the collective spirit. "Although there was a constant to-and-fro movement, with an astonishing variety of new combinations, one of these poles was not conceivable without the other," Meinecke notes. Ranke exercised a "refined collectivism" in Meinecke's words, "deducing the actions of statesmen from the large-scale necessities of States."[77] The distinction between Ranke and Hegel hinges on Ranke's insistence that knowledge of the human condition can be derived only from the study of particular events of history, while Hegel conceptualizes events as historical moments in the logical course of realizing the highest purpose of the spiritual world. Ranke argues that human life "perishes" in the Hegelian view where "the world spirit follows its course through a necessary development by sacrificing the individuals." He says further that Hegel's "leading ideas" can be understood only as "ruling tendencies" in every century.

> These tendencies can only be described, but in the last analysis they cannot be subsumed under one concept. I cannot think of the matter differently but that mankind harbors within itself an infinite multiplicity of developments which manifest themselves gradually according to laws which are unknown to us and are more mysterious and greater than one thinks[78]

It is through organic development, in Ranke's view, that history unfolds, but there is no Hegelian essentialism here, no necessary evolutionary pattern. For this reason, revolution must be avoided for it subverts the natural process of development. Also, the assimilation of one culture by another is to be avoided as this causes the potential growth of a culture to be stifled.

(3) *The Practice of Writing History.* In the practice of writing history, Ranke saw his most important task as the composition of significant narrative. Rudolf Vierhaus notes that "His considerable, quickly spreading reputation was not that of the academic teacher or the theoretician, but of the historian whose works already during his lifetime reached a

76. Leopold von Ranke, "The Pitfalls of a Philosophy of History," in his *The Theory and Practice of History*, 47–50 (49–50).

77. Meinecke, *Historism*, 501.

78. Leopold von Ranke, "On Progress in History," in his *The Theory and Practice of History*, 51–56 (55).

public far beyond the circle of historians."⁷⁹ Vierhaus points out that
pragmatic histories of the earlier Göttingen School fell out of favor with
the advent of the works of the new historicism. The older works were
"outpaced by the changing interest in history and its interpretation, by
new requirements of a historical foundation of national identity and the
affirmation of continuity in German history, as well as by new aesthetic
standards." The new historians saw their task as "the transformation of
historical facts into an interpretative narrative which made the reader a
participating observer of the dramatic process of history."⁸⁰

Ranke made his mark on German historiography through his great
histories which were well received by a broad reading public, through his
critical standards for the use of sources, through the training of several
generations of influential historians in his seminars, and through his
essays and prefaces on the theory of history. His politics were deeply
conservative. He continued to prefer the enlightened bureaucratic state of
the pre-revolutionary period and apparently failed to understand fully the
social and economic forces seeking change throughout Europe. Georg
Iggers argues that scholars younger than Ranke took his historical objectivity as a form of moral indifference. While committed to his critical
methods, they "regarded the study of the past not as an end in itself, but
as a means to achieve the political and ethical requirements of the
moment—the liberal national state. Almost all the important German
historians were politically active."⁸¹

3. *The Generation of Liberal Historians*

The liberal historians of the Prussian School sought many of the rights of
classic Western liberalism: representative constitutional government in
opposition to absolute monarchy, equality before the law, including
abolition of restrictions on Jews, trial by jury, and freedom of the press.
F. C. Dahlman, Georg Gervinus, and Jakob and Wilhelm Grimm were
among the seven scholars expelled from the University of Göttingen for

---

79. Vierhaus, "Historiography," 62.
80. Ibid., 66.
81. Iggers, *German Conception*, 91. Wolfgang Mommsen notes: "It is well
known that the German national liberal school of historians reacted strongly against
Leopold von Ranke's allegedly lifeless historiography which, while it pretended to
maintain a rigorous standard of objectivity, in fact sided with the established forces
of the *Ancien Regime*" ("Ranke and the Neo-Rankean School in Imperial Germany,"
in Iggers and Powell, eds., *Leopold von Ranke and the Shaping of the Historical
Discipline*, 124–40 [124]).

their opposition to Ernst August's suspension of the constitution on his ascension to the throne of Hannover in 1837. On the basis of their organic view of constitutional development, the Göttingen Seven protested against the arbitrary disruption of the growth of constitutional government. In the period before 1848, Karl Rotteck and Karl Welcker were members of parliament. F. C. Dahlman, Gustav Droysen, Karl Welcker, Georg Waitz, Georg Gervinus, Max Duncker, and Rudolf Haym were members of the Frankfurt Parliament during the 1848 revolution. Theodor Mommsen was the editor of a political newspaper in Schleswig-Holstein and was removed from his chair at the University of Leipzig, along with his colleagues, the philologists Moritz Haupt and Otto Jahn, in consequence of his revolutionary activities in 1848.[82] As Prince Wilhelm assumed power in Prussia in 1857, the younger historians Heinrich Sybel, Heinrich Treitschke, Hermann Baumgarten, and the philosopher Wilhelm Dilthey contributed their views to the newly founded *Preussische Jahrbücher*, demanding German unification under a Prussian constitution.[83] Wellhausen, as will be shown, was considered a "liberal." He admired both Bismarck and Mommsen, but remained outside active political involvement.

Mommsen and Gervinus were among the few who favored extending the franchise, for democracy and socialism seemed to most to offer too much power to the new industrial working class at the expense of the middle class with whom the professors shared economic and political interests. Despite their devoted efforts on behalf of a constitutional government similar in many points to those of other Western nations, these liberal historians' understanding of the nature of society and of the historical process was unique to nineteenth-century Germany. The nature of their audience and their political goals helped shape the view of history promulgated by these writers. Within a divinely ordered plan, they believed states progressed inexorably toward a condition in which harmony would exist between individual rights and the interests of the state, and power and ethics would not be in conflict.

---

82. The theologian Friedrich Vischer was also a member of the Frankfurt Parliament.

83. Thomas Wiedemann, "Mommsen, Rome and the *Kaiserreich*," in A *History of Rome under the Emperors*, by Theodor Mommsen (ed. T. Wiedemann; trans. Clare Krojkl; London: Routledge, 1996), 36–47 (44); trans. of *Römische Kaisergeschichte* (ed. Barbara and Alexander Demandt; Munich: Beck, 1992). See also Thomas Wiedemann, "Mommsen's Roman History," n.p. [cited 27 February 2001]. Online: www.dur.ac.uk/Classics/histos/1997/wiedemann.html, and Iggers, *German Conception*, 91–93.

4. *Historiography Distinct from Philosophy and Natural Science*

"By 1850," writes Michael Maclean, "historiography was the central discipline in academic life and the most consulted source in general culture."[84] By way of establishing the discipline, historians had traditionally defined their method against the abstractions and conceptualization of philosophy and the generalizing methods of the sciences. Following "philosophy's precipitous, if temporary, decline after the death of Hegel,"[85] German historians found themselves in a favorable position of advancement. At the same time the natural sciences also experienced growing public recognition and academic ascendency. While history and science had struggled, "often as allies," against idealist philosophy, it quickly became clear that, as Maclean states, the "lingering idealism of the historians was as incompatible with the increasingly mechanistic approach of the sciences as was the earlier philosophical idealism of Hegel."[86] The historical discipline felt itself threatened by a popular current of scientific materialism in the middle classes and by the influence of scientific thought on the educated public.[87] Maclean points out that "the growth of science and scientific modes of thought was most overtly subversive of traditional German historiography in two areas: as regards, first, conceptualization of the substance of the historical process and, second, the methodological prescription for its objective recovery."[88] Specifically, the scientific position fostered the notion that "history was animated by anonymous, material causal factors that transcended the wills of individuals."[89] This stood in direct opposition to the historicist view that "a spiritual unfolding...gave meaning and coherence to individual phenomenal events and...was ever productive of novelty, of progress, in contrast to nature's cyclical repetition."[90] At stake here was

84. Michael J. Maclean, "German Historians and the Two Cultures," *Journal of the History of Ideas* 49 (1988): 473–94 (489).

85. Ibid., 474.

86. Ibid., 475.

87. Maclean (ibid., 475–76) mentions that while Auguste Comte was little known in Germany until the end of the century, solid scientific achievement in Germany, several notable scientific popularizers, and the work of Darwin served to elevate the popularity of science among the middle classes. For Compte's influence in Germany, see p. 475 n. 4.

88. Ibid., 478.

89. Holborn ("The History of Ideas," 686) notes that in the Hegelian scheme, even great men are "not the real initiators of progress but only the agents of the world mind."

90. Maclean, "German Historians," 479.

the belief of the historians in the evolution of the state through ethical forces, fueled by the human will, and steady progress measured in moral and religious growth rather than scientific advancement. To conceptualize the historical process as a function of "natural" forces beyond the reach of the will was in effect to eliminate the spiritual content of history. As disagreeable as the historians found this view of the process of history, it was the methodological challenge kindled by H. T. Buckle that provoked a response that further refined German historiography.[91]

a. *The Positivist Challenge*
Buckle's *History of Civilization in England*[92] presented the positivist emphasis on the "determined, lawful regularity of history" and the demand for a more scientific method, "one borrowed from the natural sciences."[93] The German historians remained convinced that the rigorous source criticism and canons of objectivity developed through the previous half century had placed the discipline on a thoroughly scientific base. Beginning from the definition of scientific as emphasizing empirical technique in the recovery of facts through the critical evaluation of sources, interpreted by an objective researcher, historians resisted the call to become "scientific" by discovering laws in history.[94] Droysen states:

> Efforts are not wanting to treat History according to the laws which have been ascertained for nature, or at least according to the method built up for the natural sciences, and to establish even for the historical world the doctrine that to refer vital phenomena to physical laws is nothing less than a new conquest for science.

He argues that:

> To our science as to every other belongs the duty and the right to investigate and settle the conceptions with which it has to do. If it were to borrow these from the results of other sciences, it would be obliged to accommodate and subordinate itself to modes of view over which it has no control, perhaps to those by which it sees its own independence and right to exist called in question. It would thence perhaps receive definitions of the word "science," to which it would be obliged to object.[95]

---

91. Ibid., 479.
92. H.T. Buckle, *History of Civilization in England* (London, 1857).
93. Maclean, "German Historians," 479–80.
94. Ibid., 480.
95. Johann Gustav Droysen, "Nature and History," in his *Outline of the Principles of History* (trans. Benjamin Andrews; Boston: Ginn & Co., 1893), 90–105 (90–91); trans. of *Grundriss der Historik* (Berlin, 1857–58). See also, in the same volume, Droysen's review, "The Elevation of History to the Rank of a Science. Being a Review of the History of Civilization in England, by H. T. Buckle," 61–89.

b. *Understanding and Explanation*
Droysen approached this early positivist challenge to historicism through
the argument that there exists a plurality of sciences with discrete objects
and distinctive goals, which require distinctive procedures or methods.
Maclean elaborates:

> History's moral realm of constant advance required for its recovery a
> method of empathetic interpretation or understanding (*Verstehen*), while
> nature with its cyclically repetitive (and hence lawful) behaviour could be
> unlocked through explanation (*Erklärung*). Both methods were scientific;
> both had their respective spheres of cognitive competence and as such
> need not compete with nor infringe upon the domain and prestige of the
> other.[96]

Maclean further argues that Droysen's hostility to positivism is founded
not on conceptual or methodological differences alone, but in particular
on its political consequences. He explains:

> By rooting the logic of historical development in inexorable laws rather
> than in human will, positivism for Droysen obscures the genuine norma-
> tive significance of historical study and thereby threatens the moderate
> liberal practice which is its proper political expression.[97]

Unlike Buckle, for whom historical progress is material and scientific
conquest, Droysen locates progress in the ethical struggle of the human
will toward freedom. He counters positivism for the sake of the great
historical imperatives, or Ideas, which were in his view expressed in "the
political goals of moderate German liberalism: political reform and
national unification."[98]

c. *The Ethical Role of the Historian*
Droysen's response to positivism was only part of his program of historical understanding (*Verstehen*). His political motivations are apparent
also in his well-known dispute with Ranke over methodology.[99] Ranke
stressed the neutrality and objectivity of the historian in the collection of
facts. Limiting the researcher to rigorous source criticism and disinterested interpretation of the historical material, the result then must be an

96. Maclean, "German Historians," 485.
97. Michael J. Maclean, "Johann Gustav Droysen and the Development of
Historical Hermeneutics," *History and Theory* 21 (1982): 347–65 (349).
98. Ibid., 350.
99. Hayden White observes that Droysen is known as "a critic of Rankean
objectivism, celebrator of Prussian power, and defender of political relativism as a
principle of historical writing" (Review of Peter Leyh's 1977 edition of Droysen's
Historik, *History and Theory* 19 [1980]: 73–93 [74]).

account "wie es eigentlich gewesen." Ranke taught his students scrupulously to avoid "Tendenzgeschichte." To Droysen, on the other hand, Ranke was simply a collector of facts, whereas the true task of the historian was to illuminate the "direction, goal, and plan" of history. To the extent that Rankean method dominated German historicism, the "pursuit of erudition" caused historians "to lose sight of their immediate duty to disseminate an awareness of Prussia's historical mission of unification within Germany and of a united Germany's historical mission of peace within Europe."[100] The Rankean method, like positivism, in Droysen's view, denied any ethical dimension to the work of the historian. The value of the historical discipline for Droysen is not only that it offers knowledge, but also moral improvement.[101]

With Humboldt and Ranke, Droysen believed that historical study cannot use the methods of science, for in nature there is only repetition, while in history there is purpose and meaning. Understanding (*Verstehen*) of the subject is the means of discovery in history

> The possibility of this understanding arises from the kinship of our nature with that of the utterances lying before us as historical material. This act results…as an immediate intuition wherein soul blends with soul, creatively, after the manner of conception in coition.[102]

For Droysen the particular individual moments of human will and action form the visible pattern of history. It is in this pattern that the significance of history lies. He argues that at any given moment the world consists of "a maze of affairs, circumstances, interests, and conflicts." These aspects of human life may be analyzed from various points of view, politics, technology, law, art, or religion.[103] The important point, however, is that history is not an agglomeration of these details. It is the grand design that must be perceived.

Progress, Droysen says, is the manifestation of ethical forces found in concrete social institutions such as the family, church, communities, and the state. The historian's task is to understand these forces as they operate in history. "To apprehend the moral world historically means to apprehend it according to its development and growth."[104] Morality exists always in the particular society and must, therefore, be historical, relative to its time and place. The state as the sum or aggregation of communities

100. Maclean, "Droysen," 354.
101. Ibid., 352.
102. Droysen, *Outline*, 12–14.
103. Ibid., 32.
104. Ibid., 33.

expresses their common interests or purpose.[105] Restrictions on the
power of the state are unnecessary because the state must pursue interests
which necessarily coincide with the interests of society. So optimistic, in
fact, was Droysen that state power was ultimately in harmony with this
purpose and thus the interests of its citizens, he opposed popular sover-
eignty and guarantees of individual rights. The will of the people, Droysen
thought, was not the tally of each individual will, but was expressed in
the interests of the state. A constitution was not valued as a defense of
the people against government, for there is no notion of the misuse of
power by the state.

In the first moment of the *Methodenstreit*—the confrontation between
the historians and the advocates of scientific method, the positivists—
Droysen offered a solution that preceded Dilthey in deploying historical
hermeneutics. Droysen articulated a theory that emphasized the historian's duty to illuminate the ethical forces at work in history. History
could neither be subsumed by philosophy nor forced into the methodological confines of science. He endeavored to establish "understanding"
as the fundamental principle of historical study in opposition to "explaining" from law-like hypotheses as in the natural sciences.[106] History must
remain free to elucidate the process of Ideas, in particular to teach the
historical mission of Germany in the development of liberty.

5. *The Ethical Nature of the State*

This view of the historical and ethical nature of the state ultimately produced the remarkable acquiescence of those associated with the Prussian
School to the policies of Bismarck. The liberal German historians may
be seen as surrendering their principles "to nationalist sentiment and
military power," abandoning their eager hope that Germany could be
united through agreement of all the German states. Iggers points out that
when Bismarck reformed the army in violation of the Prussian constitution in 1862, those associated with the *Preussische Jahrbücher* protested,
but by 1866, following the Prussian victories over Denmark and Austria,
all but Gervinus and Mommsen had come to terms with Bismarck.[107] The
explanation for this acquiescence lies in the distinctive German notion of
the importance of historical tendencies and their development, over and

105.   Ibid., 42.
106.   Horst Walter Blanke, Dirk Fleischer, and Jörn Rüsen, "Theory of History
in Historical Lectures: The German Tradition of Historik, 1750–1900," *History and
Theory* 23 (1984): 331–56 (343).
107.   Iggers, *German Conception*, 92.

above the importance of the individual, and the value of war as the means for testing the worth of states. While none of the liberal German historians was a Hegelian because of the fundamental conflict between generalizing philosophical systems, their understanding of the unique quality of particular historical events, and the role of human agency, still these liberal historians held a view of history as successive development. Believing that history is the ultimate tribunal, they could resign themselves to history as it unfolded.

6. *The Last of the Literary Historians*

Mommsen is considered by most to be a major figure of the German historical discipline. He was much admired by Wellhausen. His style was engaging and won for him a devoted readership. Like his liberal colleagues, Mommsen was a strong supporter of the efforts to found a united Germany governed by a constitutional monarchy. He served as a deputy for the National Liberals in the Prussian Chamber of Deputies from 1873 to 1879 and he represented the Liberal Succession in the Reichstag from 1881 to 1884. He was disgusted by the popular adulation of Bismarck and by the failure of the people to continue to press for popular democracy and, almost alone among historians, he persisted in thinking that liberal, democratic principles were necessary for success.[108] Conflicts between social classes, regions, or religion left unchecked, he believed, would stifle the possibilities which might be achieved by a unified government.[109] Mommsen devoted himself to this ideal of national unity, believing that it was the historian's duty to guide readers in their understanding of and attitude toward the State; in his words, historiography is "political education" in the "service of national-liberal propaganda."[110]

---

108.   Mommsen, in a public meeting at the Tempelhof in September 1881, attacked Bismarck for manipulating public opinion. Bismarck brought charges against him for defamation of character. In his own defense, Mommsen argued, "I made no personal attack, I discussed opinions and facts, I consider I have the right to oppose every system that seems to me contrary to the people's interests. He who represents one of these systems might think himself aimed at if he wished. I did not mean one person more than another. If Prince von Bismarck feels himself insulted, there are thousands of others who are with him." Mommsen was acquitted. See Antoine Guilland, *Modern Germany and Her Historians* (Westport, Conn.: Greenwood, 1970), 137; see also Alexander Demandt, introduction to Mommsen, *Rome*, 29.

109.   Mommsen (*Rome*, 300) speaks of Rome's expansionist policies "in the service of civilization," and again of Rome's "cultural–historical mission" (p. 314).

110.   Quoted by Demandt ("Introduction," 29).

Mommsen began his *History of Rome*, modeled on Thomas Macaulay's *History of England* (1840–61), after his suspension from his Chair in Leipzig. His work achieved a remarkable literary success and became a source of pride for Germany, which until then had not produced a historian with a gift for felicitous writing. He was rewarded with the Nobel Prize for Literature and was mentioned often as the greatest historian after Edward Gibbon.[111] Macaulay apparently influenced Mommsen's efforts to relate the history of the people as well as that of diplomatic and governmental history and most certainly encouraged his fierce opposition to slavery.[112] Wiedemann also cites F. C. Dahlmann's history of Denmark as a further influence on Mommsen to include social and economic conditions in his study of Rome.[113] On the other hand, according to Ines Stahlmann, Mommsen's primary focus on the legal perspectives in Roman history "stabilized the already predominating legalistic German approach to Roman history, which neglected the economic and social basis."[114]

7. *The Move to Specialization*

Mommsen added nothing remarkable to historical theory, but altered the discipline in two areas of methodology. During the course of Mommsen's life, in large part due to the projects he initiated as secretary of the Academy of Sciences, the greater level of specialization and the sheer quantity of new historical material, made the large general histories of the past almost impossible to write. Wiedemann says, "Mommsen's view of modern scholarship as highly co-ordinated team-work meant that his pupils were world experts in limited areas, but found it hard to synthesize."[115]

Mommsen was remarkable in turning his attention to the study of Rome and it was here that he made a significant advance in historical

---

111.   Wellhausen wrote to Mommsen (December 15, 1884): "The world may be less interested in Roman emperors than in Theodor Mommsen, and less in history than in your view of it." Quoted by Demandt ("Introduction," 30).

112.   Wiedemann, "Mommsen, Rome and the *Kaiserreich*," 44. See also idem, "Mommsen's Roman History": "That condemnation of slavery was so unusual amongst German historians that Mommsen's successor Eduard Meyer said in a speech to German industrialists in Dresden in 1898 that is was 'unverständlich,' about as far as one German Ordinarius could go in suggesting that a colleague was mad."

113.   Ibid.

114.   Ines Stahlmann, "Theodor Mommsen," in *Great Historians of the Modern Age* (ed. Lucian Boia; New York: Greenwood, 1991), 299–301.

115.   Wiedemann, "Mommsen, Rome and the *Kaiserreich*," 47.

method.[116] His dissertation was on Roman law and he fully intended to practice law at home in Schleswig-Holstein. The political situation did not allow him to pursue this plan and instead he traveled to Italy to undertake a special project locating unpublished Latin inscriptions. This began his life's work—the collection of all existing Latin inscriptions from every part of what had been the Roman Empire. Through comparative linguistics, numismatics, and epigraphy, Mommsen created a body of material which had the status of archival evidence and could serve as a control on the narratives of historical writers.[117] The linguistic evidence, Mommsen felt, would provide evidence for the social structure of prehistoric Italy. Mommsen's use of religious festivals as "eine Urkunde"[118] or as *a document* for writing Roman history and his statement that comparative philology can produce evidence "wie in einem Archiv"[119] suggest a new angle of vision for writing history. Mommsen belongs to the generation of Wellhausen's near contemporaries and his addition of linguistics, epigraphy, and investigation of social practices to the repertoire of the historian marks the final stage in the development of the principles of historicism as they may affect Wellhausen's approach to history.

8. *Conclusion*

In conclusion, it is appropriate to say that history writing was transformed in nineteenth-century Germany. Leaving behind Enlightenment patterns of thought grounded in causal explanations and classical Christian doctrines of Natural Law that insisted on the static and universal claims of human nature and ethics, German thinkers and scholars forged a new view of history. Historicism developed from three basic perceptions: that humans are formed in their society; that humans can study societies, past and present, because they can know what other humans have made; and that the generalizing methods of both science and philosophy are inappropriate to the investigation of human phenomena.

116.   In Humboldt's educational program, Greece was at the center, providing a common subject of study for the various diverse regional and local groups. This focus avoided the persistent political questions of the time and could equally inspire Catholics and Protestants, aristocrats and industrialists. Greece also was not Rome with its connections to the Holy Roman Empire, which Prussia sought to supplant in popular loyalty. Because of this emphasis on Greece, Wiedemann ("Mommsen, Rome and the *Kaiserreich*," 37) holds that Mommsen's interest in Rome "was exceptional (if not unique) amongst nineteenth-century German scholars of antiquity."

117.   Wiedemann, "Mommsen, Rome and the *Kaiserreich*," 43.

118.   Mommsen, *Rome*, 161.

119.   Ibid., 14.

With the insight that humans are the products of a particular cultural situation occurs the notion that every culture is a unique composition of elements, including its religion, custom, law, and art. It follows, then, that the aesthetic or moral standards of one culture would be incompatible with another and so judgments made by one culture of another would be invalid.

Humans can know what is made by human beings as they can never know objects of study in the natural world, of which they can only make observations and calculations. The artifacts of any culture, being as they are produced by human beings and representing unique aspects of that culture, provide a "text" to be read by the investigator. Because each culture is unique, however, interpreting the data is subject to distortion introduced by the interpreter, who has a culture, a religion, a point of view of his or her own. This can be overcome only by the most serious efforts at objectivity and empathy born of in-depth encounter with the culture in question. Imagination and intuition are necessary qualities for the historian in contrast with the difficulties that arise later in regard to subjectivity.

The methods of natural science and of philosophy seek to abstract general conclusions from their data, and to formulate laws or systems by means of logic and reason. Because human activity is unique, irrational, and unrepeatable these methods force historical events into artificial schemes and exclude the vital, dynamic quality of history. The methods of history must instead highlight the singular aspect of events and the activity of the human will in producing unique patterns of events. Reason cannot organize history because history is fashioned by human agency controlled by the irrational—by such passions as desire, greed, nobility, patriotism. The historian must seek to understand the connections among the characters, events, and forces of history. These connections or "ideas" are seldom transparent, consisting instead in the inner nature of individualities, either persons or states. Individualities develop according to their inner necessities and, while this in no way dictates meaningful progress in history, still there exists a divine harmony among all the various historical entities.

These insights have the consequence of promoting extreme ethical relativism and a remarkable insularity in which institutions and world-views are thought to be supremely suited to a particular society and may not be introduced into another for fear of disrupting the proper evolution of that society. Thus, French literature is splendid for the French, German literature for the Germans, while both enrich world literature, but they should not serve as models for one another's writers. Historicism offers no means by which to criticize or judge the state or other cultures, for the development of each unfolds as its interests direct and this is by definition good. The state as an individuality may be thought of as an organism, consisting of many aspects and social functions, all necessary parts of the larger whole, which has a distinct life cycle, marked by stages of birth, maturity, and finally death. This metaphor is not original to German historicism, but has come to be seen as an integral part of its approach. It expresses the notion of the development of individualities and reflects the idea that cultures are interactive webs of social functions and traditions. Finally, implicit in the historicist approach is the notion that because of the irrationality of human behavior, it is only through the study of history that knowledge about humanity can be established. This study now takes up Julius Wellhausen's historical work and his place in the German historical tradition.

Chapter 3

JULIUS WELLHAUSEN AND THE *PROLEGOMENA TO THE HISTORY OF ISRAEL*

It was not until the final quarter of the nineteenth century that a critical history of Israel appeared, though studies of Greece and Rome, following rigorous historiographic principles, had found their way into print early in the century. Through these intervening decades Old Testament researchers, using work of even earlier generations, posited several possibilities for the division of sources in the Pentateuch. Arguments for these sources and their sequences were founded on the apprehension of stylistic and apologetical features in different strands of the Pentateuchal writings. Acceptance of the notion of multiple, anonymous writers working over several centuries did not come easily, and some scholars in biblical studies found their careers cut short or advancement curtailed, but by mid-century, tolerance in the theological faculties was growing. Thus, at Greifswald in 1878, Julius Wellhausen published his *Geschichte Israels.*[1] This remarkable work presented the hypothesis dividing the Pentateuch into four sources and establishing their relative dates. Wellhausen synthesized the previous scholarship and adduced new and persuasive arguments to form a masterful statement, which today, a hundred and twenty-five years later, still provides an initial approach to sources in the Pentateuch.

Critics attacked Wellhausen immediately on religious grounds. Particularly outside Germany his name was synonymous with the notion that biblical criticism was inevitably destructive of faith. Not long after his thesis was accepted within the academic world, newer scholarship dismissed Wellhausen for his apparent disinterest in the pre-history of the written sources. Biblical scholarship turned to topics related to oral tradition and its transmission. By the mid-1970s, scholars had challenged all

1. The second edition, published in 1883, and all later editions, carry the title *Prolegomena zur Geschichte Israels.*

reconstructions of Israel's history not based on evidence supported by extra-biblical references. Through the various trends in research down to the present time, scholars have proposed numerous modifications and adjustments to Wellhausen's hypothesis, but respected texts still present his basic division of the sources.

John Barton suggests that it is not Wellhausen's role as a Pentateuchal critic that commends him to us today, however, for while he "did indeed set the agenda for several generations…the modern agenda in Penta-teuchal studies owes little to him." Rather, it is in the history of Israel where "the greatness and continuing influence of Wellhausen appear very clearly."[2] In particular the implications of the exile, in regard to religion, institutions, community life, temperament, and identity, are assumed in biblical studies today.

I will argue that Wellhausen's historical approach to the biblical text declares his identification with historicism's premise that human under-standing is derived from history. It is not a theological interpretation that Wellhausen undertakes, but a reconstruction of Israel's past. The German historiographical tradition's emphasis on understanding the past as it occurred guides his research. His attention to hints of national unity present among the ancient tribes and to Israel's presentation of its devel-opment further signals his position within the German historiographic tradition. Following this tradition, he strives for a "presuppositionless" stance toward the material, allowing the text to direct his conclusions. Characteristics of the tradition are clear in his understanding that the expressions of a culture, whether law, custom, or belief, are related to one another and to a moment in time and that any change in situation—social, economic, or geographical—forces shifts in all aspects of culture. Wellhausen is particularly sensitive to textual clues regarding time and location in both the narrative and in the language. I will also argue that his work was addressed primarily to the academic community and those of the highly educated middle class, but through his fellows and par-ticularly through his students his reconstruction of the history of Israel reached a broader audience. This fact ultimately placed him in an unten-able position. Rather than compromise his research or to foster conflict within his students, he gave up biblical studies. The influence of the intended audience and the actual audience is a recurring issue for his-torians up to the present time.

2. John Barton, "Wellhausen's Prolegomena," in *Text and Experience* (ed. Daniel Smith-Christopher; The Biblical Seminar 35; Sheffield: Sheffield Academic Press, 1995), 316–29 (328).

1. *Wellhausen the Man*

Wellhausen was most often described with words such as frank, friendly, cordial, hospitable, and good-humored.[3] His independence was remarked by many. He was apparently strong and vigorous. His appearance was that of a farmer and Douglas A. Knight suggests that, indeed, his rural background "gave him a feel for nature and the immediacy of life, affording him perspectives on antiquity that might not have occurred to one reared in a modern city."[4] Rudolf Smend also says:

> Free and natural as he was he had a strong feeling for similar traits in the Israelites as portrayed in the early tradition…much in this tradition and its concerns was congenial to him. Its immediacy, its freshness, its straight-forwardness, its poetry claimed him as in some way kindred…[5]

We begin with this description of the characteristics which strongly impressed those who encountered Wellhausen because they reveal something of his approach to the world, to work, to companionship, and to the object of study. His boldness and openness were frequently commented on by contemporaries and, along with his sense of "the immediacy of life," formed the backdrop for his scholarship.

2. *Wellhausen the Historian*

Wellhausen was born in Hamelin in 1844. His father was a Lutheran minister, who supported the conservative position of the confessional high church movement. This movement vigorously opposed theological liberalism in the church and in the academy.[6] Rejecting his conservative views, Wellhausen, nevertheless, followed his father into the study of theology. He began his training at Göttingen in 1862. Initially he was taken with the new German studies which were an outgrowth of the research and influence of the Grimm brothers.[7] In this same vein,

---

3. Rudolf Smend quotes reports of visitors to Wellhausen's home in his "Wellhausen and *Prolegomena to the History of Israel*," *Semeia* 25 (1983): 1–20 (2–3).
4. Douglas A. Knight, foreword to Wellhausen, *Prolegomena*, v.
5. Smend, "Wellhausen," 13–14.
6. Ibid., 5. On the confessional church and its opposition to liberal scholarship, see John Rogerson, *Old Testament Criticism in the Nineteenth Century* (London: SPCK, 1984).
7. R. E. Clements, "The Study of the Old Testament," in *Nineteenth Century Religious Thought in the West*, vol. 3 (ed. Ninian Smart et al.; Cambridge: Cambridge University Press, 1985), 109–41 (128).

Wellhausen was attracted to the hymns of the church and the narratives of the Old Testament, finding them, nonetheless, insufficient for theology. It was Heinrich Ewald's *History of the People of Israel*[8] that provided the spark which turned his attention to the study of Hebrew, Arabic, and Syriac and broadly to the exegesis of the Old Testament. He later separated from Ewald over political differences stemming from the incorporation of Hannover into Prussia in 1866 on the eve of German unification,[9] but continued his interest in the problems of the history of Israel.

In 1868 he began his academic career as a *"Repetent"* in the theological faculty at Göttingen, becoming a *"Privatedozent"* two years later. Having just published *Der Text der Bücher Samuelis untersucht*,[10] he took up a professorship in 1872 at Greifswald. During his ten years at Greifswald, Wellhausen completed his "revolutionary" work in Old Testament, studies on the Pharisees and Sadducees,[11] on the composition of the Hexateuch,[12] and most importantly his history of Israel and his article on Israel for the ninth edition of the *Encyclopedia Britannica*.[13] Toward the end of his time at Göttingen, he became convinced that he was "not adequate" to the "practical task of preparing the students for service in the Protestant Church," "despite all caution" making his "hearers unfit for their office." He chose instead to resign, on finding that his interest in the "scientific treatment of the Bible" was incompatible with his responsibility to his students.[14]

Wellhausen moved to Halle as *Ausserordentlicher Professor* in Semitic languages in the philosophy faculty, continuing there from 1882 until 1885. He spent the years to 1892 at Marburg, settling then in Göttingen for the remaining years of his life. Kurt Rudolph, reviewing Wellhausen's

8. Heinrich Ewald, *The History of Israel* (trans. Russell Martineau; London: Longmans, Green & Co., 1871–76).

9. Smend, "Wellhausen," 5–6.

10. Julius Wellhausen, *Der Text der Bücher Samuelis untersucht* (Göttingen: Vandenhoeck & Ruprecht, 1871).

11. Julius Wellhausen, *Die Pharisäer und die Sadducäer: Eine Untersuchung zur inneren jüdischen Geschichte* (Greifswald: Bamberg, 1874).

12. Julius Wellhausen, "Die Composition des Hexateuchs," *Jahrbuch für deutsche Theologie* 21 (1876): 392–450, 531–602; 22 (1877): 407–79. Also published as *Die Composition des Hexateuch und der historischen Bücher des Alten Testaments* (3d ed.; Berlin: Georg Reimer, 1899).

13. Julius Wellhausen, "Israel," in *Encyclopedia Britannica* (9th ed., 1881), 13:396–431.

14. See Wellhausen's letter to the Prussian Minister of Culture, April 5, 1882, in Alfred Jepsen, "Wellhausen in Greifswald," in his *Der Herr ist Gott* (Berlin: Evang. Verlagsanstalt, 1978), 254–70 (266–67).

career as an Orientalist, like Barton, describes him as a historian. He points out that Wellhausen's historical, source-critical, and philological method in Arabic studies were quite similar to his approach to the history of Israel.[15] Again, in commenting on Wellhausen's New Testament studies, Nils Dahl notes that "Wellhausen stood in the tradition of the great nineteenth century historians."[16] R. E. Clements comments that "Wellhausen was first and foremost a historian, well worthy of comparison with the giant figures of the *Historismus* movement in L. Von Ranke, T. Mommsen and the earlier B. G. Niebuhr."[17] He continues, "The areas studied by Wellhausen show fully enough his claim to be judged as a historian, rather than as a theologian or biblical critic, and the way in which he endeavoured to use the new critical approach to history as a means of illuminating the problems of religious origins."[18] John Rogerson concurs: "Kuenen and Wellhausen were historians and not theologians. Their concern was to advance the truth, all the more so if they were opposed by theological interests that regarded the truth as a threat to traditional orthodoxy."[19] Certainly Wellhausen was a master of philology and literary criticism and was keenly attuned to theological interests, yet his studies in these disciplines served as the basis for his historical reconstructions. He is the pre-eminent historian of ancient Israel in the nineteenth century and it is as a historian that his assumptions and his methods must be investigated.

3. *Influences and Assumptions*

The thoughts of three biblical scholars initiate this study of Wellhausen's work in relation to German historiography as it was presented in the previous chapter. John Rogerson has written extensively on nineteenth-century biblical scholarship, with special attention to Germany and England. Robert Oden has written two significant articles on the German tradition. R. E. Clements' article on the transformation of Old Testament study includes insights on the debt of biblical criticism to Romanticism and historicism.

15. Kurt Rudolph, "Wellhausen as an Arabist," *Semeia* 25 (1983): 111–55 (111).
16. Nils Dahl, "Wellhausen on the New Testament," *Semeia* 25 (1983): 89–110 (106).
17. Clements, "The Study," 128.
18. Ibid., 130.
19. John Rogerson, "W. R. Smith's Old Testament in the Jewish Church," in *William Robertson Smith: Essays in Reassessment* (ed. William Johnstone; JSOTSup 201; Sheffield: Sheffield Academic Press, 1995), 132–47 (144).

a. *Empiricism and Idealism*

Rogerson begins his article on the rise of biblical criticism in Germany and England by quoting a passage in which Wellhausen claims that "philosophy does not precede, but follows [biblical criticism], in that it seeks to evaluate and systematise that which it has not itself discovered."[20] This argument that biblical criticism is philosophically neutral, Rogerson suggests, is reasonable enough when one considers the application of technical procedures of criticism to the text. For example, the conclusion, based on the alternation of the divine names and other criteria, that the flood narrative (Gen 6–9) is a composite of two earlier versions does not depend directly on philosophy or theoretical assumptions. Rogerson argues, however, that rather than guiding the outcome of research, it is the very "possibility and character" of biblical criticism that is affected by the prevailing philosophical climate.[21] He makes his case based on the differing philosophical views prominent in England and Germany in the years between 1770 and 1840. In England, according to Rogerson's argument, knowledge was regarded as something which came from outside of human beings, sense perceptions of the external world impressing themselves on the perceiving subject. Heavily influenced by Locke, the philosophical climate in England "distrusted theories about innate ideas from which, for example, the existence of God could be deduced."[22] By contrast, he offers a characterization of the climate in protestant Germany as seeking "knowledge and truth not only in what comes from outside of the perceiving subject, but especially in what is within."[23] As the previous chapter has demonstrated, the realization of ideas and the unfolding of individualities were controlling notions in historical practice and cultural consciousness. In this view, the Bible is the record of God's self-disclosure, but the evidence of revelation is to be found in the human spirit.

This German perspective on the source of knowledge promoted the study of the Bible as a historical text, for if the truth of religion was found in personal experience, then it was not dependent on the verbal inspiration of the books of the Bible. The knowledge of God as an inner conviction freed the study of the Bible from the task of supporting orthodox theological positions. The Bible contained the Word of God, certainly, but also material not necessarily pertinent to the Christian

20. John Rogerson, "Philosophy and the Rise of Biblical Criticism: England and Germany," in *England and Germany: Studies in Theological Diplomacy* (ed. S. W. Sykes; Frankfurt: Lang, 1982), 63–79 (63).
21. Ibid., 64.
22. Ibid., 65.
23. Ibid., 68.

believer. The historical investigation of the Bible endorsed historical study of theology and the church, all made possible by the understanding of religious truth as an inward phenomenon.[24] The value of the Bible is found not in the teaching of truths about the external world, but in its "commentaries on what we know to be true of human existence from reflections upon our status as redeemed persons."[25]

b. *Historicism*
To Rogerson's description of the German philosophical climate and its impact on biblical criticism, Robert Oden adds the tradition of German historicism, which he argues constitutes the very basis of biblical criticism for the past two centuries.[26] Oden states that hermeneutical issues were defined for biblical scholarship by the German tradition of historical understanding and that, furthermore, biblical scholarship has a much greater theoretical component than has been recognized.[27] He introduces his argument with a quotation from classical historian, M. I. Finley:

> Historians, one hears all the time, should get on with their proper business, the investigation of the concrete experiences of the past, and leave the "philosophy of history" (which is a barren, abstract and pretty useless activity anyway) to the philosophers. Unfortunately the historian is no mere chronicler, and he cannot do his work at all without assumptions and judgments.[28]

Oden, like Rogerson, seeks to put to rest the notion that history can be done from a position untouched by a philosophical or theoretical view. He notes that the historical-critical method of biblical study was for so long the standard approach as to make its practitioners forget that the approach "itself has had a history."[29]

To begin his description of German historicism, Oden singles out the notion of the changing and unrepeatable nature of human experience and

24. Ibid., 69.
25. Ibid., 73.
26. Oden quotes Maurice Mandelbaum, "because it is now deeply entrenched in our thoughts, it is easy to forget that the tendency to view all matters in terms of their histories may itself have had a history" (Robert Oden, "Intellectual History and the Study of the Bible," in *The Future of Biblical Studies, The Hebrew Scriptures* [ed. Richard Elliott Friedman and H. G. M. Williamson; Atlanta: Scholars Press, 1987], 1–18 [3]).
27. Robert Oden, "Hermeneutics and Historiography: Germany and America," in *SBL Seminar Papers, 1980* (SBLSP 19; ed. Paul Achtemeier; Atlanta: Scholars Press, 1980), 135–57 (137).
28. M. I. Finley, *The Use and Abuse of History* (New York: Viking, 1975), 61.
29. Oden, "Hermeneutics," 135.

the fact that, in consequence of this nature, the generalizing methods of scientific inquiry are inappropriate for the study of history. The historian should approach the material of history without abstract concepts into which to fit events. He or she must confront these concrete events and allow them to speak for themselves. Through immersion in the historical data, the creative intuition is able to "reconstruct properly the flow of history."[30] To this view of the nature of history and the proper approach of the historian, Oden joins the assumption that the life of the nation parallels that of a human organism and holds within itself a pattern of development unique and valuable. This entails that every culture, every historical period, must be judged by standards specific to itself and that any element of a culture must be understood in terms of its place within that culture. Oden concludes his remarks on the development of the German historiographic tradition with the observation that it is not the well-known empiricism, but Idealism that most strikingly marks this tradition.[31]

c. *Romanticism, Culture, and Nation*
R. E. Clements points to two other aspects of historicism important for biblical studies. In tracing the development of an awareness of the antiquity of the Bible, he notes the growing understanding that the literal sense of the text could be found only through historical criticism. The literary study which followed from this insight was heavily influenced by the thought of Herder and his friend J. G. Eichhorn. They "attached a profound importance to mythology as the natural language and form of intellectual expression which belongs to the childhood of the human race."[32] The biblical texts were increasingly treated as "human writings, full of spiritual insight, rather than as collections of texts to be used as theological proofs."[33] The Old Testament yields insights into the ideas and experiences which formed the religious life of its authors. Reading and reflection on the text itself does not uncover divine revelation, but through study of "the events and ideas which formed its subject-matter" one can find the course of history through which "God had chosen to reveal himself to his ancient people."[34] The second element of historicism important for biblical studies mentioned by Clements is the link between nation and tradition. This connection provided "the new

30. Ibid., 138.
31. Ibid., 141.
32. Clements, "The Study," 111.
33. Ibid., 122.
34. Ibid., 121–22.

scientific approach to the history of Israel" with its basic Christian interpretative standpoint. It further "allowed many of the Romantic and
Hegelian concepts of national history to intrude themselves into biblical
scholarship."[35] The history of Christianity, its religious origins, "the
situations and interests which had prompted [the Bible's] authors to
write, and the needs and problems with which they had sought to deal...
what it meant to read the Old Testament...as an oriental living in a
remote antiquity, all had to be pursued."[36] Clements claims that with
Ewald's publication of his history of Israel, history writing became "an
accepted part of the modern critical approach to the Bible... It marked
the deep intrusion into the sphere of Old Testament studies of the outlook of *Historismus*..."[37]

d. *The "Total View"*
A third characteristic of nineteenth-century historiography, particularly
in Germany, and indeed scholarship in all fields at the time, as Barton
notes, was its attraction to "total views," "vast systems, and far-reaching
syntheses."[38] It was Wellhausen's grasp of the significance of the dating
of the Priestly Source (P) that allowed him to develop a larger vision, the
"total view" in Smend's words.[39]

Scholars prior to Wellhausen had suggested later dates for P, but
Wellhausen alone saw the effect of this on the understanding of Israel's
history. In his Introduction, Wellhausen traces the history of scholarship
regarding the sources of the Pentateuch from mention in Peyrerius,
Spinoza, and Astruc to the insights of de Wette through his own contemporaries. He points out the contributions of each successive attempt to
sort out the content of the sources and their chronology relative to one
another. Wellhausen outlines the accepted division of the non-Deuter-
onomic Hexateuch into the so-called *Grundschrift* or main stock, and the
work of the Jehovist (J) (our Yahwist), noting Hermann Hupfeld's
demonstration of the presence of the Elohist (E). His attention is fixed,
however, on the material which we now designate the Priestly Code,
presenting itself as an account of the Mosaic period, imitating its
"costume" while "disguising its own."[40] He commends the scholarly
instinct which fostered research into the separation of the sources, but

35. Ibid., 126.
36. Ibid., 112.
37. Ibid., 124.
38. Barton, "Wellhausen's Prolegomena," 322.
39. Smend, "Wellhausen," 13.
40. Wellhausen, "Introduction," in his *Prolegomena*, 9.

argued that the "great historical question" had not been answered, only "put to sleep."[41] Wellhausen says in reflecting on Old Testament scholarship:

> Critical analysis [had] made steady progress, but the work of synthesis did not hold even pace with it… It was not seen that most important historical questions were involved as well as questions merely literary, and that to assign the true order of the different strata of the Pentateuch was equivalent to a reconstruction of the history of Israel.[42]

It is his summation, his intuition that the entire understanding of the Old Testament is fundamentally altered, that gives his work the claim to a "total view." Wellhausen as a historian and a biblical scholar is heir and practitioner of the German historiographic tradition. To what degree, and in what specifics, this study now undertakes to illustrate.

4. *Persistent Criticisms*

a. *Wellhausen and Hegel*
Three particular attacks are made against Wellhausen in regard to his presuppositions. The first contends that he was a Hegelian and it is this philosophy that informs his division of Israel's religious development, and thus its history, into three successive stages. Indeed, Wellhausen, as is well known, finds the earliest expression of religious life spontaneous and intimately connected to ordinary life. Successive phases are increasingly legalistic. Sacrifice, which had formerly consisted in a communal meal, in later times had become, in Wellhausen's view, nothing more than a symbol of worship. His famous statement in part contends that "the soul is fled; the shell remained…technique was the main thing, and strict fidelity to rubric."[43] That he finds three distinctive stages of religious development related to the three main sources in the Pentateuch is undeniable. The question of the influence of Hegel in this presentation, however, can be answered strongly in the negative.

The charge of Hegelianism first appeared in the 1920s in a book by Martin Kegel, in which he endeavors to refute Wellhausen point by point. Kegel argues that the theme of "development" undergirds Wellhausen's reconstruction of Israel's history: "one traces in this history construction, as before affirmed, the spirit of Hegel, and only of

41. Ibid., 10.
42. Julius Wellhausen, "Pentateuch and Joshua," in *Encyclopedia Britannica* (9th ed.; New York: Charles Scribner's Sons, 1885), 18:505–14 (508).
43. Wellhausen, *Prolegomena*, 78.

Hegel..."[44] That this influence of Hegel on Wellhausen "in a most pronounced measure depends on Vatke is known to every one familiar with the literature of Old Testament science..." Kegel claims, for "Hegel begat Vatke, Vatke begat Wellhausen..."[45] The connection to which Kegel alludes here concerns the late dating of P, the position Vatke took fifty years before Wellhausen. Wellhausen says of Vatke in his Introduction to the *Prolegomena*, "My inquiry proceeds on a broader basis than that of Graf, and comes nearer to that of Vatke, from whom indeed I gratefully acknowledge myself to have learnt best and most."[46] Apparently, Wellhausen has in mind Vatke's particular insight on the P source, for John Barton observes, "It was [Vatke's] misfortune, as Wellhausen saw it, to have linked a perfectly correct perception of the lateness of P to an impossibly outmoded philosophical framework, that of Hegel."[47] Because of Vatke's attachment to Hegel, his history of Israel attracted little scholarly attention. Lothar Perlitt argues that Hegelianism was scarcely an intellectual option in the 1870s; in fact, it was distinctly out of fashion by the time of Wellhausen's birth in 1844.[48] This refers to the ascendancy of Realism in German philosophical circles at mid-century and to the unyielding position among historians that the imposition of any philosophical system on the events of history must be rejected.

Barton comments that Wellhausen himself most effectively refutes the charge that he is a Hegelian when he discusses the well-known pattern of history presented in the book of Judges. Wellhausen says:

> one is reminded of the "thesis," "antithesis," and "synthesis" of the Hegelian philosophy when one's ear has once been caught by the monotonous beat with which the history here advances, or rather moves in a circle. Rebellion, affliction, conversion, peace; rebellion, affliction, conversion, peace.[49]

Barton remarks, "No-one who would *criticise* the biblical text by drawing this comparison could seriously be a Hegelian."[50] It has been noted

44. Martin Kegel, *Away from Wellhausen* (ed. Horace m. Du Bose; The Aftermath Series; Nashville: Publishing House of the M. E. Church, South, 1924), 294; trans. of *Los von Wellhausen!* (Gütersloh: n.p., 1923).

45. Kegel, *Away*, 285–86.

46. Wellhausen, *Prolegomena*, 13.

47. Barton, "Wellhausen's Prolegomena," 320.

48. Lothar Perlitt, *Vatke and Wellhausen: Geschichtsphilosophische Voraussetzungen und historiographische Motive für die Darstellung der Religion und Geschichte Israels durch Wilhelm Vatke und Julius Wellhausen* (BZAW 94; Berlin: Töpelmann, 1965).

49. Wellhausen, *Prolegomena*, 231.

50. Barton, "Wellhausen's Prolegomena," 320.

that one of historicism's most emphatic claims is that the abstract systems of philosophy must not be imposed on history. Wellhausen seems
to make the historicist argument here that even the Bible has forced
history into an unnatural pattern. Wellhausen's own view that Hegelian
philosophy was an unfortunate accessory to Vatke's articulation of the
dating of P and his disparaging comment on the repetitious cycle of the
Deuteronomist's (D) history demonstrate his own distance from Hegel.

John Rogerson approaches the issue from a different direction and
provides perhaps the most sensible assessment of Wellhausen's position
in regard to Hegel. Rogerson argues that Wellhausen must be viewed in
relation to the biblical scholars whose studies provided the basis for his
own work. He says that Wellhausen's work, through the *Prolegomena* in
1883, and including his prior articles on the composition of the Hexateuch, is important because his argument is based in literary criticism.
This approach and his accomplishments in reasserting a documentary
hypothesis and establishing the order of composition J, E, D, P are firmly
"within the stream" of German biblical scholarship of the nineteenth
century.[51] Wellhausen is the heir of more than a hundred years of discussion on the sources in the Old Testament. He follows a long list of
scholars in making claims for the source documents on the basis of
grammar, style, tendency, and content. Rogerson stresses the importance
of Wellhausen's studies on the composition of the Hexateuch: "It was the
literary-critical results that were presented there that were the foundation
of Wellhausen's position..."[52] This literary-critical approach was empirical in the Rankian tradition of German scholarship, which stressed assem-
bling evidence and proposing hypotheses. Wellhausen certainly was not
making "a Hegelian attempt to use history in order to demonstrate a
philosophical thesis."[53] Smend concludes the issue by observing that
"Wellhausen stood at as great a remove from Hegelian speculation as a
German historian of the nineteenth century could without falling out of
context."[54] This statement recalls points previously made regarding the
Idealist position of German historicism as distinguished from Hegelianism.[55]

b. *Wellhausen and Darwin*
A second charge brought against Wellhausen is that he portrayed the
religion of Israel in terms of evolution. Frank Delitzsch remarked that

51. Rogerson, *Old Testament*, 266.
52. Ibid.
53. Ibid., 106.
54. Smend, "Wellhausen," 14.
55. See Chapter 2, 32–33, 36–37, 40–41.

"Wellhausen's speculations" were "merely applications of Darwinism to the sphere of theology and criticism."[56] Wellhausen tells us the notion that the Priestly Code introduces cultic legislation into the record of an earlier period was attacked by critics as "Darwinian" for suggesting an evolution of the cult, not fully developed in Moses' time.[57] John Barton points to a continuing tradition in both English and American theology which argues that the sources J, E, D, and P represent an orderly progression of religious thought, a developing understanding of God, moving from an earthy, anthropomorphic concept to an increasing sense of the transcendence of the deity.[58] On this view the later P source is an advancement from the earlier sources. Heinrich Ewald's history also embodies this view. Thirty years before Wellhausen he says, "The history of this ancient people is in reality the history of the growth of true religion, rising through all stages to perfection..."[59] Barton argues that Wellhausen, to the contrary, believes that Israel's religion deteriorates over the course of its history. From the immediate communion with God that an individual can initiate with a simple sacrificial meal to the bare legalism that Wellhausen finds in the later religion where worship is practiced only in the confines of the temple by priests, he sees symbol and ritual substituted for the true spirit of religion. This development of Israel's religion is a distinct decline in the mind of Wellhausen. Rather than applying any Darwinian model of evolution which would illustrate progressive refinement of religious sensibilities, Wellhausen reaches the opposite conclusion.

On the other hand, however, it is certain that Wellhausen both organized his history into periods and stages and at the same time wrote with an eye to the larger whole. In this respect he reflected the thinking of his time.[60] The German historiographic tradition established and promulgated by Humboldt, Ranke, and Droysen emphasized the use of organic analogies in the presentation of history. The application of these analogies is based in the confidence that "entire societies and separate eras within these societies have distinct 'lives' and 'deaths,'" that they truly

---

56. Smend cites Delitzsch's remark to a Scottish visitor to Leipzig in 1882, in "Julius Wellhausen," 14, found in W. R. Smith, "Wellhausen and his Position," *The Christian Church* 2 (1882): 366–69.

57. Wellhausen, *Prolegomena*, 366.

58. Barton, "Wellhausen's Prolegomena," 321.

59. Ewald, *The History of Israel*, 5.

60. P. D. Miller describes Wellhausen's desire to schematize history: "He was in that respect a child of his times, seeing in the historical process stages in a development..." ("Wellhausen and Israel's Religion," *Semeia* 25 [1983]: 63).

conform to the social patterns of living organisms.[61] This historiographic tradition furthermore approached the study of human phenomena in the light of their origins and their development. Here, the background for Wellhausen's stages of Israel's religion is clear. Neither from Hegel, nor from Darwin, but from the tradition established by the great German historians did Wellhausen absorb his almost instinctive approach to history through stages and their development.

c. *Anti-Semitism*
A more serious accusation than those directed toward Wellhausen's periodization of history and the possibility that Hegel or Darwin formed his presuppositions, is that there are instances of anti-Semitism in his work. It is not difficult to find passages in his work which offend modern sensibilities. From the famous assessment of Israel's later religion, "The warm pulse of life no longer throbbed in it to animate it,"[62] to his comment on the Jewish attitude toward history

> It is not the case that the Jews had any profound respect for their ancient history... The theocratic ideal was from the exile onwards the centre of all thought and effort, and it annihilated the sense for objective truth, all regard and interest for the actual facts as they had been handed down. It is well known that there have never been more audacious inventors of history than the rabbins. But Chronicles afford evidence that this evil propensity goes back to a very early time, its root the dominating influence of the Law, being the root of Judaism itself...[63]

his attitude to Judaism appears unwaveringly negative.

(1) *Judgment of the Past.* Two areas of response can be offered. First, as we have seen, one of the central philosophical questions of history writing is whether or not the sentiments of the present should be the basis for judgment on the past. It is possible, if one believes that the present represents an advance in moral or ethical discernment, to conclude that Wellhausen was most certainly anti-Semitic and cannot be read with benefit by anyone living after World War II. Or one may acknowledge that nineteenth-century views are not the views of the present, that Wellhausen was formed in the culture of his time, and one must simply elect to pass over the offending passages and concentrate on the more useful or edifying sections of Wellhausen's work. The first response includes the views

61. Oden, "Intellectual History," 2.
62. Wellhausen, *Prolegomena*, 78.
63. Ibid., 161.

of Solomon Schechter in his address entitled "Higher Criticism—Higher Anti-Semitism," given in 1903.[64] In this address, Schechter argues that German scholarship in general was anti-Jewish in tone through its ignorance of Jewish religion, its criticism of Jewish historical claims, and its use of the Old Testament for its own theological purposes. In addition, Schechter finds Wellhausen's acceptance of an award from the German government sufficient proof of his particular anti-Semitic views. Lou Silberman disagrees with Schechter on the strength of the testimony of his own teacher Jacob Z. Lauterbach, who studied with Wellhausen, saying "Wellhausen was no vulgar anti-Semite." He goes on, however, to hold German Protestantism, including Wellhausen, accountable for the culture which acquiesced to National Socialism. He suggests that "practically everything written by German Protestant theologians of the period and many subsequently and to this day, is a work of anti-Judaism."[65] He bases this thesis on Luther's propagation of Paul's distinction between law and grace, characterized in the statement in Rom 5:20, "The law sidled in." This negative, not to say polemical, position toward law and what was seen, in both Judaism and Catholicism, as excessive legalism, became a tenet of Protestantism. Silberman argues that this posture "made it unnecessary for liberal Protestant thought in Germany to reassess any traditional judgment of Judaism," and intimates that this allowed anti-Semitism to grow unchecked in the era of National Socialism.[66]

(2) *Wellhausen's Anti-Institutional Bias.* The second area of response traces an anti-institutional bias in Wellhausen's disposition as the source of his distaste for Judaism. Douglas Knight suggests that it was Wellhausen's "anti-institutional posture, which turned him against the post-exilic intentions—as he identified them..."[67] Silberman agrees and argues that Wellhausen's portrayal of Judaism is based not on the sixth or fifth centuries BCE, but on a contrast between the conservative tendencies in German Protestantism in the nineteenth century and the exponents of the "higher criticism." The conservative element accused its opponents of being "negative and negating, overcritical and destructive, while at the same time claiming itself to be constructive."[68] This conservative wing of

64. Solomon Schecter, "Higher Criticism—Higher Anti-Semitism," in his *Seminary Addresses and other Papers* (Cincinnati: Ark, 1915), 35–39.
65. Lou Silberman, "Wellhausen and Judaism," *Semeia* 25 (1983): 75–82 (75).
66. Ibid., 79.
67. Douglas A. Knight, "Wellhausen and the Interpretation of Israel's Literature," *Semeia* 25 (1983): 21–33 (33).
68. Silberman, "Wellhausen," 78.

German Protestantism constituted the ecclesiastical establishment which had the power to intervene in university politics. What Wellhausen found unpalatable in post-exilic Judaism was, according to Silberman, "none other than the ecclesiastical establishment that while not attacking him made it impossible for him to retain his theological professorship in Greifswald."[69] Silberman contends that this is "not the first time nor the last [that] Judaism [was] invented in one's image of one's theological opponents so that they could be tarred with the brush of 'Judaizers.'"[70]

Wellhausen's critics accused him of Hegelianism, a sort of Darwinian evolutionary posture, and, at the least, of a cultural anti-Semitism. That he followed Hegel is clearly not so, nor even Darwin. Wellhausen's periodization of the history of Israel is an aspect of the prevailing German approach to history, which concentrated on the growth and development of stages or epochs within a larger historical sphere. As regards anti-Semitism, it is undeniable that Wellhausen held the anti-Jewish views of nineteenth-century Europe based in German Protestantism. Though Silberman holds German Protestantism, including Wellhausen, responsible for a pattern of anti-Jewish thought, including an ignorance of Jewish tradition, he concludes that finally it is Wellhausen's well-known anti-institutionalism that is the source of his derogatory statements directed at Judaism.[71] Closing the discussion of the arguments in three areas of controversy concerning Wellhausen's assumptions, this study turns to other presuppositions which influenced his scholarship.

5. Wellhausen's Liberalism

The question of German political unity was the compelling issue of the mid-nineteenth century. Wellhausen, while committed to impartial

---

69. Ibid., 78.
70. Ibid., 79.
71. Wellhausen's negative phrases have circulated for years. In some cases the context changes the emphasis, as in the following statement, which also indicates Wellhausen's sensitivity to the functional relationship between culture and religion: "It was a necessity that Judaism should incrust itself in this manner; without those hard and ossified forms the preservation of its essential elements would have proved impossible. At a time when all nationalities, and at the same time all bonds of religion and national customs, were beginning to be broken up in the seeming cosmos and real chaos of the Graeco-Roman empire, the Jews stood out like a rock in the midst of the ocean. When the natural conditions of independent nationality all failed them, they nevertheless artificially maintained it with an energy truly marvellous, and thereby preserved for themselves, and at the same time for the whole world, an eternal good" (Wellhausen, *Prolegomena*, 497–99).

scholarship, held firmly liberal views.[72] Smend notes that although Well-hausen did not join groups, political or academic, nor attend conferences or congresses, he nevertheless carefully followed the events of his period.[73] Liberalism as an influence shaping Wellhausen's assumptions is difficult to put in terms that are meaningful today. It is clear that he was an admirer of Bismarck and a supporter of German unification, but at the same time he held the values of the rural individualist. Unlike the liberal historians who involved themselves deeply in politics and worked above all else for unification, Wellhausen does not find the individual's greatest expression in the development of the state. He maintains a critical posture toward the state.

6. *The Idea of the Nation*

The idea of the nation, nevertheless, is prominent in Wellhausen's thought. He says of the Israelite tribes, "The life they had lived together under Moses had been the first thing to awaken a feeling of solidarity among the tribes which afterwards constituted the nation."[74] Wellhausen, in discussing the organic unity advanced by the monarchy, points out that the basis of the

> national personality was a thing of much earlier origin, which even in the time of the judges bound the various tribes and families together, and must have had a great hold on the mind of the nation although there was no formal and binding constitution to give it support.[75]

It is hard to read these words and fail to note their similarity to the situation of the many German states, responsive to the bonds of language and culture, but having no common constitution or common government until Bismarck effected their union under the Prussian monarch. Wellhausen speaks of the state in these terms:

72. Rudolf Smend, in a private conversation July 13, 2000, in Göttingen, insisted on Wellhausen's position as a liberal. Carlo Antoni says of the liberal position: "most had nothing but disdain for the declamations of the Paulskirche. Even before the rise of Bismarck's star this generation favoured Realpolitik" (*From History to Sociology* [trans. Hayden White; Detroit: Wayne State University, 1959], 4).
73. Antoni's description of Dilthey's view on political parties may be helpful: "For him the party struggle was an interplay of forces, each one of which had its *raison d'etre* in a given sphere of needs. Hence, it appeared to him unseemly that an historian should take sides... His aversion to party bias in any form was really an expression of his inherited anti-dogmatism" (*From History to Sociology*, 5).
74. Wellhausen, *Prolegomena*, 432.
75. Ibid.

The ancient Israelites were as fully conscious as any other people of the gratitude they owed to the men and to the institutions by whose aid they had been lifted out of anarchy and oppression, and formed into an orderly community, capable of self-defense.[76]

As he describes the constitution of the monarchy under Saul, Wellhausen is appropriately realistic about the functions of the state, including providing defense and the expenses necessary to the effort. He says, "The ancient Israelites did not build a church first of all: what they built first was a house to live in, and they rejoiced not a little when they got it happily roofed over."[77] He clearly sees the state developing from cultural bonds and national sentiment and serving to provide structure and protection. He also writes powerfully of Israel's "calling" as spokesperson for God, "a prophet on a large scale."[78] This consciousness of historical development of the nation and its larger purpose are fully consonant with the historical tradition.

Finally, the Romantic legacy of Herder and the brothers Grimm must be mentioned. Romanticism is intimately connected with historicism and the source of interest in authenticity, passion, and the sublime. Romanticism cherishes the natural, the primitive, the earliest expression of a people, seen first in their stories, their music, their beliefs, and finds in each historical age a particular "spirit." Studies of social groups in their "natural" state, their earliest periods, provide insights into their ethos or the "idea" of their culture. Wellhausen's attachment to Israel's early history is certainly, in part, a manifestation of the influence of this movement.

7. The Search for Historical Truth

The great German historians of the nineteenth century had as their primary article of faith that history must be studied in its endless particularity. History, unlike the natural sciences, was subject to no laws. No generalizations could be made, no expectations nor predictions could be based on past events. This further precluded the use of philosophical systems as indicators of the progress or outcome of history. The accumulation of evidence and its close analysis were the components of what was seen as the objective empirical method of history writing. Historians were expected to put aside their biases and assumptions and produce history without presuppositions. Wellhausen deeply admired the work of

76. Ibid., 254.
77. Ibid., 255.
78. Ibid., 400.

Theodor Mommsen, preeminent German scholar of classical antiquity, and it is from Mommsen that he acquired the notion of "presuppositionless investigation."[79] Mommsen says

> Our life nerve is research without presuppositions, research that does not find what it is supposed to find according to considerations of purpose and relevance, things which serve other goals lying outside of science, but what seems logically and historically correct to the conscientious researcher, summarized in a single word: truthfulness.[80]

The assumption that the duty of a historian is to write objective accounts of the past guides Wellhausen and leads him to comment on the process of research as an endeavor in which the facts direct the researcher. The goal is truth and should not be obscured by the purposes of the researcher or by the expectations of the culture or the time. This view seems naive to present day readers, yet German historiography both promoted this goal and debated the possibility of research without bias.

In Wellhausen's case it is clear from the foregoing that many assumptions colored his work, but he believed that he was doing scholarship free of presuppositions. He could hold to this view in part because his conclusions did not follow the current expectations. The very originality of his work suggested that he was not governed by the prevailing views. So it is to his method that this study turns to see how his assumptions affected his investigations.

8. *Method*

Law in the Hebrew Bible has two aspects for Wellhausen. First, his polemical stance toward the law has been noted. This view, derived from German Protestantism, initially rejected what it saw as the excessive legalism of Roman Catholicism. This particular aversion to the law and institutional hierarchies was easily extended to late biblical religion with its priests, elaborate cultic ritual, and legal system binding every part of life. Indeed, Wellhausen makes a direct comparison, calling the religion of the Priestly Code in its nature "intimately allied to the old Catholic church."[81] The law, however, also served as the point to begin inquiry into Israel's history. At the outset, he states the problem of the

79. Barton, "Wellhausen's Prolegomena," 326.
80. Theodor Mommsen, "Erklärung vom 15. November 1901 betreffend Universitatsunterricht und Konfession," in his *Reden und Aufsätze* (Berlin: Weidmann, 1905), 432–36 (432–34).
81. Wellhausen, *Prolegomena*, 422.

Prolegomena as "the place in the history of the 'law of Moses.'"[82] It was Wellhausen's insight that "there are in the Pentateuch three strata of law and three strata of tradition, and the problem is to place them in their true historical order."[83] He describes his procedure:

> After laboriously collecting the data offered by the historical and propheti-cal books, we constructed a sketch of the Israelite history of worship; we then compared the Pentateuch with this sketch, and recognised that one element of the Pentateuch bore a definite relation to this phase of the his-tory of worship, and another element of the Pentateuch to that phase of it.

Accomplishing his breakthrough in dating Old Testament sources by means of the relationship among the collections of law, it is important to note Wellhausen's understanding of culture as the totality of many elements in intricate relation to one another, an important aspect of historicism.

a. *Sources*

German historians, following the principles of history writing laid down by Ranke, were scrupulous in working from original sources. Likewise Wellhausen, as is well known, refused to speculate on Israelite history in the patriarchal period, holding that the sources were unreliable. Written documents were the source of history for Wellhausen as for historians in general and German historians in particular in the nineteenth century. Historical artifacts are of only incidental interest and may lend a sort of anecdotal support to the literary sources.

Wellhausen's attitude toward written sources may be seen in his criticism of Gunkel's traditio-historical approach. Wellhausen argues that, in regard to method, one can only consider what an author has written. How the author has used his or her sources in constructing the text is the concern of the historian or exegete, not an interpretation of the material's original meaning before it reached the hand of the author. He allows that the facts of history may be handed down with tolerable accuracy through a considerable period of time, but that it is only in contemporary literature that descriptions of events or conditions may be judged reliable. Rudolph quotes Wellhausen: "For proper method con-centrates on the major point at issue, and its only concern is the compre-hension of the evidence."[84] He sums up Wellhausen's position succinctly: "investigations of preliterary traditions behind written works fail to

---

82. Ibid., 1.
83. Ibid., 366.
84. Rudolph, "Wellhausen as an Arabist," 120.

comprehend the essence of such works and cannot be regarded as scientific or methodical."[85]

b. *Style and Language*
Wellhausen favored the colorful style of writing found in the histories of Thomas Carlyle and the writing technique employed by Mommsen, whose goal was to engage his audience in the events and ethos of history. Bismarck's directness of style also appealed to Wellhausen. One of the chief contributions of the *Prolegomena* is its style, says Smend:

> Of the highest literary merit, a rare exception among the works of German professors, it is written in a clear and uncomplicated language, fresh and vivid, often pungent and funny. A brilliant element is the serenely cool polemic. It gave pleasure to many readers...[86]

That Wellhausen set out to captivate his readers and to immerse them in the life of ancient Israel, to lead them through his arguments, and so to intimately understand the unfolding of history, is evident and a testimony to the influence of his chosen models.

Wellhausen's understanding of Semitic languages was renowned. Alfred Jepsen quotes from a letter of Hermann Cremer to the Prussian Minister of Education on Wellhausen's anticipated move to Göttingen:

> His command of the Semitic languages is like that of no other in his field. Languages come alive for him, he comprehends their spirit, not only their grammar. Thus though his writings are full of the most subtle grammatical observations, he never puts himself forward as a grammarian. He refuses to pay homage to the etymological trend in linguistic research, emphasizing, rightly, the gulf between etymological basic meaning and historical linguistic usage.[87]

Wellhausen says of himself that he "always employed grammar as a means to the comprehension of the literature" and that he was suspicious of efforts to discover the thoughts of the past, contradictory and irrational, which shaped language.[88]

85. Ibid., 120.
86. Smend, "Wellhausen," 12–13.
87. Letter of Hermann Cremer describing Wellhausen in Jepsen, "Wellhausen in Greifswald," 265. See also James Barr, *The Semantics of Biblical Literature* (London: Oxford University Press, 1961).
88. Rudolph quotes from Julius Wellhausen, review of H. Reckendorf, *Die syntaktischen Verhaltnisse des Arabischen, Göttingische Gelehrte Anzeigen* 158 (1895): 773–78 (777).

c. *Tradition and Culture*

Having mastered Semitic languages, Wellhausen was prepared to investigate the literary traditions according to their tendencies, contradictions, and traditional authority. This entailed establishing a source from its outlook, its interest, or its inclination, focusing on the contradictions in the text in order to separate a source from the tangled collection of traditions, and following the traditional elements through the larger text to fix the limits of a given source. He says:

> the whole area of tradition has finally been uniformly covered with an alluvial deposit by which the configuration of the surface has been determined. It is with this last that we have to deal in the first instance, to ascertain its character, to find out what the active forces were by which it was produced.[89]

With historical synthesis as the goal, these steps are but preliminary, requiring, nonetheless, the interpretative skills based on knowledge of the language and understanding of the culture and religion.

Wellhausen has a complex and sophisticated sense of the development of tradition. He is aware that tradition is interpreted anew in each generation, remarking, "Under the influence of the spirit of each successive age, traditions originally derived from one source were very variously apprehended and shaped."[90] He is also conscious of the influence that a general knowledge of traditions and older sources has on particular authors or compilers, stating that:

> Even in the case of the prophets who received their word from the Lord the later writer knows and founds upon the earlier one. How much more must this be the case with narrators whose express business is with the tradition? Criticism has not done its work when it has completed the mechanical distribution; it must aim further at bringing the different writings when thus arranged into relation with each other, must seek to render them intelligible as phases of a living process, and thus to make it possible to trace a graduated development of the tradition.[91]

He points out that:

> When the subject treated is not history but legends about pre-historical times, the arrangement of the materials does not come with the materials themselves, but must arise out of the plan of a narrator... From the mouth of the people there comes nothing but the detached narratives, which may or may not happen to have some bearing on each other; to weave them together in a connected whole is the work of the poetical or literary artist.[92]

89. Wellhausen, *Prolegomena*, 228.
90. Ibid., 171.
91. Ibid., 295.
92. Ibid., 296.

In discriminating between traditions with historical value and those more problematic for historical reconstruction, Wellhausen remarks:

> It involves no contradiction that, in comparing the versions of the tradition, we should decline the historical standard in the case of the legend of the origins of mankind and of the legend of the patriarchs, while we employ it to a certain extent for the epic period of Moses and Joshua. The epic tradition certainly contains elements which cannot be explained on any other hypothesis than that there are historical facts underlying them.[93]

Finally, in thinking about the process of fixing the traditions in written form, Wellhausen reminds us that "Even at the first act of reducing it to writing the discolouring influences are at work."[94] Though Wellhausen is remembered not for his understanding of traditions and the transmission of traditions, but for his work with written sources and his insistence that oral tradition prior to the written sources cannot be accessed to produce reliable history, nonetheless he has a clear view of the central features governing the process of building, fixing, and interpreting tradition. This view is central to his evaluation of material in the work of separating sources.

The careful work in establishing the extent of the sources and the characteristics of each provides the necessary information for the next step. The major move toward unraveling Israel's history comes in the relative dating of the sources. Rudolph tells us that "Wellhausen also saw religion in intimate relation to culture and politics."[95] It is this awareness that allows him to see the crisis of the post-exilic community in terms of its need to establish a new identity for its new situation. He recognizes that public worship provided a "firm centre," while private rituals "served to Judaize the whole life of every individual." The total program acted as a safeguard protecting Judaism from the surrounding culture and at the same time from the "disintegrating effects of individualism."[96] From this recognition it becomes possible to understand and to trace the retrojection of cultic legislation into the earlier collections of traditions. The Priestly Source then becomes the key to dating the other sources in the Pentateuch. Again the J document, on the basis of culture and politics, of

93. Ibid., 360.
94. Ibid., 361.
95. Rudolph, "Wellhausen as an Arabist," 118.
96. Wellhausen, "Israel," 499–500.

language, horizon, and other features…dates from the golden age of Hebrew literature… And the Jehovist does not even pretend to being a Mosaic law of any kind; it aims at being a simple book of history; the distance between the present and the past spoken of is not concealed in the very least.[97]

Finally, Wellhausen notes that Deuteronomy "was composed in the same age as that in which it was discovered, and…was made the rule of Josiah's reformation, which took place about a generation before the destruction of Jerusalem."[98] Wellhausen describes his method as charting "the change of ruling ideas which runs parallel with the change in the institutions and usages of worship… Almost more important to me than the phenomena themselves, are the presuppositions which lie behind them."[99] The first section of the *Prolegomena* is devoted to the relation of religion to the culture, material forces, and political pressures. It is through the analysis of these relationships that Wellhausen develops his reconstruction of Israel's history.

Beginning with linguistic study, then moving on to sort traditional material by means of attention to its *Tendenz*, its interests, and its style, Wellhausen establishes historical periods and interprets the material according to the political organization of the tribes or nation, the expression of religion, the material conditions, and culture. In constructing his hypothesis, Wellhausen first presents the history of worship. He describes the place of worship in various stories, showing that the change of location signifies changes in material culture, changes in religious practices, and changes in the role of priests and form of government. This section on worship is followed by a section on tradition. Here, Wellhausen establishes the unreliability of Chronicles. In choosing Judges, Samuel, and Kings as the valid tradition, Wellhausen understands that only after uncovering the earlier narrative tradition can the "changing spirit of each successive period" be determined.[100] He argues in defense of his method saying:

This is not putting logic in the place of historical investigation. The new doctrine of the irrationality of what exists is surely not to be pushed so far, as that we should regard the correspondence between an element of the law and a particular phase of the history as a reason for placing the two as far as possible asunder.[101]

97. Wellhausen, *Prolegomena*, 9.
98. Ibid.
99. Ibid., 368.
100. Ibid., 228.
101. Ibid., 367.

He argues on the basis of the foundational tenet of historicism that individual aspects of culture grow and develop hand-in-hand with its other facets. He concurs with the prevailing historicist argument that ideas develop out of historical experience and the material of history must not be organized by categories of logic.

9. Conclusion

Wellhausen was formed in the traditions of the nineteenth-century German academic world. That he chose the historical approach to the study of the Bible argues that this context provided him the possibility to investigate the biblical text without the constraints of theological interpretation. The signature elements of the tradition guided his work. He immersed himself in the life of ancient Israel, using informed intuition and scholarly imagination to fashion the narrative of Israel's history. The question of objectivity as it was posed in the United States was not an issue. Rather, this tradition insists that investigation be "presuppositionless" in the sense that the historian must be guided by the historical material, never by any scheme or philosophy describing the course of history or predicting future historical moments.

Romanticism, Idealism, and their influence on the concept of the nation and its necessary development, allowed Wellhausen to perceive the stirrings of national unity in the feelings of the ancient tribes. Even in the developments of the post-exilic period, which are for him a sad decline from the robust expression of the early times, he found an element of the nation preserved. The development of Israel through several stages or distinct periods in its life represents in Wellhausen's work an application of the model of national development so ubiquitous among German historians.

While producing novel results from his studies of the texts, nonetheless his theoretical and methodological approaches were compounded from the beliefs of the age. He studied the written documents and investigated the occurrences portrayed in the text, allowing them to suggest new directions in the reconstruction of Israel's past. His mastery of Semitic languages prepared him in a unique way to follow the prevailing conviction that language offers a key to understanding cultures. His awareness of the complexities of culture, the relationships among law, custom, belief, ritual, and the arts of expression, bespeak his congruence with the historiographic tradition as it had developed under the influence of Herder, Humboldt, and Ranke.

Wellhausen, as a historian, was committed to seeking truth, to the critical use of evidence, to writing history without bias. For his careful devotion to scientific principles of historiography, he was called negative, overcritical, and even destructive. Many who knew his work, particularly in England and the United States, feared his proposals as an attack on the Bible. This reaction to critical historiography will continue to be a feature throughout the following periods discussed in this study.

Chapter 4

HISTORIOGRAPHY IN GERMANY
AND THE UNITED STATES TO WORLD WAR II

The purpose of this chapter is to present a picture of the historical discipline in Germany and the United States as it forms the background for the work of Martin Noth and John Bright. In the interest of producing a solid base for understanding the influences of the contemporary historical practice on these representative figures of biblical history writing, a discussion of the challenges to German historicism at the turn of the twentieth century and responses by the practicing historians to the German defeat in World War I are included here, along with an outline of the figures and questions which were prominent in the foundation and development of the American historical discipline. I will argue that historians in both countries cast themselves as moral leaders, experts, and intellectuals offering guidance to their respective publics, and that while objectivity was associated in both traditions with scientific research, they differed radically in their understanding of both objectivity and science. For both groups of historians relativism became a central dilemma, temporarily removed to the background by the demands of World War I. Finally, I will argue that neither American pragmatism nor German Idealism found the means to formulate an adequate theoretical position regarding the writing of history.

1. *Part One: Germany*

The concluding decades of the nineteenth century in Germany and the years leading up to the First World War exhibit both high optimism for historical studies and growing pessimism in regard to the possibilities of establishing meaning in history. Optimism is reflected in cheerful confidence in science and technology and, within the field of history, in the production of fine specialized monographs. On the other hand, the apparently insurmountable difficulties of reconciling the extreme relativism of particular cultural values within any larger comprehending view drives a sense of crisis regarding the notion of historicism. German thought emphatically rejected the main currents of Western thought and in particular substituted the idea of history for the predominance of Natural Law. Historicism, as it evolved in Germany, accords specific attention to the development of a nation or civilization. While this appears to most neither an unreasonable nor an unfamiliar approach to the study of history, for those whose views are not formed by the German notion of history the further implications of this approach must be noted again. In historicism, the subject of history is always an individuality. Friedrich Meinecke distinguishes this, in a paraphrase of Troeltsch, as

> the idea of inimitable, unique individuality developing according to its own, organic laws of life, which cannot be grasped by means of logical thought, and certainly not the laws of mechanical causation, but rather must be comprehended, examined, experienced, and empathetically re-experienced with the total concert of one's spiritual powers.[1]

The uniqueness of human reality, its resistance to generalization, and the development of an historical subject according to an inherent ideal are assumptions indispensable to the practice of German historiography. The fundamental importance of the notion of individual development is often overlooked. It is from this notion that relativism springs for, because each individual pursues its own growth according to its own inner plan, no judgment may be made on the development of another individuality. Meaning in history cannot be established. In particular, German thought promotes the state as the individuality which is the true embodiment of the cultural spirit and from which each person and event draws its meaning. It definitively rejects the idea of a separate, distinct person as the locus of universal rights and ethics. This is in radical contra-distinction to the view prevailing in most contemporary Western thought that the individual person is the seat of rights and the entity for whom the state exists. In recognizing the infinite variety of cultures or states, which exist and have existed and exhibit radically different systems of values, it is inescapable that no set of absolute values can be asserted. The consequence of this acknowledgment of the relative nature of values is that the notion of the meaningfulness of history is dissolved.

The philosophic problem raised by relativism in ethics and values is reflected in the arguments about method which troubled the German

---

1. Fredrich Meinecke, "Ernst Troeltsch und das Problem des Historismus," in his *Werke*, vol. 4 (Stuttgart: Koehler, 1965), 374 (quotation trans. Gaia Banks).

historical discipline around the turn of the twentieth century. Dilthey, Weber, Troeltsch, and Meinecke represent a significant cohort of thinkers who recognized the relativistic implications of German historicism.[2] Only Weber, however, faced the obvious conclusions and let go the romantic notion of individual histories gathered harmoniously into some vague notion of spiritual continuity or eternal ideas. On the other hand, the orientation of German historians toward the state directed their emphasis to political history until after World War II. German history failed to take into account the major social and economic transformations of the nineteenth and twentieth centuries. Karl Lamprecht made an ill-fated attempt to address the socio-economic forces in history.

2. *Karl Lamprecht and the Challenge to Tradition*

The *Methodenstreit* sparked by Lamprecht's history was actually a serious and fervent debate between a mild positivism or "scientific" viewpoints on one hand, and traditional German historical thought on the other. There are certain similarities to the issues debated among historians between 1850 and 1880, particularly those enunciated by Droysen in his *Historik* and his review of Buckle's *History of Civilization in England*,[3] but the later controversy was noted for its theoretical reflections, particularly interesting among those practicing historians customarily opposed to discussions of theory.

Lamprecht published the first volume of his *Deutsche Geschichte* in 1891.[4] The guiding principle of his history was the notion that each successive period in the German experience was characterized by a dominant tendency; furthermore, the passage from one period to another was effected by developmental laws which could be compared to laws in the natural sciences. This program was deeply offensive to the contemporary historians of the Prussian School on the grounds that it contradicted the prevailing view of the unique development of the state "subject to no developmental dynamic save the logic of its own history."[5]

2. Calvin G. Rand notes that the period of productive scholarship of Dilthey, Troeltsch, and Meinecke (1880–1930) "represents the culmination of the historicist movement" ("Two Meanings of Historicism in the Writings of Dilthey, Troeltsch, and Meinecke," *Journal of the History of Ideas* 25 [1964]: 503–18 [504]).
3. Buckle published the first volume of his *History of Civilization in England* in 1858 and the second in 1861. Citations in this study are from the second edition (2 vols.; New York: Appleton, 1892).
4. Karl Lamprecht, *Deutsche Geschichte* (12 vols.; Berlin 1891–1909).
5. Roger Chickering, "Young Lamprecht: An Essay in Biography and Historiography," *History and Theory* 28 (1989): 198–214 (198).

Lamprecht offered the additional criticism that traditional German historiography had, through its attention to the state and the development of power, neglected social and economic factors necessary for a full exposition of German history. Roger Chickering suggests that this criticism was the most offensive, "for [Lamprecht] appeared to argue that the motor of historical development, of the transition from one historical period to another, lay in changing systems of exchange. This proposition smacked enough of historical materialism to add an ideological dimension" to the controversy over Lamprecht's methods.[6]

Lamprecht advocated an approach to history that replaced the descriptive method with the identification of general laws of development, concerned with cultural, economic, legal, and intellectual history. He further argued that just as science had moved beyond metaphysical systems, historians must abandon the notion of the divine element within the "ideas."[7] Indeed, advances in historical science required a new perspective on historical subjects. Lamprecht held that "pure empiricism" was "the only method adequate to the dynamics of historical phenomena."[8] Orthodox German historians countered that empiricism as proposed by Lamprecht was too materialistic, that the historians' traditional method enabled them "to gain an understanding of the entire world, while the scientist was limited to studying merely the phenomena of the physical universe."[9]

Georg Iggers argues that the real issue between Lamprecht and the traditional historians was whether political or social history was the more valid focus.[10] Even for Lamprecht, however, the state held the central role in directing society and a strong foreign policy was necessary for economic progress. Likewise, social and economic aspects figured significantly in the works of traditional historians. Lamprecht realized that individuality in some respects resists causal analysis, but he continued to insist that certain elements of social behavior are not expressions of individual freewill and thus are amenable to collective treatment. He agreed that while the historian can offer categories by which to interpret social action, he or she cannot posit rigid laws of social process.

6. Ibid., 198–99.
7. Iggers, *German Conception*, 199; see also Helen P. Liebel, "Philosophical Idealism in the *Historische Zeitschrift*, 1859–1914," *History and Theory* 3 (1964): 316–30 (324–25).
8. Liebel, "Philosophical Idealism," 325.
9. Ibid., 325. This contains an echo of Vico's argument that the material world can measured and recorded, but never known in the way that humans can know what they themselves have created.
10. Iggers, *German Conception*, 198.

Though Lamprecht's work was fully discredited on the basis of his careless research, his name is forever attached to this controversy within the German historical guild regarding its assumptions about the idealist character of history and the importance of the role of the state, and the positivists' search for repetitious aspects of historical development. It will be clear in the succeeding chapters that these issues, compelling as they were to the academic community of historians, were not topics among historians in biblical studies. Blanke, Fleischer, and Rüsen remark that the Lamprecht controversy was a

> decisive point because its outcome shows that tacit agreement predomi-
> nated about fields, aims, and methods…insofar as one proceeded from
> certain given premises against which new trends could not gain accep-
> tance. The dispute was not fully discussed—it was cut short instead.[11]

The methodological turmoil engendered by the *Methodenstreit* was an instance of the recurring question of the relationship of history to the natural sciences. Hayden White remarks that "The intellectual history of nineteenth century Germany, if indeed not all of Europe, may be conceived as centering about the problem of defining the relation between the human sciences (*Geisteswissenschaften*) and the natural sciences *(Naturwissenschaften)*." Occupying a place between the humanities and the developing social sciences, history suffered this problem most acutely. White continues, "its practitioners tended to oscillate between the conviction that history was an art, an aspect of *belles lettres*, and the conviction that it was an empirical or possibly even a positivistic science."[12]

3. *History as a Scientific Discipline*

In this regard the theoretical and methodological concerns of Wilhelm Dilthey and the Neo-Kantians must be mentioned. For these men, the task was to establish history and the cultural sciences as disciplines as rigorous in their approach as the natural sciences, yet retaining methods able to interpret meaning "embodied in history and culture."[13] Following Schleiermacher and Droysen, Dilthey hoped to "establish 'understanding' as the fundamental principle of the humanities in contradistinction to 'explaining' from law-like hypotheses in the natural sciences."[14]

11. Blanke, Fleischer, and Rüsen, "Theory of History," 334.
12. Hayden White, translator's introduction to Antoni, *From History to Sociology*, xv.
13. Iggers, "Historicism," *Journal of the History of Ideas* 56 (1995): 129–52 (132).
14. Blanke, Fleischer, and Rüsen, "Theory of History," 343.

a. *Empirical Reality and Subjective Understanding*

Dilthey's efforts, in his later writings, to resolve the contradiction he perceived between his own belief in the possibility of objective knowledge and scientific study of history, and the problem of the subjective nature of cognition, finally resulted in the notion that "life," in its many particular forms, is objectified in institutions, social groups, the family, and social products such as art, philosophy, and religion. These institutions and social expressions are manifestations of the culture or period in which an individual lives. Hajo Holborn says Dilthey

> added a new dimension to historiography by expanding it to include, apart from the rational thoughts, the imaginative visions and the conative efforts of man. Not only conflicting systems of philosophy of a period could now be shown to represent various expressions of a common living experience, but the visions of artists and the motivating ideas of statesmen could also be related to the same experience.[15]

Since these productions bear the imprint of a particular social order or experience, they are amenable to explanation only by an act of subjective understanding.[16] This does not indicate that they are mental constructions. They remain objective reality, but the means of perception and description lie within the human understanding, human comprehension through "experience (*Erlebnis*), expression (*Ausdruck*), and understanding (*Verstehen*)."[17] Finally, Antoni insists that Dilthey came to believe that "we are able to know what the human spirit is only through history, only this historical self-consciousness allows us to formulate a systematic theory of man."[18]

Iggers suggests that Dilthey was ultimately unable to resolve the contradiction between his efforts to provide "historical studies with firm epistemological foundations" and his own conclusion that "all knowledge is radically subjective."[19] Dilthey reflects on his seventieth birthday: "The Historical way of looking at things has liberated the human spirit from the last chains which natural science and philosophy have not yet torn asunder. But where are the means for overcoming the anarchy of convictions which threatens to break in on us?"[20]

15. Holborn, "The History of Ideas," 690.
16. Wilhelm Dilthey, "Allgemeine Sätze über den Zusammenhang der Geisteswissenschaften," in *Gesammelte Schriften*, 7 (Leipzig: Teubner, 1922–36; repr. 1957), 120–88 (171).
17. Ibid., 187.
18. Antoni, *From History to Sociology*, 30.
19. Iggers, *German Conception*, 134.
20. Wilhelm Dilthey, "Rede Zum 70. Geburtstag," in *Gesammelte Schriften*, 5 (Leipzig: Teubner, 1924), 7–9 (7).

4. *The Conflict of Values*

Weber confronted this compelling issue—the problem of the relativism of values and the resulting loss of coherence in history—by radically separating the arena of ethics from that of cognition. He made a firm distinction between the irrational world of values and the world of reason.[21] The scientific investigator of the social world, he argued, must establish only empirical facts and may not seek deeper or higher significance in historical phenomena. Unlike Dilthey, he supposed no concept of "life" manifest in various conflicting systems of value nor did he follow the German historical tradition by giving to providence the role of harmonizing the variety of ethical traditions. His foundational premise is that the world's various systems of value are in "irreconcilable conflict."[22] The world has no meaning, but, in spite of this, rational and objective cognition is possible.

a. *Rational Human Behavior*

Weber departs from historicism in his argument that human behavior, because it is rational, exhibits regularity and lawfulness. This regularity in human and social behavior can be observed by means of his "ideal types."[23] Weber uses the example of language. A researcher studying a particular language derives the rules of grammar and syntax from observing and recording the language as it is actually used by living speakers. The rules of language form an attempt to understand the structure of the language and to provide a guide for speech, but, as a formal description, the rules do not depict reality. This description is an "ideal" and is never really the total or true picture of the spoken usage, but is a useful device "which serves as a harbor until one has learned to navigate safely in the vast sea of empirical facts."[24] While seeking the common elements in

21. Antoni (*From History to Sociology*, 142) claims that "Max Weber is the German thinker who insisted with greatest energy upon the distinction between... science and value judgment."

22. Max Weber, *From Max Weber: Essays in Sociology* (ed. and trans. H. H. Gerth and C. Wright Mills; London: Routledge, 1993), 147.

23. For Weber, "ideal" has no relation to moral values, or to the ethical content of traditional German "ideas." He indicates rather conceptions such as those suggested by the terms Renaissance or Romanticism, capitalism, democracy, or Romanesque architecture, notions composed of many disparate, sometimes opposing elements, making up a period, ideology, or style that we somehow recognize as a whole. See H. H. Gerth and C. Wright Mills, introduction to Weber, *Essays*, 59.

24. Max Weber, "'Objectivity' in Social Science and Social Policy," in *The Methodology of the Social Sciences* (trans. and ed. Edward A. Shils and Henry A. Finch; New York: Free Press, 1949), 49–112 (104).

cultural phenomena, the social scientist does not force reality into abstract concepts as the natural scientist does, but seeks to highlight its "uniquely individual character."[25]

For Weber the individual person is the "ultimate unit of analysis" and the "sole carrier" of meaningful action. H. H. Gerth and C. Wright Mills, in their introduction to Weber's essays on sociology, observe that this view of the individual is grounded in the Enlightenment. In contrast to the prevailing German understanding of the individual as an expression of the spirit of the culture, as a document offering insight of the whole, Weber argued that human beings can understand themselves and their fellows through introspection and interpretation of their motives "in terms of their professed or ascribed intentions."[26] This is not to suggest that Weber was unaware that human actions can unquestionably bring about unintended consequences, but it is, nevertheless, through the unique approach of interpretation or understanding of motives that social science studies human beings and their actions.

b. *Science and Culture*

Weber was the student of Theodor Mommsen, and like Mommsen and the members of the Historical School, Weber was active in politics. He was a founder of the Democratic Party, an expert representative to the peace negotiations at Versailles, and it was he who wrote into the Weimar Constitution those clauses granting discretionary powers to the president in instances of crisis brought about by extremists of either the right or left. Weber resembled his fellow German liberals in their belief in the positive value of the state.[27] Iggers says that "In many ways he represented what was best in the German liberal scholarly tradition of the nineteenth century—the commitment to truth, the belief in the social and political responsibilities of the scholar, the defense of intellectual liberty," a willingness "to scrutinize all beliefs in the light of reason." Yet, his view of history as a meaningless process left nothing "but the will to power... His willingness to examine all values had shied away from the one idol which the entire tradition had worshiped: the idol of the nation."[28] Iggers concludes that "Weber's great achievement lay in understanding that it was methodology rather than its findings which gave science, including social science, its scientific character. Science

25. Ibid., 101.
26. Weber, *Essays*, 56.
27. Iggers, *German Conception*, 171.
28. Ibid., 173.

thus coincided with 'research' (*Forschung*)." Here he notes that science understood in this way stands in direct opposition "to the older historicist conceptions of history which saw history as a source of culture (*Bildung*) and assigned to historical science the task of establishing norms."[29] This shift from *Bildung* (formation) to *Forschung* (research) was accomplished during the course of the nineteenth century.[30]

c. *The Crisis of Historicism*

The issues which brought historicism into crisis are inescapable in the thought of Dilthey and Weber. Dilthey hoped to overcome historical relativism by reaffirming the idea that human actions are inevitably expressions of the *Geist* or spirit of the age or culture, instances of the larger notion he designated *life*. He had to acknowledge, finally, that he remained caught in his own contradictions and that he could find no remedy for the loss of universal human values. Weber, on the other hand, faced squarely the unavoidable conclusion that history is ultimately meaningless and sought to analyze human behavior through its rational aspects as instances of ascribed cultural meaning. While these problems were addressed in work done before World War I, what has come to be known as the "crisis" of historicism arose in Germany in the aftermath of the war. The crisis developed not because of the theoretical problems of historicism alone, but in large part as a response to the disastrous outcome of the war in Germany. As Colin Loader puts it, "the crisis arose not because of the Historicists' inability to guarantee the existence of a universal set of values, but rather because of their inability to guarantee the existence of a *unity of values* for the German nation in the 1920s."[31] Ernst Troeltsch concluded that the crisis was brought about by "the internal movement and essence of history itself... Here we see everything in the flow of becoming, in the endless and ever new individualization, in the determination by the past and in the direction of an unknown future."[32] Troeltsch saw that the only answer to relativism lay in renewed faith in the meaningfulness of history.

---

29. Iggers, "Historicism," 140.
30. Droysen (*Outline*, 12) reflects this process in his statement, "The essence of historical method consists in understanding by means of investigation."
31. Colin T. Loader, "German Historicism and Its Crisis," *Journal of Modern History* 48 (1976): 85–119 (88).
32. Ernst Troeltsch, "Die Krisis des Historismus," *Die neue Rundschau* 33 (1922): 572–90 (573).

5. *Troeltsch and Religious Relativism*

By the later decades of the nineteenth century, the transformation of Germany into an industrial nation had resulted in a "wholesale desertion of the churches."[33] Troeltsch was fully aware of the gulf between the traditions of the church and the conditions of modern life. He argued, however, that the prominence of technology and science was not the major cause. While natural science had altered beliefs in God's means of working in the world, and in miracles, these are not vital to faith. Rather, he felt, it was the work of biblical critics, employing the methods of history, who had undermined Christianity. Comparative studies had shown Christianity to be only one religion among many. The results of various studies of the texts had produced a history of Christianity, a history subject to the identical forces of trial, accommodation, and development at work in secular history.[34] Antoni concludes, "Ritschl had felt no need for apologiae, only for the exegesis of the Gospel; in Troeltsch, exegesis becomes biblical research and destroys the mysterious effect of the Word."

a. *The History of Religions*
Troeltsch struggled with his conviction that history is "the basis of all thought about values and norms."[35] While Christianity had been a historical phenomenon throughout its existence and because of this could not make a claim to the position of absolute, still, he felt, it offered insight into truth. Real values are to be found in history. The great religions offer points of similarity and study of the history of religions fosters understanding of enduring values. These truths can be known only in history and thus are exhibited in particular and time bound forms, but nevertheless, in Troeltsch's view, they exist outside history. He remains within the German Idealist sphere, still resisting Hegel's schema as a violation of the principle of individuality, but he believes that history offers instances of the development of values and this suggests an eternal value beyond history.[36]

Troeltsch's study of religion as a historical phenomenon produced *The Social Teachings of the Christian Churches and Sects*.[37] This work

33. Antoni, *From History to Sociology*, 61.
34. Ibid., 43.
35. Ernst Troeltsch, *The Absoluteness of Christianity and the History of Religions* (trans. David Reid; London: SCM Press), 3–4.
36. Iggers, *German Conception*, 178–79.
37. Ernst Troeltsch, *The Social Teachings of the Christian Churches and Sects* (trans. Olive Wyon; New York: Macmillan, 1931).

reflects the influence of his friend and colleague, Max Weber, in its use of types of religious organization and in the conception of a relation between religious life and economic cycles.[38] Here, he investigates the fundamental differences between German thought and that of the rest of the West.[39] He contrasts the Calvinist belief that the state is judged by Christian standards of morality, with the Lutheran sense of profound human sinfulness, which thus accepts force and violence as the foundation of law and justice. The state produces its own moral judgment. Troeltsch argued that this difference fostered the German Idealist rejection of Enlightenment notions, but that capitalist forces of the modern world were moving the cultures together.

b. *The Effects of World War I*
With the outbreak of World War I, Troeltsch returned to the those ideas of the German heritage which he had previously seen as responding favorably to tempering by Western Natural Law traditions. He concluded that in the West the notion that the state is an institution serving the needs of individual citizens was revealed as an illusion and that the traditional position of German liberalism—the state as an ethical entity whose interests transcend the individual and must be guided by its own interests—must be affirmed. As the war progressed, the spirit of unity and confidence in German superiority faded. By 1922, Troeltsch came to recognize the negative consequences of the German idea of individuality. He says:

> The conception of the abundance of national spirits was transformed into a feeling of contempt for the idea of Universal Humanity. The pantheistic idolization of the state turned into blind respect, devoid of all ideas, for success and power. The Romantic Revolution sank into a complacent contentment with things as they are. From the idea of a particular law and right for a given time and place, men proceeded to a purely positivistic acceptance of the state. The conception of a morality of a higher spiritual order which transcends bourgeois conventions passed into moral scepticism. From the urge of the German spirit to find embodiment in a state there arose the same kind of imperialism as anywhere else in the world.[40]

Historicism had come to its crisis by its inherent contradictions.

38. Antoni, *From History to Sociology*, 63.
39. Troeltsch espouses the view that "German sociocultural science is to be understood as an idealist, romanticist reaction to the rationalist, materialist sociocultural thought of the seventeenth and eighteenth centuries" (Guy Oakes, "The Verstehen Thesis and the Foundation of Max Weber's Methodology," *History and Theory* 16 [1977]: 11–29 [18]).
40. Ernst Troeltsch, "The Ideas of Natural Law and Humanity," in *Natural Law and the Theory of Society, 1500 to 1800* (ed. Otto Gierke; trans. Ernest Barker; 2 vols.; Cambridge: Cambridge University Press, 1934), 1:214.

As Troeltsch recognized, historicism had undermined all ethical systems by its extreme relativism. Further, by insisting that human beings are radically constrained by their own place in their culture, historicism had made any objective knowledge impossible. In *Der Historismus und seine Probleme*,[41] Troeltsch attempts to deal with these contradictions in his effort to locate absolute values. Antoni comments that as Troeltsch had

> hoped to derive from history itself the proof of the extrahistorical, absolute character of Christianity, so now he proposed to derive from the study of history the antidotes for unlimited historicism, that is, the proof of the absolute character of the values of Western Civilization in their historical formations.[42]

Humankind has no cultural unity, no unified development, thus there can only be histories of individual cultures. Each civilization or culture, however, has unity and the values appropriate to each can be discovered. Values cannot be invented, but must arise from each tradition. Troeltsch remains confident that from the civilization of the West, values emerge which properly may serve to guide the future direction of the West.[43] Antoni describes Troeltsch as "the last of the German intellectuals to remain faithful to the old gods, to the Christian order of life, to culture, to liberal progress, to history, to civilization. He was the last to believe in them, in the theological faculties of the Protestant church itself."[44]

6. *The Failed Political System and the Diversity of Interests*

Among those of the university establishment who held the historicist view, the failure of the traditional political system fostered a deep sense of unease. They felt that the organic unity of the German spirit was threatened by party democracy. The new political parties had formed to represent a diversity of interests, the material interests of particular social groups. This ascendency of material interests over the interests of the *Geist* or spirit of the nation, reflected a chaotic social sphere no longer unified in its worldview. Colin Loader argues that this new arena of competing ideas threatened the customary authority of the university establishment as arbiter of culture and became a contributing factor in the crisis of historicism.[45] The view of historicists centered on the notion that

41. Ernst Troeltsch, *Gesammelte Schriften*, 3 (Tübingen: Mohr, 1912–25).
42. Antoni, *From History to Sociology*, 76–77.
43. Iggers, *German Conception*, 194.
44. Antoni, *From History to Sociology*, 41–42.
45. Loader, "German Historicism," 101. Loader gives an example of the authority of the university establishment prior to the war: Schmoller, in his inaugural

the state was an organic unity of shared values and that their interpretation of these values was, in fact, the whole and sufficient understanding of the nation. On the other hand, Marxists and party democrats viewed the historicists as simply another interest group. Historicists were confronted for the first time with a political reality which did not coincide with their convictions.[46]

a. *The Conflict with the German Spirit*
Loader finds three responses among the practicing historicists. The first response was that of the group who continued throughout their lives to believe that democracy was something foreign to the German spirit and represented an attack on the premises of historicism which could ultimately be repelled.[47] For these men there was no need to reconsider the position of historicism on the unity of values, only to hope for the traditional political forces to reassert themselves. Men like Weber and Otto Hintze provided the second response. They not only knew that it was impossible to recover the past, but they were further aware that, in Weber's words, "Scientific pleading is meaningless in principle because the various value spheres of the world stand in irreconcilable conflict with each other."[48] Their rejection of historicism made them virtual outsiders in the university community. The third response reflected the understanding that the former political arrangement was lost and that democracy was the order of the day. In this group belong such men as Troeltsch and Meinecke.[49] They supported democratic development, but

address as rector of the University of Berlin, claimed that Marxism had no scientific validity and Marxists could rightly be excluded from the university because they could not be good scientists.

46. Ibid., 102–3.

47. Georg von Below, Dietrich Schäfer, Ernst Marcks, and Max Lenz are among this group. Iggers (*German Conception*, 230) discusses them as a Neo-Rankian cohort, abandoning the liberal positions of the Prussian School, whose historians they continued to admire, and taking up the conservatism of Ranke, who was never an imperialist, nor a nationalist.

48. Max Weber, "Science as a Vocation," in his *Essays*, 129–56 (147).

49. Still in 1924, Karl Mannheim could proclaim, "Historicism has developed into an intellectual force of extra-ordinary significance; it epitomizes our Weltanschauung. The Historicist principle not only organizes like an invisible hand, the work of the cultural sciences, but also permeates everyday thinking... For in everyday life too we apply concepts with Historicist overtones, for example, 'capitalism,' 'social movement,' 'cultural process,' etc. These forces are grasped and understood as potentialities, constantly in flux, moving from some point in time to another; already on the level of everyday reflection, we seek to determine the position of our present within a temporal framework, to tell by the cosmic clock of history what

persisted in their idealist and organicist worldview. Their task, as they saw it, was the education or formation (*Bildung*) of the German people to a new set of values in which they could be united. They continued to believe that the people, allowed to develop fully, would naturally be in one accord with the spirit of the nation. The responsibility for fostering this accord lay with the cultural elite, not the state.[50] Meinecke expresses the notion this way: "Intellectual and spiritual aristocracy is by no means incompatible with political democracy... The values of our spiritual aristocracy...have to be carried into the political democracy, in order to refine it and protect it against degeneration."[51] Troeltsch also was convinced that history could provide the lessons that would engender the consciousness of the national spirit. This bridge from past to present would support the German people in their new exercise of democracy. In contrast to Weber and his advocacy of value-free science, the historicists who attempted to solve their "crisis" continued to insist that values were central to the academic enterprise. Education leads to the realization of spiritual ideals and properly subordinates material interests. Loader puts the problem thus:

> The options that appeared open to them—either to isolate the university from society to preserve the purity of scientific decisions on validity, or to improve lines of communication with society so that the university might reassert its spiritual leadership of the nation—were equally pathetic, since both refused to abandon the premise that there could be only one "scientific" Weltanschauung...and that the university should be the judge of its validity.[52]

7. The Challenges to Classical Historicism

Two insurmountable challenges to classical historicism appeared clear at the close of the war. First, the state could no longer be viewed as an ethical entity.[53] The war had illustrated for all time the dichotomy between

time it is" ("Historicism," in *Essays in the Sociology of Knowledge* [ed. Paul Kecskemeti; New York: Oxford University Press, 1952], 84–133 [84]).

50. Loader, "German Historicism," 106–7.

51. Fritz Ringer, *The Decline of the German Mandarins: The German Academic Community, 1890–1933* (Cambridge, Mass.: Harvard University Press, 1969), 212.

52. Loader, "German Historicism," 110.

53. Meinecke addresses the problem of power and ethics in his *Idee der Staatsräson in der neuren Geschichte* (Munich: Oldenbourg, 1924); ET *Machiavellism: The Doctrine of raison d'état and its Place in Modern History* (trans. Douglas Scott; London: Routledge & Kegan Paul, 1957). Here he argues that the state, rather than being the highest ethical individuality, actually represents interests in stark contrast

power and ethics. The second problem concerns the impossibility of objectivity. All values are products of culture, no eternal values exist apart from culture and, thus, no point of judgment can be found outside of history. Individual persons, formed as they are by their particular history, can offer no objective viewpoint or criticism. Iggers recalls that Dilthey, like Ranke before and Troeltsch later, assumed that the subject matter of history had "real existence and structure."[54] Biblical historians in Germany continued to be guided by this assumption in their quest to "understand" the Israelite experience. For the new generation of German writers in the 1920s only the subjective individual existed, formed by the irrational forces of time and place. The individual's position has little to do with cognition, rather it is "an act of will and of creation."[55] From this notion it was only a step to the concept of "historicity" (*Geschichtlichkeit*) espoused in Heidegger's *Being and Time*. Iggers argues that this is effectively the end of classical historicism. Historicity, like historicism, insists that humans have no nature, only history, but historicity contends that history has no objective reality. History is an inseparable aspect of humanity. Human beings are radically free, forever confronted with decisions. He explains, "These decisions always involve choice and creativity, a choice within the framework of the concrete possibilities of the situation... The individual creates his history not upon the basis of the objective happenings of the past, but by the decisions he directs toward the future."[56] The inevitable consequences of relativism had their final effect in the destruction of eternal values and the loss of meaning (meaningful process) expressed in the unfolding of history in unified individualities.

The effects of this view were delayed, however, by the political realities of the 1930s and 1940s. Iggers points out that no new generation of professional historians took its place in the universities in these years. Promising young historians, in particular students of Meinecke, left Germany after 1933. University chairs continued to be occupied by those who held them prior to World War I. This was true of biblical faculties as well. These historians were committed to some form of traditional idealist historicism and were willing to coexist with the Nazis, whether or not they endorsed the National Socialist ideology.[57]

---

to moral behavior. He continues to hold that the state is an individuality and that it operates as a political force little affected by social and economic influences.

54. Iggers, *German Conception*, 242.
55. Ibid., 243.
56. Ibid., 243–44.
57. Ibid., 238.

8. *Part Two: The United States*

That Germany possessed the sole secret of scholarship, was no more doubted by us young fellows in the eighteen-eighties than it had been doubted by George Ticknor and Edward Everett when they sailed from Boston, bound for Göttingen, in 1814.[58]

Regard for science, for exactitude, for the mental discipline involved in scientific enterprises, was at its highest point in the United States in the decades either side of the twentieth century. In an effort to promote these approaches and their allied values in the field of history, the American Historical Association (AHA) was founded in 1884. American historians sought the authority of science for their work through the process of professionalization. By establishing rigorous objectivity in method, they emphatically separated their work from the more expansive, colorful, and popular writing of amateur historians. Through professionalism they hoped to elevate the status of the academic historian. During this period several graduate programs were established at American universities, the *American Historical Review* was founded, and the Ph.D. became the necessary credential for appointment at respected colleges and universities.

9. *The German University as Model*

The model for professionalization of the discipline in the United States was the German university. Peter Novick notes that, in the nineteenth century, thousands of young Americans traveled to German universities to receive advanced academic training. They found a university system there quite unlike anything in the United States. American collegiate education centered on moral instruction

for the inculcation of "discipline"—mental, behavioral, religious. Student life was strangled in meticulously arrayed and rigidly enforced regulations; classroom work consisted, for the most part, of mechanical recitation; intellectual innovation was viewed as a threat to Protestant piety.

In Germany, they discovered a community of researchers devoted to standards of rigorous scholarship, whose task it was to train the next generation of scholars in the methods of excellence, rather than in any "religious or philosophical orthodoxy." They also were introduced to a variety of new techniques, among them paleography, numismatics, epigraphy, and, certainly, the critical examination of texts. Possibly most

---

58. Bliss Perry, *And Gladly Teach: Reminiscences* (Boston: Mifflin, 1935), 88–89.

startling was the status and prosperity of the German professor. In marked contrast to the "shabby figure of fun they had known in the United States," the German academic might rise in the civil service to a rank near the ministerial level or even be ennobled.[59] The organization of the German university for producing scholarship and scholars, the new methods and techniques, and the concomitant wealth and status for the professorate formed an irresistibly attractive model for returning Americans.

As American scholars attempted to mold their domestic system after what they had experienced in Germany, they found the rhetorical language of science ready-made for their purpose. The authority of science was well established in the American mind and those studying in German universities were captivated by the power of the notion of *wissenschaftliche Objektivität* (scientific objectivity). This concept appeared to provide a basis for the claim of historians to an empirical and value neutral approach to their studies.

a. *The Problem of Scientific Objectivity*
Both Novick and Iggers describe the misunderstandings that occurred when Americans attempted to transplant the German idea of scientific objectivity to the United States. The term *Wissenschaft*, which seemed to be directly represented by the English term "science," in fact denoted in German any organized body of information (*eine Wissenschaft*), a discipline, or simply scholarship or learning (*die Wissenschaft*). As an illustration, Fritz Ringer notes that while in English one might argue whether or not sociology is truly a science, in German to ask about sociology's status as a science (*eine Wissenschaft*) would be to wonder whether or not it existed as a discipline separate from, say, anthropology or psychology.[60] Novick says:

> The connotations of the word were rooted in the idealist philosophical tradition within which it developed. *Wissenschaft* signified a dedicated, sanctified pursuit. It implied not just knowledge, but self-fulfillment; not practical knowledge, but knowledge of ultimate meanings.[61]

The empiricist tradition of English speakers made understanding this Idealist concept virtually impossible.

Further complicating the adoption of the standards of the German historical discipline in America was misunderstanding of the concept *Geisteswissenschaften*. Novick notes that John Stuart Mill, who rendered

59. Peter Novick, *That Noble Dream: The Objectivity Question and the American Historical Profession* (Cambridge: Cambridge University Press, 1988), 22–23.
60. Ringer, *The Decline of the German Mandarins*, 102–3.
61. Novick, *That Noble Dream*, 24.

this term "moral sciences" in English, believed that the inductive methods of the natural sciences were appropriate for historical studies. This was an outrage to German historians, for whom *Geisteswissenschaften* actually meant "humanistic disciplines" or even "spiritual studies," those disciplines particularly unsuited, in the German mind, for natural science approaches.[62] For Americans, the notion of empirical, scientific, and neutral research in history or other of the moral sciences was a given. The German *Objektivität* (objectivity) came into American usage representing research concerned only with facts, facts without bias, portrayed uncolored and indicating no preference. As an English word, objectivity had been used since the seventeenth century to speak about the philosophy and psychology of consciousness and perception. In the sense of unbiased reporting, Novick reports that "George Bancroft, writing from Berlin in 1867, responding to the observation that his history was 'written from the democratic point of view,' denied the charge, claiming that 'if there is democracy in the history it is not subjective, but objective as they say here.'"[63]

Objectivity was associated in the mind of American historians with the figure of Ranke, held to be the founder and most inspiring model of the historical profession. That Ranke was greatly misunderstood by American historians is the prevailing view of scholars in the profession.[64] For Americans, Ranke exemplified the virtues of the strict scientific investigator, whose work was untainted by either philosophical or theoretical presuppositions. Not comprehending the Idealist foundation of the German historical tradition, American historians fastened onto Ranke's technical principles as support for their scientific aspirations. It was the innovation of the seminar and the new techniques for using sources that particularly recommended Ranke to American historians striving to establish a rigorous critical environment, to attend to facts, and to avoid

62. Ibid., 24 and n. 4.

63. Ibid., 25, quotes Bancroft from M. A. DeWolfe Howe, *The Life and Letters of George Bancroft* (2 vols.; New York, 1908), 2:183.

64. Dorothy Ross argues that the complexities of the age are disregarded in the view that historians pursued a Rankean search for facts alone. She gives evidence that conscious philosophical positions guided some of the first generation of professional historians. She admits, however, that "For Americans it was easy to fall back on nominalistic empiricism as the proper ground for an authentic science. Baconian empiricism, based on commonsense realism, had early become the dominant method of inquiry in America. For heirs of this tradition, induction from observed facts and skepticism regarding preformed generalizations seemed the high road to science" ("On the Misunderstanding of Ranke and the Origins of the Historical Profession in America," in Iggers and Powell, eds., *Leopold von Ranke and the Shaping of the Historical Discipline*, 154–70 [167]).

speculation. In response, they undertook to produce monographs that carefully avoided generalizations or interpretation. To painstakingly ascertain the facts was the mark of the true historian. The application of scientifically objective method produced confident certainty in the improved quality of the historians' work. Definitive history would necessarily be the result of the scientific approach. Ephraim Emerton expressed the optimism of American historians that history was advancing in accuracy and utility when he offered this comparison:

> If one must choose between a school of history whose main characteristic is *esprit*, and one which rests upon a faithful and honest effort to base its whole narration upon the greatest attainable number of recorded facts, we cannot long hesitate... Training has taken the place of brilliancy and the whole civilized world is today reaping the benefit.[65]

b. *Ranke in the United States*
Advocating the scientific approach, Herbert Baxter Adams turned to Ranke, who is "determined to hold strictly to the facts of history, to preach no sermon, to point no moral, to adorn no tale, but to tell the simple historic truth. His sole ambition was to narrate things as they really were, *wie es eigentlich gewesen*."[66] This phrase of Ranke's, so often quoted, is one of the chief sources of misunderstanding of both Ranke and the German historical tradition. Holborn says that the statement simply denies the "intention to present lessons from the past for the present."[67] Iggers argues that the translation of the adjective *eigentlich* as "actually" in English, while not inaccurate, does not convey the more significant, contemporary meaning of "characteristic, essential." He goes on to say, "This gives the phrase an entirely different meaning, and one much more in keeping with Ranke's philosophical ideas. It is not factuality, but the emphasis on the essential that makes an account historical."[68] Americans, intent on organizing historical studies on an empirical basis, found the directive to write history as it *actually* happened much to their taste. Ranke was the "father of historical science,"[69] who "turned the lecture room into a laboratory, using documents instead of 'bushels of clams.'"[70]

65. Ephraim Emerton, "The Practical Method in Higher Historical Instruction," in *Methods of Teaching and Studying History* (Boston, 1886), 42.
66. Herbert Baxter Adams, "New Methods of Study in History," in *Johns Hopkins University Studies in Historical and Political Science* 2d series, nos. I–II (1988): 101–31 (104–5).
67. Holborn, "The History of Ideas," 687.
68. Iggers and von Moltke, "Introduction," ix–x.
69. Adams, "New Methods," 65.
70. Walter P. Webb, "The Historical Seminar: Its Outer Shell and Its Inner Spirit," *Mississippi Valley Historical Review* 42 (1955–56): 3–23 (11).

c. *Science, Facts, and Impartial Observation*
Novick describes this change in "taste" and "climate" from the warm, romantic interest in the individual in the last decades of the nineteenth century. He points to the shift toward the scientific in literature, painting, and journalism. *Facts* must be presented to the audience: observations in literature, sense data directly related by painters. Journalists were instructed to remain impartial and to attend to strict accuracy. Layers of adjectives employed in previous decades were eschewed, replaced by "cold facts."[71] Novick quotes Henri Houssaye's opening speech to the 1904 Paris World Exposition:

> if the nineteenth century began with Goethe, Lord Byron, Lamartine, and Victor Hugo, with imagination and poetry…it ended with Pasteur, Taine, and Mommsen, with science and history… We want nothing more to do with the approximation of hypotheses, useless systems, theories as brilliant as they are deceptive, superfluous moralities. Facts, facts, facts—which carry within themselves their lesson and their philosophy. The truth, all the truth, nothing but the truth.[72]

This emphasis on facts forms the background for the strenuous debates among American biblical scholars continuing into the present.

Empirical observation, measurement, verification, and, above all, objectivity were watchwords of the age. This fascination with scientific approaches was in part the product of the remarkable advances in technology and discoveries in the natural sciences, which were, in these years, still accessible to lay people. Scientific approaches were based specifically on an understanding of Bacon's views promulgated by John Stuart Mill. Their influence took on a simplified, or "vulgarized" form in the public mind. The scientific investigator ought to confront a subject with no presuppositions, and, most certainly, no question or hypothesis to direct the research. Facts should be collected meticulously and careful observations recorded. These data, when assembled appropriately, then reveal their inner connections.[73]

This rather crude "Baconian induction" insisted that empirical observation was not subject to error. Only misuse of the facts on the part of the investigator through faulty inferences might introduce mistakes or distortion. The facts themselves could not be doubted. Science was practiced as classification. Bacon's dictates were understood to mean "scrupulous avoidance of hypotheses, scorned by Bacon as 'phantoms'. It was unscientific to go beyond what could be directly observed, to

71. Novick, *That Noble Dream*, 40–46.
72. Ibid., 37–38. Charles Victor Langlois and Charles Seignobos, *Introduction to the Study of History* (trans. G. G. Berry; New York: Henry Holt, 1898), 214.
73. Novick, *That Noble Dream*, 34–35.

'anticipate' nature."[74] The scientific mind should be able to set aside personal predilections, beliefs, aspirations, and fears and attend to the truth, facing good and bad with equanimity.

The final characteristic of the scientific venture was its finite nature. In the natural sciences, research was thought to be near completion. Little was left to discover, the scientist's primary task was to elaborate the complexities of already established principles. For historians this meant that with sufficient detailed monographs completed, the comprehensive, definitive history would be written. Langlois and Seignobos, in their famous manual for writing history, noted the limited stock of written documents. This limitation also contributed to the belief that history would soon be completely written. Thus, they are able to say:

> When all the documents are known, and have gone through the operations which fit them for use, the work of critical scholarship will be finished. In the case of some ancient periods, for which documents are rare, we can now see that in a generation or two it will be time to stop.[75]

This dependence on texts, a legacy of Ranke and the German tradition, was reinforced by the use of the English translation of Langlois and Seignobos, which was the standard handbook until World War II.[76]

10. *Professionalization of the Discipline*

Among the elements influential in the establishment of the American historical discipline, the German practice of regulating the profession by means of training and formation of the succeeding generation of scholars was attractive both on the grounds that the quality of historical research would improve through dissemination of modern techniques and that the field would be restricted to professional historians. Improved scholarship and restricted access to academic jobs together were anticipated to bring higher status and increased financial benefits. These goals were not immediately realized, but the process of professionalization was set in motion in 1884 with the foundation of the AHA.

In addition to reliance on its perceptions of the German historical establishment and its existence within a strongly scientific milieu in the United States, two additional factors characterize the early stages of the organization of the American discipline: the emphasis on accumulating

74. Ibid., 34.
75. Langlois and Seignobos, *Introduction*, 316.
76. A further consequence of the pre-eminence of documents for writing history was the conviction that history could never be known for the earliest periods of human experience because no written records existed.

quantities of "second-rate" work and the inclusion of amateur historians in the new professional association are intriguing elements, which at first glance would seem to undermine the very goals of professionalization. John Franklin Jameson, one of the founders, and long-time president of the association, wrote in 1891:

> Now it is the spread of thoroughly good second-class work that...our science most needs at present; for it sorely needs that improvement in technical process, that superior finish of workmanship, which a large number of works of talent can do more to foster than a few works of literary genius.[77]

John Higham argues that the "insular and fraternal habits of professional association tended to perpetuate [a] high level of mediocrity...," and that "the protected atmosphere of the classroom" further shielded scholars from rigorous intellectual criticism.[78] Novick notes, quoting Jameson, that standardization of technique was the whole point of professional training, not "to evoke originality, to kindle the fires of genius...but to regularize, to criticize, to restrain vagaries, to set a standard of workmanship and compel men to conform to it."[79]

a. *Authority and High Culture*
This effort to enforce conformity in the profession had as its goal the promotion of academic authority. In the culture of middle and late nineteenth-century America, "charlatans" and "quacks" competed with the exponents of new scientific discoveries and promoters of other bodies of new knowledge. Higham notes that, in the final decades of the nineteenth century, most fields had established associations and societies to define and implement standards in an effort to separate "authoritative" opinion from popular or even fraudulent information.[80] In this climate,

77. John Franklin Jameson, *The History of Historical Writing in America* (New York: Antiquarian Press, 1961 [1891]), 132–33.
78. John Higham, *History* (Englewood Cliffs, N.J.: Prentice–Hall, 1965), 7.
79. Novick, *That Noble Dream*, 52; John Franklin Jameson, "The Influence of Universities upon Historical Writing," *University of Chicago Record 6* (1902): 293–300 (299).
80. Higham, *History*, 8. The American Philological Association was founded in 1869, in the 1870s state examining boards initiated regulation of the medical profession, the National Education Association was organized in 1870 and the American Bar Association in 1878. Seventy-nine learned societies were established in the 1870s and a hundred and twenty-one in the 1880s. "The great metropolitan art museums, most of which were established in the 1870s, served as weighty arbiters of taste," while "new non-partisan, nondenominational magazines—the *Atlantic Monthly*, the *Century*, *Scribner's*" offered guidance to a middle-class audience seeking reliable direction in matters of importance.

historians were a significant force in the larger drive to promote a distinctive "higher" culture for the United States. Again, with Germany as a model—here the involvement of academics in political and ethical issues—American historians, led by John W. Burgess, hoped to advance the notion of the "aristocracy of culture," by training statesmen and public officials as well as scholars. The efforts to promote "higher" cultural values, to include statesmen, and to involve amateur historians, all were characteristics of the newly organized historical profession. These characteristics were facets of an outwardly directed endeavor, whose audience was the class of educated citizenry, the general reading public. The intellectual tastes of this public were formed and catered to by the work of historians.

Herbert Baxter Adams, director of historical studies at Johns Hopkins University, early promoter of professionalization in the field of history, and secretary of the AHA for its first sixteen years, recognized the need for organization to promote the goals of professional training and intellectual authority in the field of history. Adams sought to draw together "the patrician intellectual and the academic teacher to a common center of authority." Like Burgess, he imagined historians providing the core values of a cultural flowering involving "wealth, knowledge, intellect, fashion, and political power."[81] Of the original forty-one founders of the AHA, few had any formal training. The majority were men of leisure and culture. For two decades, the presidents of the AHA were amateurs. It was not until well after World War I that the Association's presidents were college professors holding advanced degrees. From 1890–1910 only twenty-five per cent of the members were college teachers, increasing to one-third in the years from 1912–1927. From 1928 onwards most were academic professionals. Novick notes that the selection of amateurs for the AHA's presidency accommodated an important constituency, but also reflected the reality that "much of the most distinguished historical work continued to be produced by those without Ph.D.'s or professorships."[82]

In an effort to bring the country's historical resources together under the auspices of the AHA, Adams invited local and state societies to

81. Higham, *History*, p. 15. In a similar vein Thomas Wentworth Higginson called for "an educated class amongst us, to be the guardians of the traditions and feelings and aspirations of high culture, and the diffuser of an atmosphere of thought and story—a kind of barrier, too, against the gross materialism of the time, the growing tendency to estimate the value of everything in dollars and cents, and to despise or shirk all discipline of mind or body which does no promise speedy return in hard cash" ("A Plea for Culture," *Atlantic Monthly* 19 [1867]: 29–37; *Nation* 4 [February 21, 1867]: 151–52).
82. Novick, *That Noble Dream*, 49.

participate in the activities of the Association. At the same time, he attempted to stir the federal government to sponsor research, establish functional archives, and publish its historical documents. He convinced congressmen and governmental officials to attend annual meetings of the AHA and arranged for the Association to report annually to the Smithsonian Institution, securing funding for office space and printing costs. These were tenuous connections at best. The AHA petitioned the government to exercise responsibility for gathering and cataloging historical documents without success. Neither the hoped for partnership with the federal government nor the expected leadership in the area of culture materialized.[83]

Higham observes that Adams' efforts to involve government and culture in a solid partnership, reminiscent of the political interests and affiliations of German academics and their role as conscience of the state, failed along with the effort to bring "the patrician intellectual and the academic teacher to a common center of authority." The movement toward "stricter professionalism gradually pulled the academic men away from patrician associations and from the wide culture that patrician life at its best embraced." After the 1890s the number of important histories written by amateurs declined rapidly. Higham says, "There is no reason to suppose that professionals crowded them out; they quit of their own accord."[84] Industrial and commercial expansion produced a growing class of workers, the arrival of new groups of immigrants increased the diversity of the population. These shifts brought with them significant social changes and an increasingly inclusive, democratic atmosphere little inclined to support a cultural aristocracy.

b. *A New Audience*

Toward the end of the nineteenth century, as the professionalization project gained momentum, historical interest began to subside in the general population. Higham mentions several instances, in the 1880s and 1890s, of extensive historical pieces serialized in monthly magazines such as the *Atlantic* and the *Century*, which also regularly featured historical essays. The first year's sale of Macaulay's *History of England* was two hundred thousand copies, or "one copy for every fifteen white families."[85] In comparison, Henry Adams' *History of the United States during the Administrations of Jefferson and Madison* sold only three thousand sets during the whole of the 1890s. The general audience for

83. Higham, *History*, 11–15.
84. Ibid., 15.
85. Ibid., 69.

works of history declined through the first decades of the new century as issues of reform captured the imagination of the educated classes. The elite magazines worked to keep their readers by satisfying their interest in current issues related to reform. While the amateur historians, the leisured and educated intellectuals, shifted their attention to progressive topics, the academic historians found themselves without a public. Professionalism offered a new audience, improved status, and a system of rewards.

Professional historians turned to questions which were of interest to fellow historians. Not questions of broad intellectual interest, those of moral or social problems to be weighed and debated from positions of partiality, but those whose answers filled gaps in previous knowledge. Objective knowledge was the goal. The enterprise was expected to be a cooperative one and rigorous criticism and discussion were supposed to be essential to the process, ultimately expressing the collective view. The actual appeal of the notion of objective knowledge was, however, that it was "incontrovertible and noncontroversial."[86] The likelihood of confrontation and sharp mutual criticism was reduced if the results of research and study could be agreed by all to be objective, untainted by personal interest or opinion. Impartiality and detachment were the chief values of the professional historian. Here again are characteristics of the discipline that will be important to historians in biblical studies in succeeding chapters.

c. *Professional Standards and the Pressure for Orthodoxy*
As history became institutionalized as a full-time occupation, neither the market nor the idiosyncratic tastes of the public was accepted as suitable judge of a scholar's work. In their place the "visible and consensual judgment of the profession established the value of an historian and his work, and largely determined the course of his career."[87] The vehicle for the presentation of scholarly work and for professional judgment was the *American Historical Review (AHR)*. Rather than providing serious scholarly criticism or a forum for controversy, however, the journal fostered mutual respect and deference, and support for the appearance of competence of fellow professionals. Scholars often declined to undertake book reviews, not wanting to criticize their peers or those upon whom their future advancement rested. As editor of the *AHR* beginning in 1895, J. Franklin Jameson refused to publish controversial or potentially divisive work. The AHA also avoided troubling topics at their meetings.

86. Novick, *That Noble Dream*, 58.
87. Ibid., 54.

Novick comments that, "The consensus among historians in this period is in some ways surprising, for there was never another time in American history in which, overall, there was so little consensus."[88] He cites institutional pressures as a significant force for orthodoxy among historians. Wealthy donors, college trustees, and compliant administrators served as influences for traditional views against the introduction of radicalism or socialism or a view of history as other than the work of Providence. Whereas, in Germany, professors advocated their views, assuming students' freedom to accept or reject, "American educators thought of students as being in constant danger of mental seduction," from religious heresy or social propaganda.[89]

Jameson was chosen president of the AHA in 1907. He had been educated in the United States, receiving in 1882 the first Ph.D. awarded by Johns Hopkins University. He was committed to professionalization of the historical discipline in America. He rejected H. B. Adams' efforts to include amateurs and statesmen in the Association and directed his energy instead to a program of coordinating professional scholarship in American history. Novick calls him "the best placed person in the profession to evaluate the output of American historians." Jameson himself saw the 1890s as a period marked by mediocrity, a time for historians to assemble a stock of materials that later generations would find useful for their historical syntheses.[90] Indeed, the prevailing notion appeared to be that views deviating from the norm would "fail the test of objectivity." Novick suggests that while this may have had an inhibiting effect on radicalism and heterodoxy, there is no evidence that the early professional historians held any ideas in conflict with the beliefs of the propertied classes. Establishment of "new, autonomous, policy-oriented social science disciplines" allowed the more politically active historians to move away from the field of history, leaving the practitioners of history as a group even more homogeneous.[91]

d. *National Unity*
Higham describes the early professional historians as conservative evolutionists, focused on the study of institutions. The attention to institutional history allowed historians to distance themselves from the sectional divisions that had brought the North and South into conflict, and to focus on the processes of government, the structural principles which fostered

88. Ibid., 63.
89. Ibid., 67.
90. Ibid., 55.
91. Ibid., 68–69.

the growth of national consciousness. Their firm belief that the "national state, now evolving toward empire, constituted the highest form of organization mankind had yet achieved," led them to celebrate the attainment of national unity and to emphasize continuity in history. By forgoing partisan sectional interests in their studies, they were able to maintain their devotion to objectivity in their work. Their attachment to the notion of national unity led them to a particular interest in the colonial period and ultimately to locate the American heritage in English antecedents.[92] The resulting histories promoted a favorable view of Anglo-Saxonism and the belief that this was the "race" of progress and was "primarily responsible for American's political evolution."[93] A new consensus on the Civil War was based on a view of the South as victim of northern excesses and misunderstanding. Novick notes that the new historiography of the colonial period, the American Revolution, and the Civil War was "firmly rooted in contemporary racist doctrine," which elevated the Anglo-Saxon at the expense of all others.[94] Novick remarks that, in addition to the ideological function the historians rendered by promoting the ideal of national unity, they were able to appropriate a sense of confidence in their own impartiality through the achievement of broad consensus. The political affinities developing between the United States and Britain allowed them to scorn the anti-British posture of past generations and never question the "present-mindedness" of the new interpretations.[95]

11. *The Advent of Social History*

With Frederick Jackson Turner's "The Significance of the Frontier in American History," published in 1893, an important shift in approach occurred. Customary attention to political activity and institutions in respected works of history had been supplemented occasionally by brief commentary on contemporary social conditions. T. C. Smith argues that "what Turner did was to reverse the traditional procedure and to examine the conditions of life existing in communities along the western edge of settlement with a view to tracing their results in the shape of political

92. Higham, *History*, 159–60.
93. Novick, *That Noble Dream*, 81.
94. Ibid., 80–81. "Racism increased in the United States in the course of the nineteenth century, particularly in educated circles, as it acquired the authority of science. Social Darwinists were racists, of course, but so were Darwin's opponents..." (p. 74); "By the end of the century, American expansionism contributed its bit to the racist consensus" (p. 76).
95. Ibid., 83.

habits, institutions, ideals, and social structure." Turner's influence is found in the work of the many who followed his inspiration.[96] These writers saw their histories as presenting an entirely different approach to the past from that of their predecessors, whose work they criticized for their preoccupation with public affairs, a "conventional and superficial outlook," that failed to comprehend the actual forces that controlled events. Indeed, in chastising their forebears for their "partiality" and "parochialism," the new school "seemed always to praise the figures condemned" by the older writers and "to point out the flaws in the men of whom they approved."[97] One consequence of the standards of technical accuracy and objectivity should be noted. General works produced in prior generations, possessed of the unity and authority of a single author, were not possible in the new setting. The ideals of thoroughness, accuracy, and objectivity fostered individual specialization, in contrast to the creation of works of broad scope. Cooperative, multi-volume works of history were produced to provide comprehensive histories of the United States and its various regions and aspects, but the real contribution of the historians writing in the final decades of the nineteenth century through the inter-war period was found in specialized, independent works.[98]

a. *Material Interests*
Along with Turner's emphasis on the social aspects of American life for the reconstruction of history, alternative approaches were undertaken by other historians as well. Four men in particular represent the New/Progressive turn in history: Turner, John Franklin Jameson, Charles A. Beard, and Carl Becker. In his presidential address to the AHA in 1907, Jameson called for a close scrutiny of American religious sources in order to shed light on "the national character."[99] Becker, in his first book, *The History of Political Parties in the Province of New York*, published in 1909, presented the thesis that revolutionary activity arose in the lower classes in their efforts to wrest political and economic benefits from the wealthy and powerful classes. In 1913, Beard published the *Economic*

96. T. C. Smith, "The Writing of American History, 1884–1934," *American Historical Review* 40 (1935): 439–49 (441–43). G. L. Beer on British colonial policy; P. A. Bruce on colonial Virginia; C. W. Alvord, on the Mississippi Valley in British Politics; C. H. Van Tyne on the revolution; U. B. Phillips on Southern institutions; A. T. Mahan on sea power in the War of 1812; F. E. Chadwick on the relations between the US and Spain; E. D. Adams on Great Britain and the Civil War.
97. Ibid., 443.
98. Ibid., 445.
99. John Franklin Jameson, "The American Acta Sanctorum," *American Historical Review* 13 (1908): 286–302.

Interpretation of the Constitution. Beard, informed by a Marxist materialist theory of human behavior, argued that, rather than the prevailing view that sectional issues produced the struggle over the constitution, it was the personal interests of the socially prominent classes and their efforts to protect those interests that shaped the foundational document. Thus, Beard introduced a more controversial, potentially radical element into the practice of history in America, for if historical events are analyzed in terms of clashes between economic classes and the development of democracy, then "objectivity" or "impartiality" as standards for procedure are called into question.

12. *The New History, Reform, and Progress*

These shifts in approach to the writing of history, in the sources chosen to illuminate the life and experiences of past generations, in the concepts employed to organize the events of the past, were the innovations of progressive history written by the New Historians. Several factors in the contemporary American culture around the turn of the century resulted in a changed climate for historians. The fervor for reform captured the imagination of the public, including historians. Higham says:

> The crucial fact underlying both their theory and their practice was a broad sympathy with the spirit of reform then developing in the country... As progressives, the New Historians had a vivid sense that a great turning point had arrived in American experience. They wanted to participate in the transformation and to explain it.

The significant change in history writing resulting from enthusiasm for reform was the emphasis on conflict and change in place of unity and continuity. Whereas the nineteenth-century historians were concerned with the development of institutions, twentieth-century historians were captivated by change brought about by "conflicts of interest and clashes of purpose." Progress in society "was neither automatic nor secure, but had to be won at every step, over entrenched opposition."[100]

The attitudes of the Progressive Historians were informed by a conviction that the United States had flourished by shedding the constraints of older European traditions, by forging its own special identity through controversies and conflicts between various interests. Unity was not the chief value for these historians, but rather a continuing struggle for extended democracy. The historians who were in the forefront of this movement were, for the most part, from the South and Midwest. They

100. Higham, *History*, 171–72.

were interested in portraying the role that other sections of the country had in the development of the United States, and, in doing this, breaking the monopoly of Eastern historians on the writing of history. The sectional analysis of American history, first applied by Turner, produced powerful insights into causes underlying American foreign policies, including the economic interests of various groups, both north and south, in the Civil War. Ultimately, however, distinctive sections were difficult to maintain. In many situations, sections appeared to overlap or break into ever smaller units. Finally, a sectional approach was not fully suited to the sensitivities of the Progressive Historians, to whom economic conflict inevitably suggested a contest between the democratic multitude and the privileged aristocratic classes.[101] This perennial American theme was strengthened by Marxist influence then beginning to appear in American universities. James Harvey Robinson claimed that "a sober and chastened form" of Marxism "serves to explain far more of the phenomena of the past than any other single explanation ever offered."[102] Progressive Historians found that the notion of class conflict separated from socialism as a political ideology proved to be a useful analytical tool. They easily discarded Marx's dialectical model and interpreted historical materialism as simply the political importance of property. Marx's real effect on American historians was to alert them to forms of property relations.[103]

a. *Conflict and Discontinuity*
As the Progressive Historians substituted conflict for unity in their analysis of the past, so they found discontinuity a more significant feature of history than the continuity emphasized by the conservative evolutionists who dominated the profession.[104] Turner, in his frontier thesis, denied that American liberal and democratic institutions developed from the "germ" generated among the early German tribes and nurtured by their descendants in England and America, as proponents of Anglo-Saxonism held. Rather, Turner argued that the expanding frontier and the availability of free land fostered the evolution of American democratic

101. Ibid., 173–74.
102. James Harvey Robinson, *The New History: Essays Illustrating the Modern Historical Outlook* (New York: Free Press, 1965), 51.
103. Higham, *History*, 179.
104. Higham (ibid., 173) characterizes the Progressive's vision of America: "it was a livelier America, constantly in flux, full of real and vital conflicts between contending groups. It was less stable and more deeply divided than the America of the conservatives; it was less securely anchored in traditions reaching back across the centuries."

institutions. His attention to the social and economic context in which institutions developed offered a departure from traditional political and constitutional studies. This shift generated some anxiety among professional historians because discrete bodies of legal and archival materials were not available in areas of social research. The historian was forced, instead, to choose from among many materials and documents those that seemed useful, promoting the charge that investigation had been replaced by speculation. The extension of historical investigation into new areas of social study also brought with it a resurgence of the debate over methods appropriate to the study of history—individualizing or generalizing concepts. These issues, important in discussion in academic departments of history, will be remarkably absent in the debate over method in the following chapter.

b. *The Problem of Presentism*

It was the charge of "presentism," however, that was most acute in regard to the Progressive Historians. Novick mentions Beard's *Economic Interpretation of the Constitution* as a particular instance of writing history with the interests of the present in mind. Beard's explication of conflicting class interests in the early republic could hardly be ignored as commentary on the contemporary class struggles. Becker amplified the notion of history as useful to the present in his remark that "Historical thinking…is a social instrument, helpful in getting the world's work more effectively done."[105] Robinson added:

> Our books are like very bad memories which insist upon recalling facts that have no assignable relation to our needs, and this is the reason why the practical value of history has so long been obscured… The present has hitherto been the willing victim of the past; the time has now come when it should turn on the past and exploit it in the interests of advance.[106]

Turner stated, "Each age writes the history of the past anew with reference to the conditions uppermost in its own time."[107] The Progressive Historians' commitment to social reform is undoubted, as is their belief

---

105. Carl Becker, "Some Aspects of the Influence of Social Problems and Ideas upon the Study and Writing of History," *American Journal of Sociology* 18 (1913): 641–75 (642).

106. Robinson, *New History*, 22, 24.

107. Frederick Jackson Turner, *The Early Writings of Frederick Jackson Turner* (Madison: University of Wisconsin Press, 1938), 52. John Dewey's famous statement is "all history is necessarily written from the standpoint of the present, and is, in an inescapable sense, the history not only of the present but of that which is contemporaneously judged to be important in the present" (*Logic*, 235).

that history should be an aid to such reform, but the charge of "presentism" must be qualified. The Progressives remained dedicated to the professional standard of objectivity in their work. Indeed, they believed that illuminating conflict and discontinuity served as a corrective to the tendentious work of the previous generation of conservative evolutionists. Not until after the war was relativism a serious issue, nor was the discipline prepared to debate its dedication to the ideal of the objective presentation of history. Novick suggests that the Progressives, at least in part, were making "an historicist criticism directed at the pretensions of social science, which offered its propositions as timeless truth, and a protest against historians being reduced to the role as data gatherers for social scientists."[108]

c. *Relativism and Progress*
On the issue of relativism, Robinson wrote, shortly before the war, that history "should not be regarded as a stationary subject which can only progress by refining its methods and accumulating, criticizing, and assimilating new material." He insisted that increasing knowledge causes opinions to change and the resulting relativity "renders all our conclusions provisional."[109] Becker alone, however, questioned the notion of progress itself. He argued that in every age certain dominant social forces influence thought and thus history must reflect the time in which it is written; no final conclusion could be reached on historical truths. He pointed out that no standard existed for the evaluation of progress.[110] While Becker's scepticism produced no visible effect on the discipline before the war, the issue of objectivity and relativism had been introduced.

13. *The Challenges of World War I*

The Progressive Historians formed a strong minority prior to the war and shared with the conservative evolutionists the work of the professional community.[111] Both Robinson and Becker were on the editorial board of the *AHR*. Turner and Robinson served as president of the AHA, but Higham finds the balance shifting toward the Progressive view after 1910. World War I brought a series of challenges to the historical profession, challenges to the notion of progress and to the posture of

108.   Novick, *That Noble Dream*, 103.
109.   Robinson, *New History*, 25, 130.
110.   Novick, *That Noble Dream*, 106.
111.   Higham, *History*, 183.

objectivity. Controversy over the war itself caused historians to lose confidence in the belief that, by employing professional standards of investigation, historians would come to a consensus. Faith in progress was difficult to maintain. Before the United States' entry into the war, American historians had criticized their European colleagues for excessive patriotism that had set the stage for war. When the United States declared war on Germany, virtually all professional historians embraced the Allied cause and began their repentance "for having insufficiently promoted American patriotism; for having left American youth morally unprepared for their military duties."[112] The participation of historians in the war effort, they hoped, would demonstrate that historians were not taken up with obscure events of the past, but, like scientists, had useful contributions to make. Historians were involved in a great range of service, often using language and research skills, but most were employed in writing propaganda or producing "a sound and wholesome public opinion."[113]

The conclusion of the war brought disillusionment and introspection. Professionalism had provided little restraint to patriotic fervor in any of the contending countries. Particular canons of scholarship concerned with proper citation and the use of reliable documents could be followed scrupulously and still the resulting histories, pamphlets, and public school lessons would be nothing less than flagrant propaganda. Some historians in retrospect regretted their immoderation during the war years; some defended themselves by drawing attention to their painstaking accuracy and balance in a noble cause. Others found the war had tempered their materialism with an appreciation for sacrifice and fine sentiment. For the Progressives, military victory was insufficient. They had hoped for a defeat of imperialism, for the end of the capitalist exploitation of labor, and some amelioration of the gulf between the rich and the poor. Their disillusionment was intense. The cause of justice and liberty they saw overwhelmed by greed and self-righteousness at Versailles. They wondered at their own naivety during the war in supposing that their ideals would be established at the conclusion of hostilities. In reviewing the period before the war, Progressives realized that in regarding certain occurrences as important, it was possible to overlook the truly significant. It seemed clear to them that the meaning they had found in history was dependent on a view of progress that was now shattered.[114]

112. Novick, *That Noble Dream*, 117.
113. Ibid., 118.
114. Ibid., 128–31.

The disillusionment engendered by the war brought with it a general reassessment of traditional American values. Many hoped "to exorcize the crusading, self-righteous idealism of the war years" much of it associated "with New England—a land of Puritans, abolitionists, and other moral fanatics."[115] The Progressives, as mid-westerners and southerners, had long been antagonistic to the moneyed, patrician Northeast. Questioning the idealism of the crusaders of New England suggested questions about the moral character of the Civil War, and new works appeared chronicling corruption and profiteering in the Union army. Revisionists rewrote the history of the Civil War as a conflict brought on the common man by extremists. Similarly, Turner's ideal of the frontier society as the crucible of American virtue and the democratic spirit was challenged by new histories of opportunistic land speculators. The established views of Turner and Beard were attacked by newer Progressives who rejected the determinism of social forces in favor of the forces of irrationalism, unpredictable elements, chance, passion, and folly.[116]

The topics of the histories in the post-war years reflected the influence of the Progressives. Social histories and economic interpretations replaced political histories. Constitutional studies were superseded by works on religious and ethnic groups in America. Colonial history was either neglected or folded into the history of the early republic. Higham observes that "the old conservative school, although strongly entrenched in many institutions, suffered a steady and ultimately disastrous loss of intellectual vitality."[117] The ambiguous relationship between history and science developed further complications and this further altered the direction of post-war history. Neither the optimism of the Progressive view, nor the disillusionment brought about by the war and its aftermath, produced any immediate change in the practice of history in biblical studies. The field had become relatively isolated by this time.

a. *Objectivity, Knowledge, and Relativism*
Historians faithfully resisted pressures to turn to laws of human behavior or generalized theories to explain historical events, but, at the same time, had adopted methods they insisted were empirical and objective in the very best sense of "scientific." The years after the war brought remarkable discoveries in the sciences, which forced rethinking of the relation between object of investigation and the method or instrument employed in its study. Scientists declared that the object of knowledge was not a

115. Higham, *History*, 198–99.
116. Ibid., 204.
117. Ibid., 183.

reality to be revealed by a particular mechanism; depending on what question one asked, the very physical elements appeared in different aspects. For some historians this meant that history, likewise, was not simply a reality waiting to be described "as it actually happened." Written history was the product of the questions put to the past by its researchers. The term "relativist" was applied to historians in the United States who took up this view.[118] New scientific approaches were also adopted in biblical studies, and while this caused sharp debate over method between German and American scholars, the reality of the object of investigation was not doubted. The historical questions for biblical scholars, as the next chapter will show, continued to be derived from the biblical text.

b. *Everyman as Historian*
Certainly before the war, Beard, Becker, and Robinson had begun their criticism of the conservative establishment on the grounds that history ought to illuminate the issues of the present. Following the war, these men, joined by others eager for history to become more relevant to the thought and issues of the day, sought to reform the discipline in the manner of the social sciences, to become involved in interdisciplinary research, and to widen the scope of historical investigation. Becker's first allusion to the issues of relativism and the limitations of the historian came in 1910. His views had virtually no impact at the time. Higham comments on the reaction by fellow Progressives, "Doubly shielded from heresy—first by their profession's deafness to philosophical discussion, second by their own progressive faith—they too easily blamed history's difficulties on the pettifogging conservatives in their midst." In the 1920s, Becker's relativism coincided with the temper of disillusion, but it was his presidential address to the AHA in 1931 that provided the impetus for the commanding relativist movement that followed.[119] Becker gracefully sketched, by definition and example, a case for the usefulness of history. He argued that history cannot be reduced to sets of statistics or stated in terms of a mathematical formula: "It is rather an imaginative creation, a personal possession which each one of us, Mr. Everyman, fashions out of his individual experience, adapts to his practical or emotional needs, and adorns as well as may be to suit his aesthetic tastes." Mr. Everyman is not completely free in creating his own history. His

118.   Novick writes about the changes in the physical and natural sciences and its impact on historians in Chapter 6 of *That Noble Dream*.
119.   Carl Becker, "Everyman His Own Historian," *American Historical Review* 37 (1932): 221–36.

view must conform to the views of those around him in order for him to function successfully in his world.[120] Becker reminds his audience that knowledge must be adapted to the present necessities, that

> the history that does work in the world, the history that influences the course of history, is living history, that pattern of remembered events, whether true or false, that enlarges and enriches the collective specious present… It is for this reason that the history of history is a record of the "new history" that in every age rises to confound and supplant the old.[121]

It can be noted here that this very American view of history's usefulness to the present will be seen in the American approach to reconstructing Israel's history.

14. *The Passing of "Scientific" History*

Becker maintains that history is "the memory of things said and done."[122] He declares that it is the task of historians to

> preserve and perpetuate the social tradition; to harmonize, as well as ignorance and prejudice permit, the actual and the remembered series of events; to enlarge and enrich the specious present common to us all to the end that "society" (the tribe, the nation, or all mankind) may judge of what it is doing in the light of what it has done and what it hopes to do.[123]

Becker argues that the age of "scientific" history is passing. The fond belief in the possibility of objectivity is belied by the certainty that even the "most disinterested historian has at least one preconception, which is the fixed idea that he has none." He points out that the facts of history, stated in the sources, cannot be restated without reshaping them. "Left to themselves, the facts do not speak." At the very least, the historian must select facts to portray, and "to select and affirm even the simplest complex of facts is to give them a certain place in a certain pattern of ideas, and this alone is sufficient to give them a special meaning."[124] Becker concludes that it is the historian's duty "to be as honest and as intelligent as human frailty permits" and that

> neither the value nor the dignity of history need suffer by regarding it as…incomplete representation of the reality that once was, an unstable pattern of remembered things redesigned and newly colored to suit the

120. Ibid., 228.
121. Ibid., 234–35.
122. Ibid., 223.
123. Ibid., 231.
124. Ibid., 233.

convenience of those who make use of it. Nor need our labors be the less highly prized because our task is limited, our contributions of incidental and temporary significance. History is an indispensable...endeavor.[125]

In his presidential address to the AHA two years later, Charles Beard identified history as "contemporary thought about the past" and declared this to be "in accordance with the most profound contemporary thought about history, represented by Croce, Riezler, Karl Mannheim, Mueller-Armack, and Heussi..." He observed that it has "been said for a century or more that each historian who writes history is a product of his age, and that his work reflects the spirit of the times..." Contemporary thought, therefore, repudiates the notion that it is possible to write history as it actually happened.[126] Beard calls for historians to cast off subservience to "the assumptions of natural science." Giving up these deterministic and evolutionary schemes that distort history, forsaking the patterns of physics and biology, the historian is confronted by the realization that "all history is merely relative to time and circumstance..." Beard observes that the concept of relativity in history must also be a time-limited phase of thought, destined to be rejected as were the assumptions of theology, metaphysics, and science.[127] Beard suggests that writing history in the face of this knowledge is "an act of faith."[128] He goes on to say that work done in the scientific spirit is by no means useless, "the scientific method is, therefore, a precious and indispensable instrument of the human mind," but the historian must harbor no illusions that he or she is producing a science of history: "Any selection and arrangement of facts... is controlled inexorably by the frame of reference in the mind of the selector and arranger."[129]

15. *The Noble Dream*

In this address, Beard separates method from both theory and philosophy. Late the following year, in a response to T. C. Smith's defense of "objective history," Beard takes up the question of method again.[130] In answer to Smith's charge that the Association is deeply divided between

125.   Ibid., 235.
126.   Charles A. Beard, "Written History as an Act of Faith," *American Historical Review* 39 (1934): 219–31 (220).
127.   Ibid., 225.
128.   Ibid., 226.
129.   Ibid., 227.
130.   Charles A. Beard, "That Noble Dream," *American Historical Review* 41 (1935): 74–87.

those remaining true to the standards of objective history as the "noble dream" and those who do not "consider it necessary to be impartial or even fair," Beard argues that whatever the ends of the two groups may be, certainly both seek truth. "Those scholars who are placed by Smith in opposition to the noble dream may be as patient in their inquiries and as rigorous in their criticism and use of documentation as the old masters of light and leading."[131]

Insisting that a consistency in method is found in both groups of historians, Beard takes up what he calls the "all-embracing philosophy of historiography" of the noble dream. This philosophy insists that "history as it actually was can be disclosed by critical study, can be known as objective truth, and can be stated as such..." It assumes that history exists as an object outside the mind of the historian, that the historian can know this object and can describe it as it objectively existed, that for the purposes of research, the historian can divest him or herself of all "taint of religious, political, philosophical, social, sex, economic, moral, and aesthetic interests," that the events of history had some structural organization through inner relations, which can be grasped and described, and finally, that history can be grasped by purely rational or intellectual efforts, and that it is not permeated or accompanied by anything transcendent.[132] Beard argues that these assumptions are faulty and were not wholly accepted in the United States during the previous fifty years as Smith maintains. Beard supports his discussion with references to German writers and to Croce, with whom he alone among American historians was familiar.[133]

Higham believes that the contact between American New History and German neo-Idealism "did considerable violence to both." He makes three points. Beard used German ideas to place limits on the claims of science, but at the same time "clung to a positivistic conception of knowledge as a structure external to the observer." While arguing that an objective view of history is an impossibility, Beard continued to attempt an objective methodological posture. Beard's pragmatism kept him from understanding the subjectivity of Croce and Heussi. Subjectivity for them was a "mode of understanding, an identification of the observer

131.   Ibid., 75.
132.   Ibid., 76.
133.   Higham (*History*, 126) notes that American historians "lost touch with German thought after the turn of the century." Beard traveled to Germany in 1927 and established contact with leading scholars. His son-in-law, Alfred Vagts, guided his travels and subsequent reading. Through the 1930s, Beard urged his colleagues to read Dilthey, Troeltsch, H. Rickert, and Karl Heussi to no avail (Novick, *That Noble Dream*, 157–58).

with the observed." For Beard and the American pragmatists, subjectivity was related to partiality, to the historian's social goals and personal values—the opposite of objectivity.[134]

16. *Conservatives and Relativists*

Smith's article was only one instance of the controversy stirred by Beard's challenge to reconsider the nature of historiography. The annual meeting of the AHA the year following Beard's address, "Written History as an Act of Faith," devoted all three general sessions to philosophical issues. This was a remarkable departure from the fiercely antiphilosophical stance that the American historical discipline had held from its inception. The relativist movement within the New History set at odds those who were sympathetic to the social sciences and those who opposed them. The desire of the pragmatists to make history useful still tied values to a search for scientific laws. The orthodox or conservative historians denounced the relativists as defeatists who claimed there could be no objectivity and even went so far as to associate their approach with fascism. On the other hand, the relativists "implied that their opponents, puttering over harmless and distant facts, were practicing vicarious leisure and conspicuous waste."[135] While orthodox scientific historians insisted that the relativists had abandoned objectivity, the relativists were actually arguing that awareness of one's limitations could promote greater objectivity. The relativists insisted that the orthodox believed unconditionally in the possibility of objectivity, when the more orthodox historians simply pressed to eliminate all possible bias.

Ultimately, the relativist argument undermined the New History as well as the older conservative view committed to objective history. A treatise published by the Social Science Research Council, heavily influenced by Beard, gave the relativist argument a definitive statement that provided the grounds for the final controversy. Based in the awareness of the relativistic limits of history, the traditional allegiance to objective history was reaffirmed. Written history is always a product of a particular time, place, and personal view, a "frame of reference," but to reduce bias as much as possible, one should avoid absolutes and recognize one's own assumptions. For several years, historians debated the topic at professional meetings, but in speaking of objective relativism, the New Historians had revealed the contradictions and inconsistencies of their program. By the end of the thirties, most historians had come to accept

134. Higham, *History*, 126–27.
135. Ibid., 129.

some aspects of relativism and the gulf between Progressives and conservatives had narrowed considerably. The New History was no longer an issue.[136]

17. Conclusion

Throughout the fifty or so years between 1885 and the beginning of World War II, the discipline of history in the United States and Germany exhibited certain similarities in its evolution. Both traditions firmly resisted philosophical speculation. Philosophical abstractions were anathema to historical studies, which were held to be always concerned with the individual, particular, and unique instances of human behavior. Natural science was regarded with similar distaste for its generalizing tendencies. On the other hand, social science occupied a more ambiguous position. In Germany, social science was associated with positivism, efforts at generalization, and the search for laws of behavior, all of which were rejected by historians as transgressing the commitment to the concept of the individual as moral agent in history. Social science also focused attention on economic and irrational social forces which brought about change. This determinism was incompatible with the belief in the unfolding of the inner character of individualities. The notion of the continuing actualization of individual entities carried with it an impetus for studying the state, with particular attention given to political development and the institutions through which the state operated.

In the United States, social science suggested empirical research, which coincided with American historians' deep attachment to objectivity. Throughout the twenties the social sciences were acquiring greater status in the university and in the public consciousness. Academic departments in the social science disciplines were expanding and they were the beneficiaries of significant support from research foundations. American historians made dedicated efforts to work more closely with social scientists and to encourage interdisciplinary research. The concept of culture was employed to approach society as a whole, while allowing a focus on local or specialized history.[137] Social science had a very different relationship to history in the United States and Germany. Rejected in Germany for its determinism and generalizations, in the United States social science was a model of empiricism and objectivity and a path to the status of science for the discipline of history.

136. Ibid., 130–31.
137. Ibid., 117–19.

Political history and the critical use of official documents were identifying characteristics of German history throughout the nineteenth and much of the twentieth century. Because of the early affinity for German history in the United States and the German training of many American nineteenth-century historians, attention to political and institutional history was also a hallmark of written history in America well into the twentieth century. The fortunes of the state were faithfully documented and the idea of empire was positively featured in works of history in this period. In Germany, the prominent historians supported the government's colonial expansion and exhibited pride in Germany's increasingly powerful position in world politics. American historians likewise supported a growing notion of empire in the United States by emphasizing the enduring connections to Great Britain. The evolution of English institutions continuing through the American experience replaced the story of American struggle for liberty against the tyranny of the English. Based in the romantic notion of a common Anglo-Saxon heritage, American history was both racist and anti-Semitic. Germany displayed similar tendencies to denigrate Celts and Latins, Irish and French, Spanish, and Italians. Mommsen himself held anti-Semitic views and was a noted Anglophile.[138]

With the outbreak of World War I, historians in both the United States and Germany contributed unabashedly to the propaganda of their own countries. German historians quickly became disillusioned. In the United States, some historians ultimately regretted their involvement, others felt they had maintained an appropriate balance, many were frankly disillusioned.

In Germany, the pre-war uncertainties focused by relativism developed into a moral crisis. Relativism in the United States, associated with the progressive New History, produced an acute controversy over the possibility of objective history. As early as 1910, relativism was introduced by Becker, but the debate took hold only after the war. German relativism, while having implications for impartial history writing, was chiefly concerned with the problem of moral values. German historians, like American historians, saw themselves as providing moral leadership. German historians presented the moral ideal of the state through their work. The meaning of history was bound up with written history. In the nineteenth century, American historians, amateur and professional, sought to elevate the culture of the country. With the era of reform in the early twentieth century, the New Historians saw history as a means for fostering progress. The progressive agenda of the New Historians

138. Wiedemann, "Mommsen's Roman History."

appeared to conservatives to be an abandonment of the goal of objectivity. German relativism was a more philosophical dilemma, the recognition that cultural values could never be criticized by one outside of the culture. This surrender of ultimate values left German historians in a state of confusion from which they tried to salvage some meaning in history. Among historians in Germany and the United States, similarities in social function and superficial resemblances in their approach to documents were overshadowed by the differences between German Idealism and American pragmatism, yet both traditions failed in their attempts to satisfactorily define the relationship of the writer to the past. For both, the writer was inevitably captive of his or her culture or "frame of reference," capable of only a partial view. The historical discipline in Germany and the United States had to wait until the close of World War II to begin to reform their goals. In the following chapter, historiography in biblical studies in both Germany and the United States will be compared to the development just outlined in academic departments of history.

Chapter 5

BIBLICAL HISTORY AT MID-CENTURY:
JOHN BRIGHT AND MARTIN NOTH

For a long time historical presentation satisfied itself with taking up views
contained in oral and written sources, re-shaping them more or less, and
recounting them afresh; and the facts regarded through this illusion as
"transmitted," passed for valid History, much as if the history of Alexander the Great's successors should pass as nothing but a succession of
wars, because forsooth our sources for that period speak of scarcely
anything else but wars. Only since we have begun to recognize Monu-
ments and Remains as included in historical material and to avail ourselves of them methodically, has the investigation of past events gone
deeper and planted itself on a firmer foundation. And with the discovery
of the immeasurable gaps in our historical knowledge, which investigation has not yet filled up and perhaps now never can fill up, investigation
espies ever wider breadths to the domains with which it has to do, and
anticipates one day filling them with life. The presentation of the results
of investigation will be more correct the more its consciousness of its
ignorance equals that of its knowledge.[1]

In 1930, Leonard Woolley, discoverer and excavator of Ur, claimed,
"The aim of the field archaeologist is to discover and to illustrate the
course of human history."[2] The discovery of the course of human history
is the undoubted goal of the historian, as well, and the particular history
of Israel, most certainly the goal of John Bright and Martin Noth. Their
approaches to this task differed famously. Each had a remarkable
relationship with his teacher and represented, in the minds of his readers, a set of assumptions associated with his national background. The
appellations American School, or the School of Albright, and the German
School, or the School of Alt, often attached to their respective views.
This chapter will examine the particular traits of the approach and work
of each of these scholars and relate them to one another and to the

1. Droysen, *Outline*, 51.
2. Leonard Woolley, *Digging Up the Past* (London: Penguin, 1930), 33.

academic community of the first half of the twentieth century. I will argue that Noth follows in the German tradition of historical Idealism, that his intent is to *understand* ancient Israel. His methods center on the use of texts and the discovery of their meanings for the reconstruction of Israel's history. The relativism controversies that plagued the discipline in the early years of the century and following World War I have no interest for Noth because of his own belief in the metaphysical background of the life of ancient Israel. I will argue that Bright is also a figure formed in his national tradition. He remains fully confident that objectivity is possible and that meaning will emerge from the faithful presentation of "facts." Like Noth, Bright is not involved in the theoretical controversies of the contemporary departments of history. Noth addresses a scholarly audience, trained for the demands of presentation and rebuttal, an audience similarly skilled in philology and language. Bright, too, writes for the scholarly audience, but he is influenced also by the needs of a broader popular audience eager to learn the results of contemporary discoveries. Finally, Noth and Bright are separated by their respective traditions' interest in the meaning of ancient Israel. For Noth, the goal of the historian is to discover and reconstruct the meaning of the life of ancient Israel, while for Bright, it is important to learn what Israel means for people today.

John Bright was born in 1908, Martin Noth in 1903. Noth died in the Negev in 1968, suddenly and unexpectedly, at the relatively young age of 65. Bright lived to be 87, observing many challenges to the hypotheses that distinguished biblical studies earlier in his life. These two men exercised enormous influence during their lives, Noth most especially in the academic world with his hypothesis that Israel's early cultural and cultic life centered in an amphictyony similar to those later established in Greece and his proposal that Deuteronomy introduced a historical work extending through 2 Kings. In no way to denigrate his influence as critic and scholarly authority, Bright's most enduring contribution was in the education of several generations of students in both colleges and seminaries. His *History of Israel* served as the basic text in classes beginning in 1959 and continuing well into the 1990s.

These two men's names have come to stand for opposing approaches to writing Israel's history. Noth chose to work primarily within the biblical text. Indeed, he was labeled a "minimalist," even a "nihilist," by both Albright and Bright, who accused him of refusing to accept external evidence offered by archaeology. On the other hand, it was argued that Bright's dedication to the biblical view of history constrained his scholarship. These characterizations obscure the complexities of Noth's and

Bright's approaches. Fixing their views within a larger context before
examining their particular methods seems useful.

1. *Three Approaches to the Bible as a Historical Source*

Many of the so-called "assured results" of research in the first half of
the twentieth century have by now been questioned or discarded, moving
the "minimalist" position far beyond anything that Noth might have
imagined. Orthodox confidence in the inspired nature of the text has provided opposition to critical scholarship since Mosaic authorship of the
Pentateuch was first questioned and this opposition has not disappeared.
J. Maxwell Miller and John Hayes sketch three positions they believe are
available to the historian of ancient Israel.[3]

The first assumes the veracity and historical value of the biblical text.
Here the historian seeks to find adequate and reasonable explanations for
miraculous occurrences, to find means for divine intervention that are
compatible with modern sensibilities, to smooth contradictions, and to
explain repetitions in the text, all without denying anything reported in
the narrative. The Bible is treated as a history book. Whatever difficulties
the reader finds in understanding the course of events must lie in interpretation, not within the text. Contradictions in the narrative, of course,
have troubled readers of the Bible throughout the centuries. Allegorical
interpretation served to circumvent problems in the text for most of the
history of the church. From Marcion to Luther, there have been those
who were willing to put aside parts of the text that seemed incoherent,
crude, or failed to provide support to the contemporary values. As history
has achieved prominence as the favored interpretative approach to the
Bible, however, the text is expected to yield a coherent story of Israel in
the time it purports to chronicle.

Those who study the text in an effort to clarify problems in the narrative often find these very problems compounded by variant readings in
different manuscripts. Thus, the question of the historical reliability of
the Bible becomes further complicated by issues of which version, even
which passage, is accepted. For anyone approaching the Bible as the
accurate and authentic history of Israel, research into its background in
an effort to overcome its awkward passages inevitably uncovers additional obstacles in terms of textual variations, anachronisms in the narrative, artificial time periods, conflicting genealogies, and contradicting

---

3.   J. Maxwell Miller and John H. Hayes, *A History of Ancient Israel and Judah*
(Philadelphia: Westminster, 1986), 74–79.

accounts of historical events. How to present a coherent history based directly on the text is a formidable task.

The second and opposing position regarding the historical value of the biblical text holds that it has none, that it is useless as a source of history. This is not simply to argue that the Bible is not a book of history. Whether or not the Bible's chief purpose is to record history, the historian is free to sift the text for clues or information about the past. Documents of all kinds have been scrutinized fruitfully for what details or facts that may be useful to the task of writing history. For those who exclude the Bible, and particularly the Pentateuch, as a source for history, even purportedly ancient materials are so compromised by their later incorporation into the documents where we now find them that they do not constitute any source for writing history.

These scholars, who find little or nothing of historical value in the Pentateuch, date all its documents late and refer to Wellhausen's observation that the sources have more to tell about the time in which they were written than about the time they write about. They argue that the stories are constructed artificially to foster an identity for a post-exilic community, that much of the legal system described in the Pentateuch is inappropriate to tribal society, that archaeological investigation has shown that the conquest described in the text never occurred. They point out that Israel and Judah are not known from chronicles or correspondence from surrounding territories, that the single mention, before the monarchy, of the word "Israel" on the Merneptah Stele is ambiguous. This extreme view of the historical unreliability of the text insists that only material which is confirmed by external documents can be accepted as authentic. By this reasoning, the history of Israel begins with the Omride kings.

The third possibility suggested by Miller and Hayes is a compromise position, neither accepting the biblical account as actual history, nor rejecting the Bible totally as a historical source.[4] The question of method is a complex one. If it is not allowed that the text simply and directly tells the history of the people of Israel and, likewise, the position which denies that the Bible tells history is rejected, then how one will discover historical evidence in the text, by what means it will be evaluated, and how the conclusions will be verified become the significant issues. Thus, decisions must be reached on the function of archaeology and the use of extra-biblical documents. Standards for literary-critical analysis must be established. Judgment must be made on the appropriate use of historical and sociological models.

---

4. Ibid., 76.

John Bright and Martin Noth belong to this compromise position. Though differing substantially from one another, they, nevertheless, avoid both extremes described by Miller and Hayes. Neither accepts the biblical chronology of events uncritically and neither rejects the Pentateuch as a source for historical information. For both, questions of method assume very real significance. Martin Noth's work will be the first subject of investigation, then attention will be turned to the writings of John Bright and, finally, their points of difference and agreement will be discussed.

2. Part One: Martin Noth

During the years 1921–1925, Noth studied at the Universities of Erlangen, Rostock, and Leipzig. In November 1925, returning from three months of study in Jerusalem, he took up an unpaid assistantship at Griefswald. There he completed his inaugural dissertation the following year and his Habilitationsschrift in 1927. These two works examined the significance of Israelite personal names in a larger Semitic context and developed the work he had first undertaken in Leipzig in the area of History of Religions. This research was published in 1928, as *Die israelitischen Personennamen im Rahmen der gemeinsemitischen Namengebung*. Noth began teaching at Griefswald in the summer of 1927, moving to Leipzig for the two years 1928–1930. By the end of 1929, he had a call to Königsberg as a full professor.[5]

While at Königsberg, Noth published in 1930 *Das System der zwölf Stämme Israels*, the famous presentation of his amphictyony hypothesis, followed in 1938 by his commentary on Joshua. 1940 brought both *Die Gesetze im Pentateuch* and *Die Welt des Alten Testaments*. During his years at Königsberg, 1930–1944, Noth published an additional thirty articles, characterized by Christopher Begg as having "a clear focus, reflective of the continuing influence of Alt, on questions of the history, topography and archaeology of the ancient Near East, Syria–Palestine in particular," only occasionally addressing other matters such as linguistics or theology.[6] Noth's *Überlieferungsgeschichtliche Studien* was published in 1943. Smend mentions that during his time in the army in World War II, Noth carried a small Hebrew Bible with him and studied the Pentateuch when he was able. Through this study, without the aid of any

5. Christopher T. Begg, "Martin Noth: Notes on his Life and Work," in *The History of Israel's Traditions: The Heritage of Martin Noth* (ed. Steven L. McKenzie and M. Patrick Graham; JSOTSup 182; Sheffield: Sheffield Academic Press, 1994), 18–30.
6. Ibid., 20.

secondary literature due to the circumstances, he was forced to derive questions and answers from the text itself. This led to an original, though "closed and imposing" view of the text.[7]

At the close of the war and the partition of Germany, Noth left Königsberg in the east and took up the Old Testament chair in Bonn, which he held until his retirement in 1967. He was twice rector of the University. Noth continued his remarkable productivity, publishing *Überlieferungsgeschichtliche des Pentateuch* in 1948 and his *Geschichte Israels* in 1950. Commentaries on the book of Exodus and Leviticus followed in 1959 and 1962, respectively. His enduring interest in history, geography, topography, and archaeology is clear in his writings from the post-war period, in some forty periodical articles and articles in collections, eighteen encyclopedia entries, and a hundred reviews and responses to the work of other scholars.[8] Noth continued to write on specific elements of the Deuteronomistic History and to answer criticisms of his hypotheses. Begg points out Noth's role in the establishment of major collaborative projects in scholarship on the Hebrew Bible, in particular *Vetus Testamentum* and the *Biblischer Kommentar* series, and his presidency at the fourth Congress of the International Organization for the Study of the Old Testament in 1962.[9] Noth took leave from the University of Bonn in 1964 to accept the directorship of the Deutsches Evangelisches Institut in Jerusalem. His commentary on the book of Numbers appeared in 1966. His work on Kings for the *Biblischer Kommentar* series was complete only to 1 Kgs 1–16 at the time of his unexpected death on May 30, 1968.

Noth was, first of all, a historian. His encounter with Karl Barth after the war in Bonn made a strong impression on him; still Noth increasingly distanced himself from Barth's theology of the Word as he recognized that such a theology opposed the notion of history. With Gunkel, Noth understood history writing to be the product of nations, a literary genre most often confined to the court or to official circles. He believed that the oral period of tradition production was the creative stage and that the oral genres evolved according to fixed laws. Against the view of Wellhausen that the traditions of the Pentateuch were unreliable for writing Israel's history, Noth argued that the pre-literary traditions could be studied by

---

7. Rudolf Smend, "Nachruf auf Martin Noth," in *Gesammelte Studien zum Alten Testament: Martin Noth*, vol. 2 (Theologische Bucherei Alten Testament 39; Munich: Kaiser, 1969), 137–65 (157–58).

8. A complete bibliography of Noth's work compiled by Hermann Schult is found in *Gesammelte Studien zum Alten Testament: Martin Noth*, vol. 2.

9. Begg, "Martin Noth," 21.

means of Gunkel's form criticism and made to yield significant historical material. From these principles Noth generated particular premises
regarding the process of tradition transmission and the nature of Israel
and her history.

3. *Assumptions and Approach*

Examination of the presuppositions which undergird Noth's work begin
with his understanding of the inexplicable element in history. He states:

> An element of the inexplicable is in fact present in *all* human history and
> is bound to be present not merely because it is not even remotely possible
> to embrace the whole profusion of cause and effect even in the historical
> present, let alone in the past, and least of all the remote past, but above all
> because history is not merely a constant repetition of complicated con-
> catenations of cause and effect if God is really active in history not
> simply as a prime mover, but as the ever present Lord working within the
> superficial interplay of cause and effect.[10]

The assumptions of historicism are evident here. Certainly, the notion of
the irrational, and the unique and particular quality of every aspect of
history are integral to the teachings of the Historical School. Noth draws
attention to the inexplicable in all human history and insists, in company
with the traditional German historians, that history may not be forced
into causal schemes. Though Noth's view of the divine working through
history to effect its necessary ends initially may appear more overtly
Hegelian than members of the Historical School, it is actually based in
his belief in Israel's special election, which he affirms throughout his
work.

a. *The Limitations of Sources*
Implicit in Noth's statement is the methodological principle that all
history writing is, and must be, selective. The limited availability of
sources constrains the possible reconstructions of the past resulting in the
impossibility of embracing the whole past, while the position of the
historian in time and place serves to further restrict the interpretation of
the sources. Noth added a caution, however, that this must not provide an
excuse for assigning "all the obscure events in the history of 'Israel' to
this 'unhistorical' sphere, since deeper historical insight and new possibilities of comparison with events in other areas of world history may

10. Martin Noth, *The History of Israel* (2d ed. with rev. trans. by P. R. Ackroyd;
New York: Harper & Row, 1960 [1954]), 2.

easily throw light on what is at first apparently incomprehensible." He describes the historian's task as "seeking for possible comparisons and explanations," while keeping in mind the presence of the "unhistorical."[11] As an heir to the tradition of German historicism, he insists on the critical evaluation of sources. Also, as part of this tradition, he knows that the way to the past is through immersion in its world and intuitive interpretation of the available material.

b. *The Subject of History*

In distinguishing the subject of his history, Noth describes the entity "Israel" as a "historical reality with its own historical period, during which it was intimately involved in the multifarious life of the sur-rounding world." The proper means then to comprehend this "Israel" is through historical research and all methods of historical research must be employed, "precisely because 'Israel' is without question a historical reality."[12] He argues emphatically for viewing Israel in the context of the ancient "Orient," pointing to a remarkable store of discoveries over the past century illuminating the background of the history of Israel: "There is hardly any event in the history of 'Israel' that is not clearly related to this ancient Oriental background." He speaks of "far-reaching context and reality" for the Old Testament tradition, "surprising possibilities of comparison," and the close involvement of Israel with the "varied life and historical movements of the ancient Orient."[13] Notwithstanding the significance of Israel's connections to the larger world of the ancient Near East, Noth marks out a special place for Israel, calling it a "stranger wearing the garments and behaving in the manner of its age, yet separate from the world it lived in." He claims that for Israel there is no parallel, "not because the material for comparison has not yet come to light but because, so far as we know, such things have simply never happened elsewhere."[14] This unique character of Israel is an important premise for Noth's stance toward its history and exceeds the traditional German position that every historical entity exists as a singular individuality. Taken with the strength of his statement about the divine interventions in Israel's history, his view of Israel's uniqueness is based, not on a theoretical position only, but upon an understanding of Israel's sacred destiny.

11. Ibid., 2.
12. Ibid., 1.
13. Ibid., 2.
14. Ibid., 3.

c. *Israel's Identity Found in History*

The reality depicted by the term "Israel," Noth claims, was a "unique phenomenon," not truly a nation as described in the Old Testament tradition, but a group a tribes acting as a unit only for the brief period of the monarchy and living again as tribal groups subject to later imperial powers.[15] These tribes were held together by a common language, though not a language exclusive to them alone, and by geographical proximity, but most significantly by a "similar historical situation and hence by a common historical experience."[16] This historical experience was articulated and promulgated in the cult and it is only when the tribes were established as a confederacy around the cultic center, having occupied the agricultural land, that one may speak of an entity "Israel." At this point only can a history of Israel begin. Noth's insistence on the singular character of Israel is not based on the notion of amphictyony, however, for the concept is itself borrowed from the sacral leagues known from Greece and Rome, but on the function of the historical experiences represented in the ancient traditions, which constituted the identity of Israel. He calls attention to something akin to *essence*, which he identifies within both Israel, and, later, Judaism. While careful not to regard them "as one and the same," Noth suggests that "the historically unique element in Judaism must have been present in embryo in the 'Israel' from which it evolved,"[17] as historicism finds the spirit of an individuality manifested in its continued evolution.

As the designation "Israel" is first appropriate only for the group of tribes established in the land, forging a common bond through the recitation of traditions in cultic gatherings, it continues to be authentically applied to the state as it develops under the monarchy and as it evolves into two separate kingdoms. After the destructions of 721 BCE and 587 BCE, the question occurs as to the status and identity of this "Israel." Noth argues that the demise of the political entity "no more signified the end of Israel than the development of political forms of organization marked the beginning of its life."[18] He holds that the term "nation" is not the proper or adequate term for Israel, that the tribes seldom acted as a unit and never for long, the period of the state artificially combined the existing tribes, and finally that "the tribes continued to live as subject groups in various provinces of successive large empires."[19] He chooses to

15. Ibid., 5.
16. Ibid., 4.
17. Ibid., 5.
18. Ibid., 6.
19. Ibid., 5.

speak simply of "Israel."[20] By this means it is possible to follow the *Geist* or spirit of Israel through the period of Hellenization, and into the Roman era.

In Noth's view, then, Israel existed as an actual historical reality, and this existence was totally unique among all the nations or peoples of all times. Having chosen as the subject of inquiry the history of Israel when it was established in the land, Noth allows that, nevertheless, Israel's prehistory is part of its history. Noth states, "The history of the Pentateuchal tradition is itself a part of the history of Israel."[21] The important element to investigate is the life of twelve tribes within the sacral league. This life, Noth suggests, is ordered and regular, not interrupted by notable events which require reporting. The historian must seek traces of the internal life of the tribal groups within the traditions. Noth continues, "In this narrative is reflected a stage of the life and behavior of the united tribes of ancient Israel, and therefore from this point of view too the history of the Pentateuchal tradition must be considered."[22]

d. *The Traditions*
The sources for writing history, Noth tells us, are literary traditions, which chronicle events and describe people and places. He states:

> If we begin by enquiring about the source of the information which enables us to establish the outward course of the history of Israel...we must refer, in the first place, to the Old Testament with its wealth of historical material, but also to a great mass of sources outside the Old Testament.[23]

He points first to the Deuteronomistic History with its compilation of different sources, developed from material of varying backgrounds and from different periods and composed for different purposes. He includes the Chronicler's work citing its use of the Deuteronomistic work and additions of new material from other sources for the period after 587 BCE. The Pentateuch has qualified usefulness for writing history, for it "did not originate and was not planned, at any rate from the outset, as a historical work at all... It is a great collective work which conveys historical information...[but] it can only be used with many provisos."[24] Because of Israel's existence within the larger context of the ancient Near East, Noth adds the historical documents of that world as sources for

20. Ibid.
21. Martin Noth, *A History of Pentateuchal Traditions* (trans. and with an introduction by Bernhard W. Anderson; Atlanta: Scholars Press, 1981), 252.
22. Ibid., 252.
23. Noth, *History*, 42.
24. Ibid., 43.

writing Israel's history, citing royal inscriptions and other official records from Egypt, Assyria, Babylonia, and Persia. The two books of Maccabees and Josephus complete his list of sources for the later period. Archaeological discoveries "give colour and life to the literary traditions and greatly assist our understanding of them," and while it is no longer possible to ignore the "abundant and, to a very large extent well authenticated, results of Palestinian archaeology," they can "only be understood and appreciated in relation to information from literary sources."[25]

e. *The Value of Artifacts*
In assessing the value of artifacts for writing history, Noth separates written documents recovered through excavation from other artifacts. He asks, "what knowledge of any real accuracy and historical substance… would we possess if we had all the material remains except literary relics" recovered by archaeology? He answers that these concrete remains of past history represent "isolated details," which must be constantly fitted into the historical contexts once they are reconstructed. He argues that it is "the innumerable written documents which have come to light as a direct or indirect result of the excavations" that provide the bulk of the contribution made by archaeology.[26] In the case of Israel's history, these contributions are primarily the documents of Mesopotamia and Egypt. The political character of Israel was not such that it produced the quantity of documents necessary for the great governmental and trading powers. In the circumstances of its weather, for example its winter rains, written documents of the Iron Age have failed to survive. Syrian–Palestinian archaeology[27] is unfortunately "wholly silent" in regard to the Israelite period.

Sources available and appropriate for writing Israel's history then, consist in documents, all tablets, inscriptions, papyrus records, and potsherds uncovered in the ancient Near East, and the histories and traditions included in the Hebrew Bible. Other artifacts, properly interpreted and fitted into historical contexts provided by documentary evidence, serve to "color" the resulting historical picture. Noth states, "Everything that can make any contribution, direct, or indirect, is to be welcomed

25. Ibid., 42.
26. Ibid., 46.
27. Noth (*History*, 47) mentions "enthusiastic" and "intense" excavations carried out in the past "from purely Biblical motives," but notes that "Syrian–Palestinian archaeology has long since developed from an auxiliary discipline of Biblical studies into an independent science with methods of its own and aims evolving from its own work." He cautions that "it has still not entirely overcome the improper search for direct Biblical connections."

wholeheartedly," but "*the* source of information on this subject is simply the witness of the Old Testament..."[28] At this point Noth adds a dimension which he says would be "unscientific" to disregard. He says that the history of Israel may be given a

> unified meaning by declaring outright that God, the Lord of the whole world, here used a people as his instrument so that in it "shall all families of the earth be blessed"...to ignore this question as to the deeper meaning of Israel's history is to leave out of account a certain fact—the fact that the main traditional source of information in the history of Israel, beside which all other sources are purely supplementary, is indissolubly bound up with this testimony.[29]

This is a remarkable statement that indicates Noth's emphasis on the biblical text is not solely the result of methodological considerations. From this acknowledgment of his own assumptions, it is a short step to the question of objectivity in history writing.

f. Standards for Using the Biblical Traditions
Differences of opinion persist among historians handling the identical materials describing the origins and early life of Israel. Noth's approach to this problem argues that systematic study of the traditions has not been yet been accomplished by those who attempt to reconstruct Israel's history. Instead, uncertainties abound in the utilization of the traditions. With the lack of standards of judgment, scholars dispute the historical credibility of certain passages according to their own discretion, and fail to challenge the consensus regarding the accepted "historical nucleus." The only criterion customarily offered as warrant for historical credibility is that of the age of a given tradition, established through the work of source criticism. Noth insists that the historical assumptions lying behind each individual tradition must be determined, from the very earliest to those within the later historical complexes and then each unit of tradition must be assessed "as objectively" as possible to see what they can tell us about the course of Israel's history. He says historical analysis must include origin, motive, and development of the tradition: "Only when we have grasped the circumstances under which they arose and what they are driving at, can we answer the vital question as to how they arrived at their particular selection from the wealth of events and why they presented it in the particular way they did." Then it is possible to see what subjects are enlightened by the text and "the weight which may be

28. Ibid., 49.
29. Ibid., 9.

attached to what they say and to what they suppress."[30] Noth insists that
these questions must be asked of the text, knowing all the while that
answers will not achieve mathematical clarity. Too many uncertainties
remain even in the very best analysis to expect complete assurance. He
remarks that the charge of "subjectivity" may be brought against such
results, but he enunciates the philosophical position that "objectivity" is
not available in history writing: "Every exposition of history is inevitably
'subjective' even if it is imagined to be 'objective,' since the fact is that
the available traditions shed a purely accidental light on the course of
events."[31] Noth offers the conviction that if all accessible information is
scrutinized carefully, the resulting conclusions will be convincing. Here,
he seems to be arguing for persuasive reconstruction of Israel's history,
knowing full well that the material itself may often be inconclusive.

g. *The Period for Study*
The major works on the history of Israel prior to and contemporary with
Noth begin with descriptions of life in the Bronze Age, the political and
cultural development in the Fertile Crescent, the migrations of ethnic
groups, including the patriarchs, and the series of events which led up to
settlement of the Israelite tribes in Palestine, the years in Egypt, the
exodus and wanderings, the occupation of the land, and the continuation
of Israel's history through the exile and return.[32] Noth specifically
excludes all events up to the settlement, when he holds that one may
begin to speak with confidence of an entity "Israel." The conclusion of
Israel's history he places beyond the record of the Hebrew Bible at the
final suppression of the Maccabees in 135 CE. He provides his reasons
and arguments for this demarcation in his introduction to *The History of
Israel*. He uses the greater part of the fifty pages in the English translation of this introduction, however, for his own exposition of the
background to Israel's corporate life. He describes in depth the geography, its situation relative to the sea and to the significant powers in the
region, and the physical characteristics of the land, its climate, its water
sources, and its natural resources. He remarks that the land had "a long
and eventful history" before the foundation of Israel, and this must "carefully examined" for it is "bound to be of direct and substantial importance

30. Ibid., 46.
31. Ibid.
32. Douglas Knight mentions in this regard Wellhausen, Sellin, Jirku, Olmstead,
Lods, Oesterley and Robinson, Kaufman, Albright, Ricciotti, Gordon, Orlinsky,
Bright, Neher, Mowinckel, and Metzger (*Rediscovering the Traditions of Israel*
[Chico, Calif.: Scholars Press, 1975], 167 n. 88).

for the early development of Israel."[33] He includes an inventory of the specific documents of the Bronze Age that are pertinent to Israel's prehistory. Life in the cities, their commerce, arts, technology, and regulations are outlined, as well as that in rural districts, where farming and small cattle breeding were practiced. The elements of the wider population are traced through their migrations by means of international correspondence, language traits, and archaeological evidence concerning occupation of various areas.

Following the introduction, which describes the land itself in some detail, the history of the area to 1200 BCE, and the sources for writing history, Noth divides *The History of Israel* into four parts. Part one is devoted to the confederation of the twelve tribes. Part two concerns Israel's assimilation to the land, relations with its Canaanite neighbors, and its fortunes from the period of the judges through the time of the monarchies. Part three deals with the final years of the kingdoms as they succumb to the great international powers, while Part four concludes with the Maccabees and the final demise of Israel at the hands of the Romans. Parts two, three, and four follow the biblical histories and Noth's own studies in these areas, strongly supported by scholarly studies of place and personal names, the records of surrounding kingdoms, and the results of archaeological research. Part two is a section unusual in a history of Israel, for here Noth bases his history on his previous conclusions derived from tradition criticism.

4. The Traditio-Historical Approach

Here, then, is Noth's characterization of the appropriate subject of a history, the sources available for and pertinent to writing this history, and his delineation in time and space of the particular subject of the history of Israel. It is necessary now to investigate his method, beginning with the influences on the development of his traditio-historical approach. In the first chapter of *A History of Pentateuchal Traditions*, Noth outlines the task of traditio-historical studies. He calls attention to the fact that the large collection of traditions now found in the Pentateuch are set into a complicated literary structure. These traditions found their way into this final text through a long process "nourished by many roots and influenced by manifold interests and tendencies."[34] Originally, this traditional material was circulated orally; indeed, it was in the oral stage that the creative forces worked to give form to the traditions. "It is the task,"

33. Noth, *History*, 18.
34. Noth, *Pentateuchal Traditions*, 1.

Writing the History of Israel

Noth remarks, "of a 'history of Pentateuchal traditions' to investigate this whole process from beginning to end...," though the "major interest is in the origins and first stages of growth" for much work has been done on the final form and thus it requires less in the way of examination.[35] The study of the history of traditions is necessary to understand the structure and content of the Pentateuch. Noth contrasts the materials of the Pentateuch to those of the Deuteronomistic History and the history of the Chronicler, which, according to Noth, originated as literary compositions of a particular author despite their dependence on traditional materials.[36]

a. *Cultic Themes Shaping the Form of the Pentateuch*
Noth argues that the Pentateuch not only had no author, but even the authors of the various sources found their material already substantially arranged into an order on the basis of a series of themes rehearsed in the cult. He cites Gerhard von Rad's work on the themes, which von Rad holds constituted the confession of the Israelite tribes. Originally separated and unrelated, these themes, when arranged into a narrative sequence, over time gradually accumulated additional material, filling out the thematic structure and eventually resulting in the final literary form of the Pentateuch. It is the development of the early stages, the process of arrangement and accumulation, that must be investigated if we are to understand the meaning and construction of the Pentateuch.

Wellhausen claimed that the patriarchal traditions offered no valid information on the time they purported to depict. He believed that Israel was formed and existed largely independent from the surrounding cultures. Nineteenth-century archaeology seemed to him to offer little that was pertinent to understanding the development of Israel. His orientation to the biblical text was by means of literary criticism, the study of literary features, the unique characteristics of sections of the Pentateuch by which the major sources were to be identified. The notion that the significant steps in the formation of the text might have taken place at an oral stage did not engage Wellhausen. Noth's position directly opposes Wellhausen on this issue, yet he accepted the results of Wellhausen's source criticism, as may be seen in this statement: "Noth takes his point of departure in the accepted, assured results of literary criticism...his precise literary analysis of J, E, and P in the Pentateuch betray his debt to Wellhausen."[37] B. W. Anderson places Noth in a direct line from Wellhausen on the basis of their common historical interests and adds that

35. Ibid., 1.
36. Ibid., 2.
37. Knight, *Rediscovering*, 146.

"Noth's study of the Pentateuch does not support the notion that... the Higher Criticism symbolized by the name Wellhausen has been rejected..."[38]

b. *The Contributions of Form Criticism*
Gunkel's work on the preliterary stages of oral tradition is also important to Noth for its account of the final form of the individual sagas and saga cycles. Gunkel did not oppose the use of source or literary criticism and, as Douglas Knight points out, he analyzed Genesis on the basis of the customary division into sources.[39] Gunkel finds in the opening Genesis creation narrative traces of ancient myth. He argues pointedly, however, that the sources are not works of a particular author; for example, he disputes the notion that the Priestly writer composed this account of creation and argues that it was at the level of oral tradition this mythic creation account was carried into the traditions of the early Israelite tribes. From this interest in the history of religion, the questions of the transmission of tradition come to Gunkel's attention. Knight goes on, "Gunkel is intent on uncovering all details of [a unit's] historical development...this means determining the probable foreign origin of each and also describing the process of adaptation or 'Israelitizing' which it underwent in Palestine."[40] This process includes discovering the well-known *Sitz im Leben* or original setting where a given tradition was at home, often the evening campfire, or within the cult, or in a legal situation. Locating the setting and determining the function of a unit of tradition is important to understanding what group would have an interest in passing it on. His work on the principle of transmission of elements of Genesis from a generalized regional culture and their subsequent interpretation in an Israelite setting, and his work on the character and function of individual units of tradition, were both important to Noth's development of the traditio-historical method.

Anderson observes that "Gunkel's work was informed by a kind of poetic universalism." He believed that one of Wellhausen's weaknesses was his exclusion of the study of religious literature from surrounding cultures from his efforts to understand the religion of Israel. Gunkel followed Herder in locating the spirit of a people in its intuitive perception of experience. Anderson states, "The romantic stress upon feeling, emotion, imagination, and communion with nature led into a broad

38. Bernhard W. Anderson, introduction to Noth, *Pentateuchal Traditions*, xiii–xxxii (xviii).
39. Knight, *Rediscovering*, 74.
40. Ibid., 79.

universalism which finds no essential place for the election of Israel, special revelation or inspiration of Scripture in the orthodox sense."[41] It is at this point, Anderson insists, that Noth leaves Gunkel and returns to Wellhausen, drawing his conclusions about the Old Testament from within the text itself. For Noth, like Wellhausen, history is the important focus, though Noth reaches back into the oral period to locate the traditions. The traditions represent real historical memories of individual tribal groups and it is in the oral stage that the traditions were drawn together, but only within the cultic experience of the confederated tribes.

c. *Scholarly Influences on Noth*
Noth, himself, singles out Gunkel's commentary on Genesis and Hugo Gressmann's discussion of the Moses sagas as "extremely important and successful works" in the study of traditions. Knight describes Gressmann's work as confined to tradition criticism, insisting that each level in the formation of a unit of tradition must be scrutinized carefully to determine its own history, its purpose, and its use. Gressmann, however, "refuses to carry out the tradition-historical step—diachronically arranging his critical results into a relative chronology" in order to demonstrate how the final form was reached.[42] His emphasis on the need for a better understanding of oral tradition and its place in ancient cultures, religions, and literature added to the movement away from classical source criticism.

The shift away from emphasis on the practice of source criticism and from Wellhausen's view of the limited historical value of the patriarchal narratives embodied in the Gunkel's and Gressmann's work, opened new possibilities for scholarship. In a similar way, Albrecht Alt's effort to improve "the historical foundations upon which Old Testament studies are built," through assessment of archaeological finds, topographical studies, studies of tribal territorial boundaries, and the settlement of the tribes had significant impact on research in the field.[43] Alt's thesis dealing with the settlement forms the background for Noth's work.[44] Alt took the study of tradition beyond Gressmann's efforts to isolate the earliest form of tradition by excising all secondary material. Using tradition criticism

41. Anderson, "Introduction," xx.
42. Knight, *Rediscovering*, 86.
43. Ibid., 92.
44. Albrecht Alt, "Die Landnahme der Israeliten in Palästina" (1925), reprinted in his *Kleine Schriften zur Geschichte des Volkes Israel*, vol. 1 (Munich: Beck, 1953), 193–202. See also, in the same volume, the essays "Der Gott der Väter" (1929) and "Die Ursprünge des israelitischen Rechts" (1934).

and knowledge of comparative cultures to establish the *Sitz im Leben* of religious and legal traditions, Alt hypothesized the cult of the God of the Fathers and distinguished customary and cultic law. His proposals remain part of the vocabulary of biblical studies.

5. *The Historical Compositions*

Noth's own development of the traditio-historical method, then, produces his thesis that the ancient traditions were recited, collected, and elaborated in the sacral league of the twelve Israelite tribes.[45] From this premise, he moves on to argue that "The whole of the historical tradition in the Old Testament is contained in a few large compilations."[46] He names the Pentateuch, the Deuteronomistic History and the Chronicler's History. Noth argues that in order to investigate the individual elements of the historical tradition, to examine the sources critically, and to derive an account of the history of the Israelite people, it is necessary first of all to understand the "extent and nature of these collections and of the degree to which they have re-worked the older, traditional material, or, at least, have coloured it in some special way by insertions into a particular passage."[47] The Pentateuch, he avers, holds a special place, as its intention is to present specific themes, which are the foundations of life and faith. To do this, many historical details are incorporated, but collecting historical reports is not the aim of the Pentateuch. The Deuteronomistic History and the History of the Chronicler, on the other hand, represent "compilations in the strict sense of historical traditions..." The Deuteronomistic work is the "first collection and editing of historical tradition within Old Testament literature...it is only within this work that an abundance of priceless, old historical tales and reports are preserved..." without which "our knowledge of Israelite history would be pitifully small."[48]

Beginning with a defense of his proposal that the Deuteronomistic History is a unity, Noth analyses the traditional elements of the work and argues that, rather than working simply as an editor or redactor, the Deuteronomist composed material to provide the settings for the

45. Martin Noth, *Das System der zwölf Stämme Israels* (BWANT 4.1; Stuttgart: Kohlhammer, 1930).

46. Martin Noth, *The Deuteronomistic History* (JSOTSup 15; Sheffield: JSOT Press, 1991), 13; trans. of *Überlieferungsgeschichtliche Studien* (2d ed.; Tübingen: Niemeyer, 1957), 1–110.

47. Ibid., 13.

48. Ibid., 14.

traditional literature which was available to him, and that his arrangement of the available material constitutes an original interpretation. Noth firmly separates the Deuteronomist's history from the literary sources found in the Pentateuch. The Pentateuch presents the themes foundational to the faith, while the recapitulation of those themes serves only as an introduction to the historical contents of the Deuteronomist's history and represent no continuation of Pentateuchal sources into Deuteronomy.[49] It is on the basis of literary criticism that Deuteronomistic elements were identified throughout the various books. Noth has no argument with the accepted conclusions. His argument concerns the unity of the composition and the creative use of the available traditions by the Deuteronomist.

Noth approaches the Chronicler's history as a unified work and comments that it is "generally accepted" as such.[50] Therefore, he expends no effort on the demonstration of the work's unity, as he has in the case of the Deuteronomistic History. Rather, he says that it is essential to determine the "original contents as they left the hand of the work's main author."[51] He declares the fault of previous research on this work to be the failure to ascertain the original shape of the Chronicler's history. This history is presented by means of compiling information from various sources, often in exact transcriptions, but sometimes excluding material which offers context or consequence. The language is inconsistent, even careless, a witness to the varied sources. These factors make it difficult to conclude through linguistic means what may be additions to any particular unit. Nevertheless, he describes the task of determining the original form of the Chronicler's work as "a purely literary-critical task."[52] Neither analysis of the work's historical reliability nor the use of sources should complicate the initial task. This search for the original form is achieved by attention to certain features of the work's construction. Finally, after analysis of the sources and a determination of the date of the composition based on the date of the latest sources, Noth turns to the aim of the Chronicler or the "nature of the composition." He reminds us that it is inevitable that any author is the product of his or her time, that his or her outlook is "determined by the historically conditioned institutions and conceptions" of his or her day. Noth maintains that "A brief consideration of the historical situation at Chr.'s time is therefore

49. Ibid., 119.
50. Martin Noth, *The Chronicler's History* (JSOTSup 50; Sheffield: Sheffield Academic Press, 1987), 29; trans. of *Überlieferungsgeschichtliche Studien* (2d ed.; Tübingen: Niemeyer, 1957), 29–106.
51. Ibid., 30.
52. Ibid., 31.

indispensable for an accurate assessment of his work."[53] Here, however, Noth reads the history of third-century Judea from the interests of the Chronicler.

6. *Traditio-Historical Criticism of the Pentateuch*

Noth's method, applied in studies of the two great history collections of the Hebrew Bible, is centered in criticism of the literary features of the text and was compatible with the traditional methods of the German historians. The shift in method comes with the development of traditio-historical criticism in his research on the Pentateuch. Noth starts with the acceptance of source criticism as the foundational practice, but one insufficient to the study of elements of the pre-literary tradition. He says, "Especially in a traditio-historical study of the Pentateuch, whose scope *also* includes the history of the early literary stages of the final form of the Pentateuch, this literary problem cannot be disregarded, even though the primary interest is the preliterary stage."[54] He lays out carefully his understanding that P provides the framework for the larger narrative and J as the basis for the combination of the JE narrative with their common background source. He insists, however, that these literary records cannot be included "within the 'creative stage' of the history of *traditions*, even though in the theological *reworking* of the whole they have taken completely new and individual paths."[55] So, to begin the study of the preliterary traditions in the Pentateuch, Noth isolates five major themes, which he believes, like von Rad, had their home in the cultic life of Israel. These themes may represent historical occurrences as they are recalled in the religious life of the community, but as they appear in the present text they have developed separate and individual histories which must be traced. First, in the process of development, additional material accumulates around the original theme. For the tradition historian, interest in the "filling out" of a particular theme is restricted to "that which is concrete and nonrecurring" leaving aside the general motifs and schemes which are the staple of narrative quite generally among peoples everywhere.[56] The Pentateuch contains many examples of these motifs presenting the everyday concerns of human life and these are, indeed, secondary additions to the original themes, but such motifs are the stock

53. Ibid., 83.
54. Ibid., 5.
55. Ibid., 44.
56. Ibid., 65.

of storytellers universally and certainly existed before their attachment to any of the Pentateuchal figures. Noth argues that the Pentateuchal figures were not created for these schemes and motifs, "Rather, the great themes given in this tradition, together with the individual figures already contained in them, were narratively elaborated and further developed through the application of such schemes and motifs."[57]

The added materials which are of interest to the scholar tracing the history of a tradition are, instead, those which enrich the basic theme with details, events, and explanation. Noth concentrates on the stories of the plagues and the Passover celebration as additions to the theme of the Guidance out of Egypt. For the theme "Guidance into the Arable Land," it is the sequence of stories about the occupation of tribal lands. The Jacob tradition provided the original framework of the theme "Promise to the Patriarchs," with later incorporation of Isaac and Abraham drawing together narratives of central, southern, and eastern tribes. The "Guidance in the Wilderness" theme has no roots in cultic celebrations. It is not a truly independent theme, but neither is it simply an elaboration of one of the other themes and thus requires investigation on its own.[58] Here the problems of hunger, thirst, and enemies are the subjects of the added narrative, along with the motif of the people's murmurings. Finally, the "Revelation at Sinai" theme is completed with material about the Midianites, covenant, and apostasy. Noth takes care to explain that these themes did not develop chronologically, but concurrently, though nothing can be said about the chronology of events in the history of traditions.[59]

a. *Tales of the Pentateuch*
The analysis of the individual themes and their accretions Noth augments by particular attention to the chief figures in the traditions, each patriarch and the eponymous figures of the Israelite tribes and their neighbors, and the women figures. He devotes study to the character of the materials, the "circle of ideas and interests" which enriched the traditions. He points out that the narrative elaboration did not simply carry the traditions along in the way they were headed, but with its growth the Pentateuch "entered into a sphere of life which differed from that in which the basic themes

---

57. Noth refers to Märchen or folktale motifs and cites Hermann Gunkel's *Das Märchen im Alten Testament* (Religionsgeschichtliche Volksbücher 2; Tübingen: Mohr, 1921) and André Jolles' *Einfache Formen: Legende, Sage, Mythe, Rätsel, Spruch, Kasus, Memorabile, Märchen, Witz* (Halle: Niemeyer, 1956).

58. Noth, *Pentateuchal Traditions*, 115.

59. Ibid., 65.

had been formulated."[60] Here, the strange behaviors of their neighbors were related in stories absorbed into the traditions. He mentions the several stories of sexual depravity and the perceived dangers to a man traveling with his beautiful wife. Problems arising between shepherds and settled people over the rights to water, relations with neighboring tribes, and even stories from far-away Mesopotamia and details of the very different world of Egypt are included in growing narratives.[61] The reality of daily life is included in many situations needing further explanation. Aetiologies of names and places and explanations for unusual local phenomena found their way into the unfolding of the themes as they moved away from their original foundation in the cultic setting.[62]

As the process of the growth and development of traditions takes place and the stage is reached when the traditions become interwoven, "we come very close to the stage of the oldest literary fixations, and often it can no longer be determined whether a certain traditio-historical occurrence is to be assigned to the oral stage or the literary stage of work on the Pentateuchal narrative."[63] Classifying the traditional materials according to their priority must be accomplished successfully in order to formulate the developmental history of the present narrative. Noth follows certain guidelines in locating the earliest units of tradition. Anderson sketches these guidelines,[64] beginning with the earliest traditions, which are small units in concise style, attached to places, often giving an aetiology of the place name. They are religious or cultic and tend to portray typical and anonymous characters, while in later traditions, characters are named and are assigned distinct individual traits. The older traditions are noticeable in the text as we now have it, depicting "shadowy" characters like Isaac. Finally, like Gunkel, Noth argues that traditions which have been brought together artificially by means of connecting passages, genealogical relationships between characters, travel itineraries bridging time and space and tying together two or more themes, show later development. The connecting material is later than the traditions which are connected.[65]

---

60. Ibid., 165.
61. Ibid., 191–95.
62. Ibid., 190. Noth calls attention to the fact that only the first theme, "Guidance out of Egypt," continues its elaboration along cultic lines. The other themes focus on "remarkable phenomena in the world and in the environs of the Israelite tribes settled in the arable land..." (p. 191).
63. Ibid., 98.
64. Anderson, "Introduction," xxii–xxvii.
65. Ibid., xxiii–xxv.

7. Reliability

Anderson questions the reliability of Noth's guidelines on several grounds. First, that the development of tradition does not follow predictable rules; indeed, instead of developing consistently from simple to complex, on occasion the trajectory of development is sometimes observed to move from elaborate to refined. The fixing of tradition to a specific place may be less consistent with semi-nomadic or unsettled peoples. The notion that cultic material precedes secular is questionable because very old secular traditions may only be excluded by the selection process as it functions in a cultic context, and, finally, Noth is less than persuasive regarding the dating of connecting material in several of his chosen examples.[66]

These principles regarding the relative antiquity of traditions have significant consequences for the reconstruction of history as they are used in traditio-historical research. For example, Noth eliminates Moses from history through a process of applying traditio-historical principles, specifically the conclusion that Moses is a late addition to the Exodus story, which originally featured anonymous elders negotiating with the pharaoh. Traditio-historical criticism in Noth's research finds that the original elements of the Pentateuchal tradition consist in the five major themes, the testimony of the twelve Israelite tribes settled in the land. These themes recount what had been done for them by their god and were repeated and celebrated in the ceremonies of the sacral league. Following the principles of the Myth–Ritual School, these sacred ceremonies within the cult fostered the elaboration of the themes with new narrative material.[67] This material provides the only glimpse into the life of pre-state Israel. Several points may be observed.

First, Israel is presented as a unity, despite traces of traditions peculiar to individual tribes. A common Israelite consciousness constitutes the fundamental premise of the sacral league. Noth maintains that the awareness of the twelve tribe confederation lingered as an influence even into the period of the monarchy and after.[68] Second, the expanding narrative "enables us to penetrate into the thought-world of the ancient Israelites and to see how they viewed with their own eyes the milieu in which they were living." Third, the "bedrock of the tradition" is found in the

---

66. Ibid., xxv–xxvi.

67. The Myth and Ritual School, most especially S. H. Hooke and J. G. Frazer, held that pre-literate peoples invented stories to explain their ancient rituals and beliefs, having long since forgotten the original foundations for these ceremonies.

68. Noth, *Pentateuchal Traditions*, 254.

"fundamental content of the individual themes as still disconnected from one another." The elaborations and connections which link the traditions as they are brought into association with one another tend to present history in a simplified or less complex form than any actual set of historical occurrences. Noth states, "A proper presentation of history can rest only on a knowledge of historical connections..."[69] Since, in the absence of accurate, historical connections, artificial links have been forged to connect the traditional materials, the content of the traditions cannot be included in a history of Israel. Finally, the events reported in the traditions may or may not have happened to the group or groups mentioned. The historical connections are lacking in the original traditions. Therefore, it is not possible to reconstruct a direct chronology of events from the traditions as they are. Noth argues that despite the apparently negative results of this investigation for the purposes of history, it is better to limit our scope to what "we can actually and cogently establish historically...than to rear a historical construction on a foundation incapable of bearing it."[70]

8. *Conclusion*

In conclusion, Noth's approach to historical problems and his use of methods are rooted in the long tradition of German historicism, though his conviction that Israel's destiny is designed by God sets him apart from his forebears in this tradition, even from Troeltsch who steadfastly refused to relinquish the notion of meaning in history. In fact, Noth's basic premise, the very idea that the identity of Israel was formed through its historical experience, is at the foundation of the German tradition. That Israel is bound together by its common understanding of its own traditions is at the heart of historicism's view of the spirit of a people. His hypothesis would not have been possible were it not for his formation in the tradition that argues for the spiritual unity of a nation, a people, an individuality, constituted by its history. Indeed, in this tradition, it is the idea or the spirit, rather than any material element, that animates history. Neither physical interests, nor defense, not blood relationships, not language, but history is the unifying principle in the German historical tradition and Noth builds his hypothesis on this notion.

---

69. Ibid., 258.
70. Ibid., 259. Knight (*Rediscovering*, 208–9) states that Noth "sought only to attain sold ground and reliable reference points," which Knight refers to as a "critical minimum."

Historicism was seen by its practitioners as a decisive turning point in the understanding of reality. Its marks are the awareness of the time-bound quality of all historical phenomena, the consciousness of the relativity of every sort of belief, and the recognition that history is an evolutionary process from which all events draw their meaning. From the notion of the radically contextual nature of all historical beings and events, proceeds the concept of the individuality of every historical phenomenon. Noth is well aware of Israel's existence in the particular context of the ancient world, but he further insists on Israel's novelty within this world. Israel's singularity, for Noth, is not the uniqueness of an historical individuality, but is directly the result of God's election of this people for a particular task. Israel's individuality functions easily within Noth's generally historicist approach, but it is derived from a source quite different from individuality in historicism.

A fundamental aspect of the historical tradition is relativism. Taking its beginning from Ranke's statement that every epoch is immediate to God, relativism became increasingly problematic by destabilizing deeply held values. The factor that kept relativism from overwhelming all sense of meaning was the notion of a metaphysical force or will that drew all history into a unified harmony in a plane outside of historical time. All recourse to metaphysics was finally abandoned in the early twentieth century, ultimately producing the crisis of historicism. After World War I, Germany in general, and proponents of historicism in particular, were forced to confront issues of value, the morality of power, and the dominance of the interests of the state. Relativism did not present a problem for Noth, however, because he had never forsaken the notion of the divine will guiding the course of history. His statements, quoted earlier, "[God] is active in history not simply as a prime mover, but as the ever present Lord working within the superficial interplay of cause and effect," and "God, the Lord of the whole world, here used a people as his instrument," give a vivid sense of his commitment to a view of history ultimately controlled by divine will. Here, Noth stands at a great distance from German historiography and especially from the contemporary discussions of subjective cognition and its impact on the perception of the reality of history.

In Noth's choice and application of methods there is a substantial connection to his traditional training. Underpinning historicism is the thesis that every historical individuality exhibits an "idea" or spirit that persists and unfolds through its history. This premise is necessary to Noth's work on traditions, for in tradition criticism units of text are investigated for the clues they might yield about the time and place in which they developed. Because a particular spirit is recognizable in its progress in time, it is possible to find Israel's unique character in the oral traditions of the Pentateuch. Israel's spirit expressed in the ancient tradition may be successfully distinguished from the more universal folk motifs that have attached to them over succeeding generations. Regardless of the source of Israel's unique character, the method for tracking its development is found in the principles of historicism.

Documents are the primary sources for historical research. Since Droysen and Mommsen, artifacts have been admitted as historical evidence, though the preference for texts continued. Noth says, "tradition of the Old Testament is not our sole source of information about the conditions which confronted the Israelite tribes when they entered Palestine"; indeed, the many documents recovered by archaeologists allow scholars to describe this early period "fairly concretely and accurately."[71]

The critical use of documents was famously established by Ranke and Noth takes up this task with competence and enthusiasm. His statement, "the main traditional source of information in the history of Israel, beside which all other sources are purely supplementary, is indissolubly bound up with this testimony," namely, that God selected Israel to bring blessing to all the earth, however, calls Noth's objectivity into question. His critical work on individual texts is inspiring, but his presupposition regarding the meaning of Israel's history sets him outside the longstanding tradition of German historical research.

Noth may be seen as a critically competent scholar, formed in a tradition which offers him the opportunity to develop an understanding of Israel as an historical entity defined and self-understood as a unity based on its historical experience. His method proceeds along traditional lines. He discovers the faint outlines of the ancient character of the people and traces the unfolding of this character through the life of Israel. A firm belief in the reality of God's guidance in history relieves Noth of the extreme consequences of the relativism which afflicted the German historicists and finally brought about historicism's demise, but most certainly separates him from the German historical tradition.

9. Part Two: John Bright

Bright received his Ph.D. in 1940, from the Johns Hopkins University. His dissertation, "The Age of King David: A Study in the Institutional History of Israel," was followed by a series of ten articles and three books in the next two decades before the publication of his *A History of*

---

71. Noth, *History*, 1.

Israel in 1959. One of the books and four of the articles dealt with the topic of history. In *Early Israel in Recent History Writing: A Study in Method* (1956),[72] Bright directly challenged the methodological approach of Martin Noth. The final section was reprinted as an article, "The School of Alt and Noth: A Critical Evaluation," in 1969.[73] He wrote also on theological themes, on prophets, Jeremiah in particular, and on education for the clergy and theology for the church. *A History of Israel* was published in German in 1966, and Italian in 1970, and was translated into Japanese in 1968. Another book, a dozen essays, and numerous contributions to commentaries, dictionaries, and encyclopedia followed. He taught at Union Theological Seminary in Richmond from 1940 to 1975, except for a period in World War II when he served as a chaplain in the US Army in Europe.

10. *Assumptions*

Certain broad assumptions guide the scholarship of John Bright. He begins his Foreword to the first edition of *A History of Israel* with a justification for writing the history. He says, "Because of the intimate manner in which the message of the Old Testament is related to historical events, a knowledge of Israel's history is essential to its proper understanding."[74] History functions for ancient Israel as the matrix in which divine revelation occurs. The great events of Israel's past are recalled in her ceremonies and at moments of crisis as reminders of God's identity, "the God who brought you up from Egypt," "the God of your fathers." For the modern reader the historic events take on symbolic status as signs of God's compassion, ongoing interest, and promise of protection. Bright's emphasis lies in the contemporary reader's understanding of Israel's history, rather than ancient Israel's own conception of its past. This focus on present interpretation of the events of Israel's past is a decided effort to make the "message of the Old Testament" pertinent to student of today in keeping with his view that the descriptive work of the historian serves the theologian in his or her task.[75]

72. John Bright, *Early Israel in Recent History Writing: A Study in Method* (SBT 19; London: SCM Press, 1956).

73. John Bright, "The School of Alt and Noth: A Critical Evaluation," in his *Old Testament Issues* (ed. Samuel Sandmel; London: SCM Press, 1969), 157–93.

74. John Bright, *A History of Israel* (3d ed.; Philadelphia: Westminster, 1981 [1959]), 17.

75. Krister Stendahl, "Biblical Theology," *IDB* 1:418–32.

a. *Israel Unique in History*

"The distinguishing factor that made Israel the peculiar phenomenon that she was, which both created her society and was the controlling factor in her history, was of course her religion." Israel's unique religion and the fact that Israel was "at all times set off from its environment as a distinctive cultural entity," are further convictions that stand behind Bright's work.[76] The singular character of Israel among her neighbors and, indeed, in history, has consequences for research on her history. Cross-cultural comparisons and the use of sociological models are ruled out by her uniqueness. Atypical events or one-time occurrences may be supported by this view of singularity.

11. *Sources*

a. *Israel's Traditions*

It is equally important to Bright that Israel was not indigenous to the land. To assume an autochthonous people forecloses the possibility that the patriarchal narratives hold authentic memories of the ancestors of Israel. To the contrary, Israel "had come from elsewhere and was well aware of that fact. Through a body of sacred tradition quite without parallel in the ancient world, she remembered...how, centuries earlier still, her ancestors had come from faraway Mesopotamia to wander in the land" she later called her own.[77] Bright admits that while "to attempt to use these traditions as historical sources presents severe problems that cannot be shirked, the traditions are by all means to be taken seriously."[78] This is a rather circular sort of argument, for if it can be compellingly demonstrated (here archaeology is called on for support) that Israel settled in the land, coming from elsewhere, then the traditions must have some validity. If the traditions are thus valid, then Israel's ancestors came from outside the land they settled. So Bright's argument that Israel was not indigenous to the land of Palestine buttresses his belief that the biblical traditions contain accurate historical memories.

Bright qualifies his belief by noting that "If it is correct to say that history can be written with confidence only on the basis of contemporary records...the patriarchal narratives are certainly not historical documents contemporaneous with the events of which they tell" and as such cannot be used for reconstructing Israel's origins.[79] Nevertheless, Bright argues

76. Bright, *History*, 17.
77. Ibid., 147.
78. Ibid.
79. Ibid., 68.

that extra-biblical sources now confirm some of the traditional material and have led to a more positive evaluation of the patriarchal narratives. Though it is generally "conceded that the traditions might contain historical reminiscences," and thus that Wellhausen's "judgment was much too severe," still it is difficult to offer any convincing support for the historicity of any particular tradition.[80] Bright reminds us that when the documentary hypothesis was developed there was no real awareness of the long history of the civilizations of the ancient Near East, no cultural background known to offer perspective for the patriarchal traditions. Without any frame of reference for judging these traditions, it was not surprising that they were rejected as having no historical worth.

b. *Regional Culture*

Bright points out that millennia had passed before Israel appeared, that in addition to advanced pottery techniques, irrigation, and improvements in agriculture and animal husbandry, writing, legal systems, literature, and art were well developed. More innovation had occurred before Israel's appearance than for centuries after—in fact, until the modern era. Alongside the sophistication of technology, law, and the arts, commerce fostered connections among cities and empires. The entire area of the Fertile Crescent formed a world in which literature, religion, military, and political organization took similar forms.[81] The emphasis on the dynamic regional culture serves two purposes for Bright. First, the stress on the regional character of the culture sharpens the distinction of the unique features of Israelite society and religion. Second, details of the culture serve to indicate the remarkable amount of knowledge that has accumulated about this part of the world in very ancient times. This is in high contrast to what was known in the nineteenth century, by Wellhausen and his followers in particular, and supports the argument that the current state of knowledge allows a more generous view of the patriarchal traditions.

c. *Scope of Study*

Bright expresses his confidence in these traditions by asserting, "Surely the Bible need claim no immunity from rigorous historical method, but may be trusted to withstand the scrutiny to which other documents of history are submitted."[82] His optimism is based on his broad understanding of the ancient Near East. The origins of Israel must be found within

80. Ibid., 68–69.
81. Ibid., 24.
82. Ibid., 68.

this world and the Bible offers hints of this same world. Therefore, any and all rigorous study of the biblical texts can only succeed in drawing the connections more firmly. Before the thirteenth century, when Israel's presence is "attested by archaeological data and contemporary records" there are only "seminomadic wanderers elusively roaming the map of the years, unattested by contemporary record and leaving behind them no tangible trace of their passing."[83] These nomadic peoples are not technically part of Israel's history, but of her pre-history. Bright argues that "the prehistory of a people... is really a part of its history."[84] Here he follows the view of Arnold Toynbee. Toynbee argues that no nation or state, taken by itself, constitutes an intelligible field of study, but the wider causes or influences of the broader culture of which a nation is a part must be included in the study. The extension of a society in the dimensions of both space and time must be explored. He continues, "The intelligible unit of historical study is...a certain grouping of humanity which we have called a society."[85] In the space dimension, "The 'intelligible field of study,' in fact, appears to be a society containing a number of communities of the [same] species..."[86] In the time dimension, tracing a society back to its origins, one finds the last phase of a preceding society, a parent culture. Certain continuities stand out though the function of typical structures may shift. The ancient Near East during the three millennia before the common era, then, constitutes an appropriate field of study in Toynbee's terms. Bright says, "to begin with 2000 BCE, as though nothing had happened before that time, would be unwise."[87] After sketching the neolithic and chalcolithic cultures which occupied the region, Bright describes the cultures of the third millennium in the Fertile Crescent as the background for the emergence of ancient Israel.

The controlling assumptions for Bright's study of the history of Israel are, then, that history is the descriptive discipline which provides material necessary to the "proper understanding" of the biblical text. The historic background of a people or nation is in some sense part of the history of

83. Ibid., 47.
84. Ibid., 147.
85. Toynbee, "The Unit," 114.
86. Ibid., 104. By way of example, he points out the situations of four Greek city-states between the eighth and fourth centuries. He argues that, taken separately, the conclusions one would draw about each city would indicate that they had been very different from their foundations. Archaeology, however, confirms their similarity. Studying them together as a wider unit, one discovers their common difficulties brought on by an increasing population and the consequent pressures on available resources.
87. Bright, *History*, 23.

that people. Our greater knowledge and awareness of the cultures of the ancient world, extending several millennia into the past, significantly shifts our perspective on the culture and development of Israel from that of Wellhausen's day. In particular, Israel became a recognizable entity as a tribal confederacy. Israel's religion was the creative element in her formation and her history, and made her unique among contemporary peoples throughout her existence.

d. *The Use of Archaeology*
Two other areas remain to be addressed in regard to Bright's assumptions: the place of archaeology in the work of the historian of Israel and Bright's own relationship to biblical theology. Knowing that neither the characters in the patriarchal narratives nor the ancient traditions are mentioned in any contemporary text, that no reference is made in any other ancient document to the entity "Israel," with the single exception of the Merneptah Stele, until well after the time of David and Solomon, Bright relies on material recovered by archaeologists to support the existence of the patriarchs and their way of life. He assumes that artifacts offer more objective evidence than texts, that archaeology provides straightforward testimony of habitation, of warfare, of technical advances at particular dates. Not to overstate this, for Bright was not unsophisticated, but for him archaeology supports a view of history as events, rather than developing an anthropological perspective, a picture of a culture or way of life. William Dever points out that biblical archaeology gathered evidence "selectively," "conclusions were drawn and debated, and interpretations advanced—all on the basis of an appeal to 'history'... but what history *was* and how a modern historiography was possible using archaeological data, were questions scarcely raised."[88]

e. *Reaction to Liberal Theology*
Biblical theology, as a movement which flourished between 1945 and 1960, was, according to James Barr

> a strong reaction against the way in which the Bible had been studied under the "liberal" theology, with its dry historical exegesis, its analytic tendency and dependence on source criticism, its tendency to understand biblical material in terms drawn from the environing culture, its evolutionism, its complacently universal theological positions, and its lack of theological concern and existential fervor.[89]

88. William Dever, "Syro-Palestinian and Biblical Archaeology," *ABD* 1:354–67 (62).
89. James Barr, "Biblical Theology," *IDB*, Supplementary vol., 104–11.

Bright's *History*, as noted above, takes a firm position on Israel's unique religion, its distinctive culture set off from its environment, and the continuities of Israel's religion from earliest times. He seeks to overcome the problems resulting from source criticism. He finds Wellhausen "too severe" in his judgment that the patriarchal narratives are in no way records of the second millennium. Bright hopes to counteract the view of Israel's religion as "the crudest sort of animism or polydaemonism,"[90] a view that has its roots in the History of Religions School, the evolutionism and universalism which Barr noted. Bright plans to "accord religious factors their proper place in and alongside political events,"[91] which, like Wright, he takes as real history understood by faith.[92] To study the ancient narratives as traditions is, in a very real sense to Bright, to exclude the possibility of writing history. For if the framework of the Pentateuch is derived from cultic celebration rather than historical experience, then the questions which can be addressed to the text are those about the cult, not about history.[93] Bright's assumptions are akin to those of the biblical theology movement opposing the minimal stance toward the historical value of the Pentateuch and the unremarkable origins of Israel fostered by historical and source criticism. His *History* proceeds from the position that the Hebrew Bible contains memories from which history can be reconstructed with the aid of external and comparative materials, that the message of the Hebrew Bible is deeply intertwined with historical events, and that to understand the message, one must understand the history.

12. *Method*

Having established the assumptions Bright brings to the task of writing Israel's history, we now turn to his method. Bright chooses to investigate the sources of Israel's history by a means he calls *the balance of probability*.[94] The judgment on the reliability of texts is not one of proof, he says, but *"where is the balance of probability in the matter?"* This is

90. Bright, *History*, 23.
91. Ibid., 17.
92. G. E. Wright, "Modern Issues in Biblical Studies," *Expository Times* 71 (1959): 292–96 (293).
93. Ibid., 293.
94. J. Alberto Soggin expresses great expectation for this "new" concept. He notes, however, that for Bright, archaeological evidence, while not proving anything directly, "still inclines the balance toward the biblical account" ("Ancient Biblical Traditions and Modern Archaeological Discoveries," *Biblical Archaeologist* 23 [1960]: 95–100 [99]).

indeed, the area in which the historian usually labours. He weighs the evidence, *and does not brush aside the more probable for the less probable.*"95

Historians in modern times have been exceedingly skeptical of their sources, unwilling to accept uncritically the reports of witnesses. Before the historical-critical method gained favor, the task of the historian was to collect as many witnesses to past events as possible and to transcribe what they reported. In the case of disagreement among the witnesses, the historian made a judgment for the more authoritative source. Modern historical consciousness shifted authority from past witnesses to the historian in the present. The historian is now responsible for the accuracy of historical reporting.96 The Bible, as the witness—at many points the sole witness—to Israel's past, thus requires the judgment of the historian on its authority and trustworthiness in portraying history.

Bright places most historians of ancient Israel, including himself, in the middle ground between those who accept the patriarchal narratives as fully historical and those who allow the narratives no historical value. That is to say that he assumes most of those writing on the history of ancient Israel take up a critical position regarding the Bible as witness. He observes, however, that these historians of the middle position reach no agreement on how the traditions should be evaluated. The variety of reconstructions put forward on the basis of the same traditions, he argues, must be the result, not of the evidence clearly, but of the evaluation of evidence.97

13. *Theology Based in History*

Bright begins his essay on method, *Early Israel in Recent History Writing*, with the question: "by what method may one evaluate the historical worth of these traditions, and in what manner, and to what degree, may one use them, together with other evidence, in reconstructing the origins and early history of the Hebrew people?"98 In beginning to answer this question, he comments that it is not only an academic matter, but has theological significance as well, for Old Testament theology is a theology of events, and "the interpretation of those events in the light of

95. Bright, *Early Israel*, 88.
96. Joseph Albert Deegan, "Noth, Bright and Mendenhall on Early Israel: A Critique of Historical Explanation" (Ph.D. diss., Claremont Graduate University, 1978), 23–24.
97. Bright, *Early Israel*, 15.
98. Ibid., 11.

faith."⁹⁹ He goes on, "although, one may say that the theological interpretation is of greater significance than the events themselves, the actual history can never be a matter of indifference to the theologian... Old Testament theology rests in history." He argues that one's reconstruction of Israel's early history and religion colors the subsequent history—political, institutional, and spiritual. The degree of continuity which "one is prepared to find in Israel's religion" has direct impact on "the unity that one may allow to Old Testament theology..."¹⁰⁰ Thus, theology and religion are always to be kept in mind and are ultimately served by any effort to write Israel's history from the Hebrew Bible.

a. *Material Culture*
With the principle that theology is dependent on a proper understanding of history established, Bright proceeds to outline the method for determining the origins of a culture. To study an indigenous culture, Bright tells us, one must examine the archaeological evidence and trace the material culture. This will include seeking possible contacts with other cultures, breaks or gaps in culture under investigation, shifts or waves of population. Traditions must be studied, presumably all literary production is of interest here, and linguistic clues are sought for indications of connections or affiliations with other peoples. More difficult to study is a people who have no origins in the land where they first come to prominence. Bright points to classical Greeks and Hittites who have no memory of their origins, though modern research has established the directions of their migrations. Again, he insists that archaeological, linguistic, and cultural material comprise the evidence to be evaluated. For those nonindigenous groups who hold traditions of migration or origins elsewhere, their traditions are to be added to the evidence, "not to be used uncritically; but neither are they to be ruled out of court."¹⁰¹

b. *Evaluation of the Text*
Evaluation of the traditional account of Israel's origins poses a problem on the general principles which Bright has established. For how will the period between the events described and the time they are recorded in the form we have them be bridged? First, Bright begins with the "accepted results of literary criticism" from Wellhausen and those who followed, and includes "all objectively achieved results" of form criticism and studies of the transmission of tradition. Here he notes the work of Noth.

99. Ibid., 11.
100. Ibid., 12.
101. Ibid., 122.

One must "especially include the numerous comparative studies of individual units of tradition, of a linguistic, topographical and archaeological nature, such as those in which the schools of Alt and Albright have been so prolific."[102]

c. *Use of Evidence*

Bright has moved from his general principles of investigation, that is the evidence to be used in particular varieties of cultures, to the particular types of evidence available to the historian of ancient Israel. Sources, forms, traditions, language, topography, and artifacts are appropriate material for study. The historian is to be objective and refuse "to make unwarranted deductions which exceed the evidence." The historian proceeds always "by a balanced examination of internal and external evidence" pondering the intrinsic probability by inquiring whether or not the story, report, lore, or recollection seems reasonable. One should check for bias, tendency, or apology in the text. The form of the unit of text may suggest that its use or purpose may have influenced its shape, its embellishments, even its contents. Bright acknowledges the subjective quality of this endeavor and exhorts the historian to be aware of his or her own predilections and also those reflected in the documents.

Against the subjective nature of the investigation of the texts, he advocates the use of external evidence from archaeology. Bright acknowledges that the evidence provided by archaeology is circumstantial and he appeals again to the balance of probability in the application of this evidence. In particular he notes that archaeology may be significant in the evaluation of individual traditions, supporting and clarifying particular features or actions, and in regard to the larger text of the Hexateuch, providing a context for the whole of the patriarchal traditions.[103]

In summary, Bright argues for a methodology which takes into account all the available evidence, including the earliest traditions. The results of literary criticism and the analysis of tradition history must be included in the method. The historian, furthermore, must make every effort to identify and exclude bias and partiality in both the researcher and in the text. The conclusions of this investigation are then compared to the historical picture provided by archaeology and weighed against the reasonable possibilities. The final outcome of this process of gathering and weighing of all available evidence, before any theory is formulated, is simply a probability more likely than not, or more likely than other possibilities. Bright's approach follows closely the American historical

102. Ibid., 123.
103. Ibid., 125.

tradition. Evidence is collected, including the "results" of literary criticism and tradition analysis, and compared and checked against external material. From these "facts" conclusions may be drawn. The scientific procedure is protected by excluding bias and subjectivity. Bright says in several places that given what little we can prove conclusively about Israel's ancestors and origins, the widely differing reconstructions of Israel's early life are based on the pleasure and credulity of the writer. His outline of a methodology for the evaluation of the traditions is an attempt to establish some "objective controls" for evaluating the early traditions of Israel.[104]

14. *Criticism of Alt and Noth*

The well-known criticism of Alt's and Noth's approach to Israelite pre-history was initiated by W. F. Albright in the April 1935 issue of the *Bulletin of the American Schools of Oriental Research*. Albright's challenge continued through the 1939 article, "The Israelite Conquest of Canaan in the Light of Archaeology." Albright specifies three troubling principles employed by Alt and Noth: first, analysis of the oral traditions through the operations of *Gattungsgeschichte* or form criticism; second, the function assigned to aetiology; finally, the *Ortsgebundenheit* or the notion that names and stories cling tenaciously to particular sites.[105] Albright notes that oral traditions, conforming as they must to certain customary patterns and conventions, can never be conclusively evaluated by the literary framework in which they are found. He adduces several examples of confused aetiologies to support his view that an aetiological statement can only be judged in light of external evidence. He observes that "Traditions connected with places are notoriously shifting."[106]

Bright takes up this argument in his *Early Israel in Recent History Writing*. At the outset he identifies the problem of using early traditions for the reconstruction of history as one of method. He points out that early biblical criticism had little extra-biblical data to draw on to develop an understanding of early Israel. Certain assumptions concerning the evolution of primitive religion guide researchers in describing the development of Israel's religion through stages of fetishism, polytheism, to monotheism. Bright suggests a Hegelian basis for this scheme and argues that, even when that philosophical view receded, the developmental view

104.   Ibid., 15.
105.   Knight discusses these criticisms in *Rediscovering*, 199–202.
106.   W. F. Albright, "The Israelite Conquest of Canaan in the Light of Archaeology," *BASOR* 74 (1939): 11–23 (14).

of Israel's religion persisted. This, Bright insists, had a serious effect on the valuation of early traditions, which are seen, on this view, as cult legends.[107]

Bright reiterates and amplifies Albright's earlier arguments against the principles of Noth's method. First, dependence on the analysis of oral and written literary forms is too great. Because, he says, of the conventional forms in which the early traditions are found, nothing final may be concluded about the historicity of the traditions without the corroboration of external evidence.[108] Furthermore, once the ancient traditions are used as indications of the stages in the evolution of Israel's religion, there is "a consequent devaluation" of the biblical account.[109] Bright acknowledges that there are many aetiologies in the biblical text, but, unlike Noth, insists that narratives answering the question "why?" are generally understood to belong to a genre of fable, not meant to be taken literally.[110] To illustrate, he observes that in cases where the origin of a tradition can be confidently traced, as with certain events in American history, one finds that aetiology is only one among several elements of the tradition and does not necessarily undermine the historicity of the tradition.[111] He insists that "the only possible test of Noth's theories *re* aetiology must be made precisely where the facts are in our control."[112] Bright's criticism of the notion of *Ortsgebundenheit* claims that traditions are tied not to places, but rather to people. He offers the example of Appalachian folk songs that remain remarkably consistent in content over time, yet substitute local place names for the original English ones, "with the result that English lords and ladies wander and plight their troth somewhere by the Forks of Big Sandy."[113]

The debate between Bright and Noth over these particular issues takes the form of a methodological dispute, but, Alberto Soggin believes, the contenders are "nearer each other than one might *prima facie* believe."[114] Soggin bases his argument on the close agreement of Noth and Bright on the results in several areas of research. The Mari and Nuzi texts, they agree, are particularly relevant to understanding of the origins of Israel as

107. Bright, *Early Israel*, 22.
108. Ibid., 90.
109. Ibid., 23.
110. Ibid., 92.
111. Bright (ibid., 95) uses several examples from American tradition. Thanksgiving, he points out, is based on a legend which preceded the custom, which according to Noth's theory, it should have been invented to explain.
112. Ibid., 97.
113. Ibid., 103.
114. Soggin, "Ancient Biblical Traditions," 100.

far as names and customs are concerned. Both recognize the large scale of destructions in the thirteenth and twelfth centuries documented by archaeological data. They agree that biblical authors did not write for the purpose of recording history and that reconstructing history without contemporary records presents sometimes insurmountable difficulties.[115] These points of compromise on particular issues, pointed out by Soggin, are the results of years of research and debate, the very progress promised by scientific inquiry. They are concessions in regard to results only, however, and have little to do with differences in approach. These differences are usually attributed, as by Bright himself, to methodology. It is clear, as Soggin points out, that Noth and Bright both accept textual criticism and archaeological evidence as basic data for biblical studies, but their differences are more profound, based in their respective historiographic traditions.

15. *Conclusion*

For Noth the history of Israel is the "idea" of the people as it comes to full consciousness in the land. It is the expression of their spirit effected through the design of God. The identity of the people is entwined and ultimately dependent on their historical awareness and self-understanding. Noth, following the classic German historicists, deeply immerses himself in the culture of ancient Israel. He favors documentary evidence over material and, from his intimate involvement with the form and function of ancient traditions, he discovers the *real* meaning of the biblical history. Noth continues in the historicist tradition of the idealist historiography. The German crisis of relativism produced no particular effect on Noth's worldview. The metaphysical underpinning of biblical history remains intact for him and keeps the questions of relativism at bay.

Bright is less influenced by the possible metaphysical background for the development of history than Noth. His commitment is to the accurate

115. Ibid., 77–79. J. Maxwell Miller notes that both "Altians and Albrightians recognized that the biblical presentation of Israel's history is not entirely accurate as it stands; both were confident nevertheless that historically useful data could be derived from the biblical materials; and both insisted that the nonbiblical sources should be granted an integrity of their own rather than simply harmonized or explained away in deference to the biblical account... Alt and his followers tended to be much less confident than the Albrightians regarding the reliability of the biblical materials for historical reconstruction, and the reconstructions they proposed tended to depart more radically from the biblical account" ("Israelite History," in *The Hebrew Bible and Its Modern Interpreters* (ed. Douglas A. Knight and Gene M. Tucker; Chico, Calif.: Scholars Press, 1985), 1–30 (21).

recounting of events. The American historical tradition of "objectivity" stresses facts. Facts impartially assembled speak for themselves. Meaning in history will emerge from the objective presentation of facts. Indeed, the meaning of the Bible is subject to its reliability as an accurate account of history. For Bright and for those formed in the assumptions of the biblical theology movement, history is critical for belief. G. E. Wright puts it most succinctly: "In biblical faith everything depends upon whether the events actually occurred."[116]

While Noth, in the German tradition, seeks to *understand* the experience of the Israelite confederacy in the formation of its identity, Bright strives for a more detached approach. He has adopted the position of the conservative or orthodox cohort of American historians. While objectivity can never be absolute, all efforts of the historian must be directed to the elimination of personal bias and reasonable success in presenting an impartial reconstruction of history can be expected. As for the historians of the American pragmatic tradition, Bright's audience is made up of interested and informed readers, readers who eschew dry, analytical treatises and seek life and color and a contemporary relevance for history. This audience eagerly responds to the promise of new discoveries for illuminating the biblical past and to the presentation of the facts of the biblical history.

The American historical tradition emphasizes the usefulness of history for the present. Within this tradition, the story of Israel's history produced by Bright addresses his audience's desire for a satisfying account of life in ancient Israel, an account which pays close attention to the events of the biblical record. The events, or *facts* of history, are essential to the meaning of history. The work of nineteenth-century critical scholarship, the History of Religions School, and, subsequently, tradition critics, on the other hand, participate in the German historical tradition, which gives attention to the particular stages or developments in the biblical tradition. They are especially interested in the function or contemporary significance of each unit in the tradition rather than in the question of the actual reality of an event. It is biblical thought or biblical religion that commanded German scholarly attention and thus generated opposition among Americans who sought enduring theological meaning and relevance for the present. American biblical scholars pursued eternal truths in Israel's history, whereas German historicism taught that truth is always relative to the context of a particular society. It is not

116. G. E. Wright, *The God who Acts: Biblical Theology as Recital* (SBT 8; London: SCM Press, 1952), 126.

methodology, but the theoretical background of their respective traditions, which produce profound differences in approach.

Despite the differences between the approaches of Noth and Bright to the problems of Israel's history, both manifest the significant remove of historiography in biblical studies from that in academic departments of history. In the previous chapter, the distinctions between American pragmatism and German Idealism were explored, but, finally, it was pointed out that neither tradition was able to come to terms with the problems of relativism, value and meaning, or to provide a satisfactory explanation of the relation of the historian to the past. Historiography in biblical studies did not confront these issues. In the next chapter, questions about the character of history and the position of the scholar and researcher become more insistent for academic historians.

Chapter 6

HISTORIOGRAPHY AND CONTROVERSY
IN THE RECENT PAST

> To be sure every historical account is a construct, but a construct arising
> from a dialog between the historian and the past, one that does not occur
> in a vacuum but within a community of inquiring minds who share crite-
> ria of plausibility.[1]

Following World War II, serious challenges to notions of progress and
development, coupled with fundamental changes in culture and society,
began to have an impact on the work of practicing historians in the
United States and Europe. History oriented toward events and individuals, the life of the state, and the importance of the modern Western world,
was increasingly accompanied and displaced by histories attending to
social and economic factors and to the lives of larger groups within the
general population. Whereas before the war relativism undermined the
notion of objectivity and scientific history, now social scientists insisted
that history must be more "scientific" and, like all sciences, offer general
conclusions and causal *explanation* rather than *understanding*. In
response, historians undertook quantitative studies of economic trends
and influences, studies of structural forces within societies, social motivations and limitations, class divisions, and ideological and rhetorical
pressures. To these endeavors eventually were added studies challenging
the prevailing notions of time. Long periods bound by natural patterns
and social frameworks exhibiting only gradual change when examined
beside quicker-paced political events exposed the fact that even a particular epoch or interval did not present the coherence once imagined. A
single narrative following a sequence of events could not follow the web
of conditions that existed simultaneously. Particular groups, too—women,
various ethnic identities, immigrants, workers—noted that conventional

---

1. Georg Iggers, *Historiography in the Twentieth Century: From Scientific
Objectivity to the Postmodern Challenge* (Hanover, N.H.: Wesleyan University
Press, 1997), 145.

histories had excluded them and sought to place their histories alongside the existing treatments of the past.

By the 1960s a new critical perspective emerged, influenced by the Holocaust and the implications of World War II. The horrific possibilities of technology and the negative potentialities of economic growth for certain communities undermined the notion of progress. The idea of national consensus promoted by historians for several decades broke down as works appeared stressing the diversities within societies. Awareness of economic, educational, and political disparities suggested that different groups had different histories. The subjects of study proliferated dramatically. Works appeared documenting the particular histories of unnoticed or neglected groups, "histories from below." These histories claimed no stance of objectivity; rather, they offered a perspective promoting the interests of the group chronicled. They opposed the studies of social structures and forces promoted by social scientists in favor of more intimate and personal studies of culture, everyday life, and everyday experience.

The historical discipline in the nineteenth century operated from the conviction that history dealt with meanings and intentions, the agency of human actors, and that this realm was sharply distinct from the realm of nature and thus not amenable to generalizations. With the ancient writers of history, the professional academic historians presupposed that history corresponded to real events that occurred in time, and that history would be written as a temporal sequence. The professionalization of the discipline was primarily an institutionalization of history writing, a division between the academic practitioners and the learned amateurs, and the defense of the disciplinary boundaries within the academy against philosophy, natural science, and poetry.

The question of objectivity, as it was debated through the nineteenth and early twentieth centuries, was grounded in the belief that history writing was a scientific discipline. While avoiding the aspects of causality and generalization characteristic of the natural sciences, historians tried valiantly to establish history as science with rigorous methods and criteria of judgment and validity. Philosophy with its own generalized schemata and teleologies was also shunned. Disquiet, even disillusion, with contemporary Western civilization produced pronounced reaction to the scientific agenda of the modern world. Within the humanities, this rejection of science made questionable the notion that there existed objects of research discoverable through clearly defined methods. Instead, it appeared that the interests and predilections of the researcher determined the object of research. In this view, the historian was no longer a scientist but a writer of fiction.

Georg Iggers explains:

> The idea that objectivity in historical research is not possible because there
> is no object of history has gained increasing currency. Accordingly the his-
> torian is always the prisoner of the world within which he thinks, and his
> thoughts and perceptions are conditioned by the categories of the language
> in which he operates. Thus language shapes reality but does not refer to it.[2]

The difference between the German and American historical traditions
and the positions loosely called "postmodern" is seen most clearly in the
older traditions' confidence that the historical subject exists and somehow remains free of the historian's prose, while the newer thinkers insist
on the "metaphorical, nonreferential character of every historical text."
Indeed, the whole of modern historical scholarship may be seen as "an
aberration from the older, premodern conception of history as a form of
rhetoric."[3] Iggers points out that even those historians writing before the
professionalization of the discipline "viewed themselves as rhetoricians
for whom history was to contain exemplars, lessons for life, and were at
the same time committed to telling a truthful story." The impact made by
the radical critiques of the methods of historical inquiry on the practice
of history writing has nonetheless been limited. To fully accept these critiques would be to decline to write history and, certainly, this has not
happened. Practicing historians have continued to recognize that history,
while indisputably a form of narrative, seeks to report a real past, to
reconstruct a reality that existed before and outside the text.[4] This is the
position held by historians in biblical studies, though they have been
spared, for the most part, critical debate over the reality of past and the
constraints of language. The function of narrative will be a feature of the
discussion of biblical history in the next chapter, the intention of the text
will be argued, and standards of objectivity will be disputed, but theoretical questions regarding the existence of the historical subject do not
figure in the controversies within the field.

This chapter will investigate the challenges to Western traditions of
history writing as they gained force following World War II. I will argue
that these challenges represent stresses within the culture regarding the
ideas of progress and development and the place of science, and that
historians, while exercising caution in their claims to reconstruct the past,
remain committed to producing a reliable narrative based on honest and
systematic inquiry. At the same time, I will argue that the professional
character of the discipline has undergone some significant modification.

2. Ibid., 9.
3. Ibid., 11.
4. Ibid., 11–12.

The questions regarding audience, social function, professionalization, and the scientific character of history that have guided the earlier sections of this study continue to be important in the present. The broad audience of educated readers of the nineteenth century has disappeared for professional historians. The academic character of the audience is increasingly important, to such a degree that a writer finding a popular or non-academic readership is marked as a lesser scholar. The role of the nineteenth- and early twentieth-century historian as one charged with the task of improving the general level of culture has faded entirely. The part historians played in providing propaganda in the two wars subsequently proved embarrassing. The fact that many historians wrote with obvious conviction at the time added strength to the argument that objectivity is not possible. So, the function of history as edification has given way to history as the voice of particular segments of the culture. The relation of history to science continues to be debated with many quantifiable factors included in studies of the past alongside studies of the minutiae of everyday life.

1. *The New Scientific History*

Ranke's practice of scientific history entailed careful evaluation of source material. The resulting sets of facts were to be interpreted by knowledgeable and empathic scholars. This endeavor was "scientific" in that it followed rigorous standards of criticism and impartiality. It opposed, however, any sort of positivistic vision that reduced human behavior to general laws. While German historiography resisted social science approaches to historical study for several generations, eventually quantification became part of the accepted methodology. In the United States and the rest of Europe, these approaches gained strength in the effort to make history more objective. Scientific historians were confident that the major problems of historical explanation would be solved, "such baffling questions as the causes of 'great revolutions' or the shifts from feudalism to capitalism, and from traditional to modern societies."[5] Lawrence Stone identifies three models of "scientific history" that were prominent in the twentieth century: the Marxist economic model flourishing from the 1930s to the late 1950s, the French ecological/demographic model, influential in 1950s to the mid 1970s, and the American "cliometric model," a major force in the 1960s and 1970s.[6]

5. Lawrence Stone, "The Revival of Narrative: Reflections of a New Old History," *Past and Present* 85 (1979): 3–24 (7).
6. Ibid., 5, 7.

a. *Marxist History*
The Marxist economic model, based in dialectical process, understood history as a clash between social classes. These classes are products of the forces which are brought into being by the evolution of the means of production. Social and economic determinism, prominent in this model, fostered interest in societies rather than individuals. Methodology from the social sciences appeared imminently suitable for study that "would in time produce generalized laws to explain historical change."[7] Furthermore, Stone argues that ideological commitments among western intellectuals supported the Marxist type of scientific history. He says, "It seemed desperately important at the time to know whether or not the Marxist interpretation was right..." Questions about the rise or decline of the gentry in seventeenth-century England, the real income of the working class in the early stages of industrialization, and the causes, nature, and consequences of American slavery were all debates driven by ideological concerns. He suggests that "the decline in the thrust of historical research to ask the big *why* questions" is related to the decline in intellectual Marxism.[8] From the 1930s to the late 1950s, this notion of scientific history was promoted and defended by traditional Marxist historians, but the new generation of neo-Marxists have relinquished the tenets of economic determinism and the claim to "scientific history."

b. *The* Annales
The French historians of the *Annales* school also produced "scientific history." German economic history initially influenced the founders of the journal *Annales*. Very soon the traditional topics of investigation—politics, law, literature, religion—were integrated into the study of culture as experienced by the whole population. Economic aspects of history were understood to be closely tied to social and political structures, to patterns of thought, and to geography. Collective consciousness, norms, customs, and belief were incorporated into approaches linked to sociology and anthropology. The *Annales* sought to provide a forum for new theories and new directions. Still on the margins in the 1930s, following the war *Annales* historians were established in a new section of the Ecole Pratique des Hautes Etudes. In 1972, this section was reorganized as the Ecole des Hautes Etudes en Sciences Sociales, "committed to integrating history and the social science disciplines within a comprehensive 'science of man.'"[9] Here, in addition to economics, sociology, and anthropology,

7. Ibid., 5.
8. Ibid., 9.
9. Iggers, *Historiography*, 54–55.

the study of linguistics, semiotics, literature, arts, and psychoanalysis became approaches to the study of history.

In abandoning traditional conceptions of time, the *Annales* historians present a "plurality of co-existing times," both among different civilizations and within each civilization. The almost imperceptible changes in the land, the geographic conditions, the climate, exist beside the slow changes in the social and economic structures, fixed by custom, law, habit. Alongside these elements, the time of political events moves along rapidly. The old notion of unified historical development is not compatible with a non-linear view of time. The nation, which provided a sense of identity for many in the nineteenth and twentieth centuries, is not a historical focus for the *Annales* historians. Regions or localities and their everyday life are the topics of these researchers. Without the concept of linear time, progress becomes a problematic idea and confidence in the advanced state of Western culture is challenged. The role of the individual as historical agent is eroded by the notion that the external world, climate, and technology, strongly determine the activity of human beings.[10]

In the 1960s, the French historians were affected by the general fascination with science and increasingly chose to call themselves scientists. To their enduring interest in geography and demography was added quantification. Emmanuel Le Roy Ladurie stated simply that "history that is not quantifiable cannot claim to be scientific."[11] For Le Roy Ladurie the chief variable in history is the relative balance between food supplies and population. Economic and demographic determinism directed the historical research of this period. Social structure and intellectual, religious, cultural, and political factors were largely ignored. With attention placed on the material conditions of the masses instead of the politically and socially elite, Stone says, "it became possible to talk about the history of Continental Europe from the fourteenth to the eighteenth centuries as 'l'histoire immobile.' Le Roy Ladurie argued that nothing, absolutely nothing, changed over those five centuries." Remarkable developments such as the Renaissance, the Reformation, and the Enlightenment were passed over along with "transformations of culture, art, architecture, literature, religion, education, science, law, constitution, state-building, bureaucracy, military organization, fiscal arrangements, and so on, which took place among the higher echelons of society in those five centuries." In addition to these problems, quantities of statistical

---

10. Ibid., 57.
11. Emmanuel Le Roy Ladurie, *The Territory of the Historian* (trans. B. Reynolds and S. Reynolds; Chicago: University of Chicago Press, 1979), 15.

analysis produced histories "without people."[12] The individual as historical agent was not a part of this approach. The inadequacy of deterministic approaches, the emphasis on a single segment of society, and the lack of the individual human dimension eventually encouraged a shift toward history of the everyday life and thoughts of real people.

The investigation of everyday life was further enhanced by semiotic studies and psychological research in the effort to reconstruct the most intimate and personal details of the real life experiences of concrete human beings. Criticism of the *Annales* argues that these approaches are unsuited for the study of modern times. Though much of this work has been concerned with the Middle Ages, in fact, there has been considerable work done on industrialization and the mass movements of the late nineteenth and early twentieth centuries. The *Annales* contribution to historical studies has been its focus on culture and symbols, the consciousness or *mentality* of individual societies. Iggers holds that "no scholarly movement in the twentieth century has had such an impact internationally as a model for new paths of historical investigation of culture and society." He suggests that the *Annales* attention to the pre-modern kept them free from assumptions about the superiority of scientific and technological orientations of Western thought and made them especially attractive when social science approaches began to be questioned in the 1970s.[13]

c. *American Historians at the Close of World War II*
John Higham suggests that during the war American historians became both increasingly knowledgeable about European history and impressed with the common American–European experience:

> The war supplied to historians as to so many other Americans a standard of relevance that conferred a kind of automatic unity upon activities previously disparate. Affecting America and Europe alike with the direct perception of its protracted span, scope, and effect, this war inspired a crisis literature that lumped the pasts of all segments of Western civilization together into a common transmission of society toward the present.[14]

Higham goes on to argue that at the same time the war produced a sense of continuity between the United States and Europe, it also fostered certain disruptions through the changed position of the United States relative to the rest of the world. He says, "The United States graduated

---

12. Stone, "The Revival," 8.
13. Iggers, *Historiography*, 62–64.
14. Higham, *History*, 289.

from the status of partnership, which characterized World War I, into the status of leadership over all the Allies but the Soviet Union…" and "this leadership was in large part the function of the expansion of the main military and political arena beyond Europe into the far reaches of Asia and the Pacific."[15] The impact of these factors on historians was more immediate than the typical indirect effect of political developments because of "the mass employment of historians, *qua* historians, in the government."[16] Whereas leading historians had provided public information on a volunteer basis in World War I and had contributed service as short-term consultants, the generation of historians during and just after World War II contributed "years-long full-time activity in military and political intelligence and planning for the government by all ranks of the profession, ranging from the most prominent to the novice."[17] Historians formed by this experience constituted the single identifiable cohort among practicing historians in the post-war period. The ultimate effect of the wartime role of American historians was a heightened sense of the common destiny of Europe and the United States tempered by the consciousness of the US's divergence from both the totalitarian impulses and the social radicalism found in Europe and their immediate awareness of the new relationship between the United States and the rest of the world based on its dominant position during the conflict.

The broader framework for European history in the United States brought with it a devaluation of the focus on the histories of specific nations. Significant movements or events involving several nations provided subjects for historians. Such topics as economic development, the effects of industrialization, and the impact of the history of science on society transcended national specialization. Intellectual histories, biographies, and studies of urban centers offered locations from which to view the larger society. These approaches, which Higham calls "microcosmic," were convenient vehicles where quantities of material are too great for competent analysis and they further respond to demands for precise research within the context of broader interpretation. The larger processes—social, cultural, political, or even providential—formerly assumed to lie behind history and form the basis for meaningful understanding, were replaced by categories constructed of immanent and discontinuous factors only just sufficient to invest events with meaning "intelligible to outsiders."[18] In particular, the liberal values of the West were shown to

15. Ibid., 290.
16. Ibid.
17. Ibid., 291.
18. Ibid., 305.

have origins in greater complexity, variety, and ambiguity. The "fragmen-
tation of the liberal tradition that has furnished American historiography
with its dominant values and interpretive criteria" has revealed the
historical process to be "open, plural, discontinuous, devious, volitional,
and immanent in the actual events of history."[19]

d. *History as Social Science*
"Perhaps at no time since the Enlightenment have theoretical discussions
bridged national lines so much as in the last three decades; nor have
historians in various Western countries been so aware of each other's
work," claims Georg Iggers.[20] Yet there are important distinctions in the
traditions as they developed in the 1950s and 1960s.

In the aftermath of World War II, the assumptions inherited from the
New Historians were called into question.[21] The new generation of historians, formed in wartime service, saw the United States, "in contrast to
Europe, as a truly classless society, free of ideological divisions, which
with the exceptions of the Civil War had been free of serious conflicts...
They believed that an expansive capitalistic market economy had elimi-
nated the final elements of class conflict."[22] The realities of the modern
world, industrial efficiency and a mass consumer market, demanded a
new history, one of quantifying methods based in computer technology.
This technology was obviously useful in studying economic trends, but
was soon employed in the analysis of various aspects of culture, opinions
and attitudes, voting behavior, and religious practice. Demographic data
was processed to yield information about family make-up, births, deaths,
marriages, and the disposition of property. Human relationships, which
finally must be apprehended qualitatively, were exposed to study through
quantitative research. Iggers quotes Geoffrey Baraclough's 1979 study,
written for UNESCO, on historical trends: "the search for quantity is
beyond all doubt the most powerful of the new trends in history, the
factor above all others which distinguishes historical attitudes in the
1970s from historical attitudes in the 1930s."[23]

		19.	Ibid., 311.
		20.	Iggers, *Historiography*, 65.
		21.	While the New Historians had borrowed from the social sciences to produce
their histories of economic factors, the influence of religion, and role of social and
regional conflicts, they continued to resist positivistic social science. "The New
Historians were filled with optimism regarding the evolution of society toward a
democratic goal, but they...were not seeking to discover laws of irreversible
progress" (Iggers, *Historiography*, 43).
		22.	Ibid., 43.
		23.	Ibid., 45.

e. *American Cliometricians*

Defined by methodology, rather than by any agreement on the nature or cause of historical change, the "cliometricians"[24] argued that only their particular quantitative approach could be called truly scientific. All other historians employing statistical or scientific methods they lumped together with traditional historians writing political, diplomatic, and constitutional histories. They built "paradigmatic models, sometimes counter-factual ones about worlds which never existed in real life" and tested "the validity of the models by the most sophisticated mathematical and algebraical formulae applied to very large quantities of electronically processed data."[25] To accomplish the work necessary to process volumes of information, team work was essential. Research assistants were employed to encode data, program the computers, and run the system. The results were published as statistical tables, accompanied by analytical argument, often laden with jargon.

Several problems became apparent with these studies. Questions concerning the reliability of the original data caused doubts about the subsequent conclusions. Lack of confidence in the accuracy of the encoding process causes further skepticism concerning these studies. In order to prepare data for processing, variation and detail must be reduced to manageable categories, thus significant individual characteristics are lost. Mistakes in program design or in the logic of the procedure invalidate results. Verifying information is virtually impossible since the data were stored on computer tapes and cannot be effectively reproduced in footnotes. Stone argues that "On any cost–benefit analysis the reward of large-scale computerized history have so far only occasionally justified the input of time and money."[26]

On the other hand, these studies have had some positive results. They have provided data in the areas of demographic history, social mobility, economic history, voting patterns, and voting behavior in democratic political systems. The presentation of precise numbers in historical studies has strongly discouraged historians from using vague or relative terms to describe increase or decrease, more or less quantity, or to indicate growth or decline.[27] These pressures for precision are laudable, though difficult to maintain.

24. This term is fashioned from the name of history's muse, Clio, and the word metrician, an expert or specialist in measurement. The word was first used by Stanley Reiter in 1960 (Online: http://cs.sba.muohio.edu/Clio/index-About.html).
25. Stone, "The Revival," 6.
26. Ibid., 13.
27. Ibid., 10.

2. Critical History in Germany

Late to experience industrialization and resistant to democratic reforms through much of the nineteenth century, the burger and academic classes in Germany, as well as the aristocrats, feared social change. This fear led to the rejection of social science approaches, which were associated with Marxist thought in Germany, even while these approaches were adopted in most countries during the early twentieth century. Opposition to social studies and investigations of society and culture persisted even after World War II. The patterns established as historical studies became professionalized in Germany continued to direct historians toward studies of the state and the conduct of political affairs. Approaches related to anthropology, demography, geography, and sociology were consistently avoided. Social history appeared only in economics departments, which were more historically oriented than such departments in English-speaking countries.[28]

Interest in social science eventually appeared among scholars trained after World War II and "was closely linked to their eagerness to confront the German past critically and their commitment to a democratic society."[29] Their attention was centered on the study of modern times and particularly the causes of imperialism, expansionism, and the disaster of the Nazi years. Unlike their predecessors, however, they did not limit their research to politics and diplomatic topics. They were acutely aware of the technological and structural forces of modernization and the attendant changes in society, and their impact on the political world.

While historiography in the West was becoming sharply critical of modernity, historical studies in Germany was taken up with the examination of the immediate past. The notions of the Frankfurt School were influential in arguing that the historian has a political responsibility to further the establishment of a reasonable society through critical examination of the past. Modernization was affirmed "as a process of permanent transformation in which science and technology develop hand in hand with increasing freedom, political maturity, and responsibility among a society's members."[30] This view has roots in the universal values of the Enlightenment and shapes the discussion of Germany's failure to modernize along lines similar to the rest of Western Europe. Here is a

28. See, for example, Weber's study of the agricultural system in east Prussia, given as his inaugural address as Professor of Political Economy at the University of Freiburg in 1895.
29. Iggers, *Historiography*, 67.
30. Ibid., 70.

sharp break with the national tradition that insisted that an individual state would follow its own distinctive path. On the other hand, the notion that the historian has responsibility to further the development of the society falls easily in the pattern of educator and guide affirmed by traditional German historiographic thought.

The establishment of the University of Bielefeld in 1971 as a center for interdisciplinary studies provided Critical Social History with an institutional base which was enhanced by the new monograph series, *Critical Studies in Historical Science*. The journal *Geschichte und Gesellschaft* followed in 1975, occupying a place in the discipline in Germany similar to *Past and Present* in Great Britain and *Annales* in France. Significant differences existed, however, in the German approach. German scholars showed little or no interest in pre-modern societies, but remained focused on the stresses in modern industrial societies and the study of structural transformations, and the interrelations between politics and society.[31]

Quantitative methods were engaged cautiously in keeping with the traditional German suspicion of social science. Class formation in the nineteenth century was studied through economic and structural approaches. Theoretical models in Weberian style were applied to problems of social change. By the 1980s German historiography included reconstructions of individual everyday life. While the emphasis found elsewhere on sexuality, family, religion, is largely absent from German work, still the study of social transformation in modernization and industrialization has broadened to include, along with quantitative material, data on the qualitative aspects of everyday life from such sources as interviews, letters, biographical material.[32]

3. *Decline of Social Science*

The attention given to economic and demographic facts by the social science approaches left aside other aspects of history. The experiences of groups in history and the *mentalité* of cultures were illuminated through the interpretation of data from parish records, municipal statistics, court documents, but intellectual, religious, literary, artistic, and political developments tended to be only lightly touched upon, if at all. The isolation of social history from other facets of culture produced works that failed to take account of the exercise of power, political authority and decision making. Stone claims that many historians began to "believe that the

31. Ibid., 71.
32. Ibid., 76–77.

culture of the group, and even the will of the individual, are potentially at least as important causal agents of change as the impersonal forces of material output and demographic growth." It had become clear that there was no theoretical reason that demographic forces and prevailing production models should necessarily dictate culture or the fate of the individual. The opposite could equally be argued and, indeed, the "linkages between culture and society are clearly very complex..." and vary "from time to time and place to place." Many assumptions based on economic determinism regarding family, literacy, privacy, failed to hold up to subsequent investigation.[33]

Quantification as a method suffered increased criticism regarding the difficulties of verification and, especially, the reliability of the primary data and their subsequent encoding. The arcane language used to present many studies was a barrier to scholarly review, limiting debate to a select few. Stone points out that major historical questions remain unanswered. By way of example, he suggests that quantification

> had the beneficial effect of focusing attention on important issues such as the diet, hygiene, health and family structure of American Negroes under slavery, but it also diverted attention from the equally or even more important psychological effects of slavery upon both master and slaves, simply because these matters could not be measured by a computer.[34]

He argues that ultimately quantification has proven disappointing. Historians have come to recognize that "variables are so numerous that at best only middle-range generalizations are possible in history."[35]

Through the application of methods derived from science and the limitations that became clear through the endeavor, the philosophical issue of the relation of history to science was explored at a practical level. A growing cohort of historians recognized that the preoccupation with a specific methodology—structural, collective, and statistical—obscured other possible questions. Stone argues that the attempt to produce a coherent scientific explanation of change in the past has come to an end, that economic and demographic determinism has been shown to fail as an explanation of change. Structuralism and functionalism, likewise, do not account for all the possible variables. Quantitative method can only answer a certain limited set of questions. "Understanding based on observation, experience, judgement and intuition" has recommended itself as a means to a broader view of past cultures.[36]

33. Stone, "The Revival," 9.
34. Ibid., 12.
35. Ibid., 13.
36. Ibid., 19.

4. *Universalism or Particularism*

The notion that historical truth is universal, accessible to all, was one of the foundational tenets of historiography as it was practiced on both sides of the Atlantic in the nineteenth and early twentieth centuries. Commitment to any group or position, ideological or religious, was rejected as compromising objective historical writing. Neither the German emphasis on *Verstehen*, empathic understanding, nor American obsession with objectivity left room for any but the most detached investigation. In the United States especially, universal norms were promoted as an antidote to regionalism and to ethnic identifications. Whereas, in most other countries the professional historians wrote their own national histories, historians in the United States were more cosmopolitan, writing histories of countries with which they had no personal connection. Historians of the United States were a minority in every major history department. Novick argues that the inclusion of large numbers of Jews in the profession in the 1950s and 1960s was the result of universalist norms. Jews, entering the profession, insisted that they were "committed to a sensibility which was not just integrationist but usually assimilationist as well."[37] This dedication to universalism was challenged from the late sixties onwards, beginning with African-American and feminist historians.

Novick points out that the new historians were not scholars "who happened to be African Americans or women," but *black* and *feminist* historians with agendas that called for a "thoroughgoing transformation of historical consciousness." They stressed the distinctiveness of their views and were often critical of the central values of the profession.[38] What Novick identifies as assertive particularism has implications for the notion of writing truthful history and for the ties of loyalty and solidarity within the profession. Against older assumptions that scholarship was not correlated with sex or race, that approved academic style promoted universalism and objectivity, "serious claims were made for distinctive discursive and cognitive styles among blacks and women—differences which might possibly, in some distant future, be synthesized with those of white males, but ought on no account to be assimilated to them."[39] This position set colleagues at odds, undermining professional ties of loyalty.

Women's history and African-American history both had their origins in movements outside the academy and rapidly grew into major historical fields. While women had been included in the historical profession from the beginning, they had been marginalized, employed in women's

37. Novick, *That Noble Dream*, 470.
38. Ibid., 470.
39. Ibid., 471.

institutions, allowed token representation on committees of the major historical associations, but rejected by departments in major universities.[40] For African Americans, the issue was who would have "the power to define and interpret black history."[41] Both groups were constituted by a deeply felt public need and were seriously committed to providing their constituencies with a "usable past." Their work, however, "cast in an academic idiom, and appearing in academic media, rarely reached a lay audience."[42] From their place within the academy, African-American and feminist historians had their greatest impact on the notion of universalism. As individual historians struggled with conflicting interests, those of their constituent groups and those of academic professionalism, it became clear that irreconcilable values would continue to challenge the conventional character of the discipline.

5. *Professionalism and Public History*

J. Franklin Jameson's wisdom in seeking to professionalize the historical discipline early in the twentieth century, admired and defended for decades, came under attack in the 1970s and 1980s. The national standards established for the field were devised to overcome provincialism and regionalism and to promote quality based on objectivity. Amateur historians were displaced by professional academics supposedly immune to the pressures of local or particular interests.[43] Academics, like the traditional professionals, doctors and lawyers, were increasingly becoming salaried employees of large bureaucratic organizations. The university, however, had less and less actual control of the classroom experience or of scholarly writing, which was judged by experts in the individual disciplines. While objectivity was not guaranteed by this system, "it was generally seen as one of its principal social preconditions."[44]

---

40. Ibid., 491.

41. Ibid., 474. Novick remarks that African-American and feminist historians "anticipated theses advanced by Michel Foucault about the relation between power and knowledge: the 'disciplining' of subordinate groups through being made the object of 'disciplines'; arguments by Edward Said about the occidental construction of 'the Orient'; concern by ethnographers about the legitimacy of their franchise to describe and define non-Western cultures" (p. 471).

42. Ibid., 510.

43. The ideal of the professional held that an individual practitioner should be engaged by a client but that the service provided was determined by universal professional standards rather than the interests of the client. Novick (ibid., 511) says: "it was the professional, and not the client, who determined how the services were rendered: what pill to prescribe, what motion to file."

44. Ibid., 511.

With the academic job crisis beginning in the 1970s, larger numbers of academics were employed outside the university in government and industry. For historians, the field of "public history" included work for local historical societies and museums, work on variously funded oral history projects, work as historical consultants in film making, and historical work for government agencies and businesses. Often these organizations and employers had very clear interests and goals that were in direct contradiction to the standards of detachment and objectivity. Some historians' work was concerned with policy analysis, bringing the lessons of the past to present policy making, some in straightforward advocacy. They argued the historic rights of a certain Indian tribe to disputed lands. They offered expert testimony in water rights cases and in the area of historic preservation, argued for or against landmark status for client's buildings.[45] Much of this work proceeded without critical review or even public scrutiny. Novick remarks that "various efforts were made to draft codes of ethics for public historians, but the resulting texts demonstrated the difficulty in balancing professional responsibility to clients and scholarly norms." The pressures on historians employed by municipalities, public or private agencies, or businesses were unquestionably greater even than those felt by scholars in fields like women's history or African-American history where academic expectations balanced tendencies to present particular agendas.[46]

The very concept of history as a profession became problematic in the 1970s with a general decline in the status of the "professional."[47] Historians began a discussion of the distinctions between client-oriented professions and research-oriented academic disciplines. Favor rested with the notion of "learned disciplines" and a return to the original term for graduate programs as "advanced" rather than "professional" study.[48] With the increase in the numbers of public historians, the discussion took another turn. Joan Hoff-Wilson, shortly before she took the position as the executive secretary of the Organization of American Historians, sharply criticized the domination of the field of history by academics. She recalled Herbert Baxter Adams' efforts to include all historians, amateur and academic, in the AHA. Hoff-Wilson argued that "the

45. Ibid., 513.
46. Ibid., 514–17.
47. Calls to limit professional power came from cultural critics, sociologists, deregulationists, and academic historians, while "respect accorded to lawyers plummeted in the wake of Watergate. Declining faith in the authority of physicians was reflected in the growing number of malpractice suits" (ibid., 518).
48. Ibid., 518.

independent scholar must, as at the turn of the previous century, either share equally or dominate both the leadership and rank-and-file."[49] She attacked Jameson's legacy and the promotion of professionalism at the expense of amateur and less exclusive historians. Professionalism, as a chief characteristic of American academic history, supporting universalism and, finally, objectivity, suffered serious attack in the 1970s and 1980s.

European universities, founded and funded by the various states, had been subject to certain influences toward professional conformity like their American counterparts. While academic freedom flourished within the universities, the recruitment and hiring of academics necessarily reflected a certain uniformity in viewpoint acceptable to the state. Iggers remarks, "What is striking is how professionalization, with the development of the scientific ethos and scientific practices that accompanied it, led everywhere to an increasing ideologization of historical writing."[50] Evidence from archives was employed in support of national interests and class preconceptions. As the focus of historiography shifted from political history concerned with major events and great personalities to a greater awareness of the role of society, economy, and culture, two basic assumptions that had endured into the 1970s suffered decline. A challenge to the professional character of the discipline was precipitated by the economic situation that forced many academically trained historians into the public sector. This development, coupled with the ideological component of history written by scholars committed to a particular group or audience, compelled a new look at old assumptions regarding objectivity and scientific detachment.

6. *The Postmodern Challenge*

The trend toward the study of everyday life in its concrete manifestations, seen in both the United States and Europe, is the outcome of the confrontation of assumptions that guided historical studies since its professionalization. In the 1970s, historical studies were transformed by the rejection of the concept of scientific rationality and the notion of progress. The aura of consensus that prevailed in the United States after the war, the belief in the United States as a truly classless society, were shattered by a series of works starkly revealing the divergence in American society. Iggers points to John Kenneth Galbraith's *The Affluent Society*,

49. Joan Hoff-Wilson, "Is the Historical Professional an 'Endangered Species'?" *The Public Historian* 2 (1980): 4–21 (6, 7–8, 9, 16).
50. Iggers, *Historiography*, 28.

Daniel Bell's *The End of Ideology*, and Michael Harrington's *The Other America*, as examples of works featuring the segments of American society which were not part of the perceived consensus.[51]

In 1979, Lawrence Stone published a now famous essay, "The Revival of Narrative," in which he states that a basic shift had occurred in historiography. Scientific approaches to the study of the past, in particular the belief that a coherent scientific explanation of change in the past was possible, were discredited. Interest had turned instead to culture and individuals as agents of historical change. Stone pressed further by asking again the vexing question whether or not history could be seen as a science. Here, he challenged both social science historiography centering on quantitative approaches, and older concepts of scientific historiography such as the German tradition emphasizing the impartial investigator employing rigorous method in the study of an actual past. In Chapter 7, it will become clear that both scientific approaches and the tradition of the objective researcher remain important elements of historiography in biblical studies.

Stone suggests that the quality of contemporary consciousness influenced the shift in historical priorities in the 1970s. Animosity toward institutions and corporations, toward authority and structure, fostered a climate where personal interests superceded public issues, where individual ideals and desires were accorded prominence. Similar interests in the "feelings, emotions, behaviour patterns, values, and states of mind" of the individuals of the past reflect the changing attitudes.[52]

From a different perspective, the disillusionment with quantification brought about a move toward the intellectual, psychological, and cultural. Anthropological methods allowed "a whole social system and set of values [to] be brilliantly illuminated by the searchlight method of recording in elaborate detail a single event, provided that it is very carefully set in its total context and very carefully analyzes for its cultural meaning." Clifford Geertz's model of "thick description" is the familiar example.

7. *The Linguistic Turn: The Historian as Rhetorician*

Stone began his article, "The Revival of Narrative," with the claim, "Historians have always told stories. From Thucydides and Tacitus to Gibbon and Macaulay the composition of narrative in lively and elegant prose was always accounted their highest ambition. History was regarded

---

51. Ibid., 98.
52. Stone, "The Revival," 14.

as a branch of rhetoric."[53] Writing in 1979, he drew attention to the "current revival of narrative" in response to "disillusionment with the economic determinist model of historical explanation."[54] He argued that the turn to narrative marked "the end of the attempt to produce a coherent scientific explanation of change in the past."[55] A similar point is made in the next chapter in response to a proposal for a "narrative approach" to the study of Israel's history.

The shift from "scientific" modes of history writing to those informed by "linguistic" approaches involves a broad range of theories and assumptions. Hayden White argued that there can be no criteria of truth by which to judge historical narrative. He does not say that it is impossible to discover historical facts, only that to record them is a moral or aesthetic act, involving the judgment and choice of the writer.[56] More problematic than this for historiography is the criticism of thinkers who insist that there is no unity between word and its referent. Because "there is no Archimedean point from which a clear meaning can be assigned," there exist an infinite number of signifiers without clear meanings. Iggers concludes, "For historiography this means a world without meaning, devoid of human actors, human volitions or intentions, and totally lacking coherence."[57] White goes on to argue that the lack of meaning in history is an important impetus to action in the present. In his view historical narratives are produced in established centers of power by those with approved credentials. Those "subordinate, emergent, or resisting social groups" are advised to "view history with the kind of 'objectivity,' 'modesty,' 'realism,' and 'social responsibility' that has characterized historical studies since their establishment as a professional discipline..."[58] He claims that modern ideologies

> impute a meaning to history that renders its manifest confusion comprehensible to either reason, understanding, or aesthetic sensibility. To the extent that they succeed in doing so, these ideologies deprive history of the kind of meaninglessness that alone can goad living human beings to make their lives different for themselves and their children, which is to say, to endow their lives with a meaning for which they alone are fully responsible.[59]

53. Ibid., 3.
54. Ibid., 8.
55. Ibid., 19.
56. Hayden White, *Metahistory: The Historical Imagination in the Nineteenth Century in Europe* (Baltimore: The Johns Hopkins University Press, 1973), 433.
57. Iggers, *Historiography*, 121.
58. Hayden White, "The Politics of Historical Interpretation: Discipline and De-Sublimation," in his *The Content of the Form: Narrative Discourse and Historical Representation* (Baltimore: The Johns Hopkins University Press, 1987), 58–82 (81).
59. Ibid., 72.

Relativism is recognized as the consequence of the historian's inability to write "objective history" by those noting the rhetorical aspects of historiography, but with White the meaninglessness of history resulting from relativism is a positive good, forcing people to confront the present.

As the historical discipline professionalized in the nineteenth century, its pretensions toward scientific recognition rested in large part on efforts to become "objective," to free the language of history writing of all rhetorical elements. Science and rhetoric were supposed to be in opposition. There was no awareness of the rhetorical qualities of scientific writing, indeed that all language has a rhetorical dimension.[60] Dominick LaCapra pointed out that even the "plain style" supposed "to be entirely transparent to its object" did not exist and he encouraged historians to cultivate the rhetorical quality treasured since antiquity.[61]

8. *The Modes of Historiography*

This "linguistic turn" in the field of history has fostered new thinking concerning the nature of history, the audience of the writer, and the notion of objectivity as a goal of method. White claims that history is necessarily "philosophy of history," that "the possible modes of historiography are the same as the possible modes of speculative philosophy of history." These modes "are in reality formalizations of poetic insights that analytically precede them and that sanction the particular theories used to give historical accounts the aspect of an 'explanation.'" There are no grounds by which one can claim authority for any mode being more "realisitic" than another, and thus any choice for a particular perspective on history is aesthetic or moral rather than epistemological, including the scientific perspective so long favored by historians.[62]

Indeed, "reality" is the problem. Gabrielle Spiegel calls the difficulty with reality

> the post-modern dilemma, the hallmark of which has been a growing awareness of the mediated nature of perception, cognition and imagination, all of which are increasingly construed to be mediated by linguistic structures cast into discourses of one sort or another—the famed "linguistic turn" that has raised such troubling problems for the study of history and literature alike.[63]

60. Iggers, *Historiography*, 122.
61. Dominick LaCapra, "Rhetoric and History," in his *History and Criticism* (Ithaca, N.Y.: Cornell University Press, 1985), 15–44 (42).
62. White, *Metahistory*, xi–xii.
63. Lawrence Stone and Gabrielle M. Spiegel, "History and Post-Modernism," *Past and Present* 135 (1992): 198–208 (195).

A language-based conception of reality has come to replace traditional notions of an external reality intelligible in ideas and phenomena represented directly through verbal signs. Post-structuralism has "shattered this confident assumption of the relation between words and things, language and extra-linguistic reality." Language, to the contrary, is "the very structure of mental life" and it is not possible to regard reality from a position beyond language. Within these constraints history becomes impossible. The past cannot be recovered because texts, documents, literature, traditional sources for writing history, do not reflect reality, only other texts. In this view, study of the past cannot be distinguished from literary studies. Historical evidence does not reflect the past, but mediates it. Spiegel says that there has been a "shift from the notion that texts and documents transparently reflect past realities, as positivism believed, to one in which the past is captured only in the mediated form preserved for us in language." She makes a distinction between the classical definition of mediation as an analytical device that seeks to establish a relationship between two different orders or levels of phenomena, and the modern concept, articulated by the Frankfurt School, that mediation is within the object, not between two objects, a process that constructs reality through language: "In studying history, then, what we study are the mediatory practices of past epochs (in effects, discourses) which, then as now, constructed all being and consciousness."[64] She concludes that "one of the features of the 'linguistic turn' in the humanities has been to replace the classical notion of mediation with the modern, and to undermine our faith in the instrumental capacity of language to convey information about the world." Spiegel suggests an alternative view in which it can be admitted that "language can function instrumentally by mediating between us as perceiving, knowing subjects and that absent past that we wish to describe." She argues that language need not be limited to the reflexive, but ought to include a descriptive use, as well, "as there clearly is in our everyday linguistic habits," without denying the "performative" use, "even when that language is embodied in past texts (including documents) and thus possesses something of the literary character that post-structuralism has taught us to apprehend."[65]

This intermediate view of mediation recommends itself as a position that acknowledges an external reality that can be conveyed through language. Here, language is recognized as a product of a particular social world and through that language it is possible to recover some sense of

64. Ibid., 198–99.
65. Ibid., 201.

the material world of the past.[66] Spiegel does not suggest that language is transparent, but she resists the opposite view that the structures and events of the past cannot be distinguished from the documents of the past or historical discourses that portray them. She says that historians have always held that their "arduous, often tedious labour yields some authentic knowledge of the dead 'other,' a knowledge admittedly shaped by the historian's own perceptions and biases, but none the less retaining a degree of autonomy, in the sense that it cannot be made entirely to bend to the historian's will."[67] This point provides an important caution in the debate over the mediated nature of perception, that the denial of a material reality that once was believed could be known and written about scientifically. Spiegel offers a middle ground, opting "for a mixed and potentially richer understanding of language and its mediatory possibilities" where "both concepts of mediation and language [are] put into play simultaneously."[68]

9. Relativism and Objectivity Again

Hayden White's claims that when choosing among "alternative visions of history, the only grounds for preferring one over another are moral or aesthetic ones,"[69] distressed historians committed since the professionalization of the discipline to seeking the objective facts. Novick points out, however, that it is an error to suppose that White suggested that one view was as good as another. White's view was based on the conviction that a specific historical inquiry is less concerned to find that certain events occurred than to find what certain events might mean to particular groups.[70] As White blurred the distinctions between history and fiction, LaCapra argued that the autonomy of history constituted a problem. He sought the unification of history and criticism, but not in White's presentist sense. LaCapra had no agenda to press people to assume full responsibility for their lives; instead, he sought to open inquiry, not to end an argument, but to open the way for counterargument, "new avenues of criticism and self-reflection."[71]

Novick notes that American historians failed to respond to these new currents of thought, citing as an example *New Directions in American*

---

66. Ibid., 204.
67. Ibid., 201.
68. Ibid., 202.
69. White, *Metahistory*, 433.
70. Novick, *That Noble Dream*, 601.
71. Ibid., 605.

Intellectual History, 1979, edited by John Higham and Paul Conkin, which made no mention of Baktin, Barthes, Derrida, Gramsci, Goldmann or Lukacs. He claims that the neo-objectivist position which countered these "rhetorical relativists" arose in response to the excesses of the student insurgencies of the 1960s:

> Black Studies, Women's Studies, and affirmative action programs; "ideological" scholarship (of the left), and any scholarship not pursued "for its own sake"... Bitter memories of the 1960s, and often-exaggerated estimates of its residue, were lumped together with various relativistic, postmodern currents into an undifferentiated and monstrous Other which had to be combated if liberal rationalism was to survive.[72]

10. *The Task of the Historian*

The use of history and the role of the historian are topics of endless discussion. In times of crisis within the field, the discussion often takes on a polemical tone. Appleby, Hunt, and Jacob in their book *Telling the Truth About History* disparage the "heroic model of science" and argue that the democratization of the educational establishment has led to an interest in previously neglected areas of history and in the lives of groups hitherto unexamined. The role of the historian in bringing attention to these groups is a positive one. Furthermore, they point out the use of history in the constitution of society. They outline history's function in bolstering governments and institutions and in bringing discredit to fallen regimes. They claim that "Because history and historical evidence are so crucial to a people's sense of identity, the evidence itself often becomes the focus of struggle." They note that citizens rush to find historical evidence of the previous government's misdeeds "in order to fortify the will to reconstitute their nation."[73] They draw attention to textbook controversies regarding Eurocentric, racist, sexist, and homophobic biases. They ask, "Must history be continually rewritten to undo the perpetuation of racial and sexual stereotypes? Or should it stand above the tumult of present-day political and social concerns? Is the teaching of a coherent national history essential to democracy?"[74]

In answer Appleby, Hunt, and Jacob allow that, while skepticism and relativism are part of a contemporary worldview, it is possible to move beyond a position that holds that "knowledge about the past is simply an ideological construction that serves particular interests, making history a

---

72. Ibid., 605–7.
73. Appleby, Hunt and Jacob, *Telling the Truth*, 4.
74. Ibid., 5–6.

series of myths establishing or reinforcing group identities" and that science is only a social construction, or simply a series of linguistic conventions, an elaborate power game coded mathematically to ensure Western dominance over the earth's riches."[75] They note the tendency of historians to leave the questions of philosophy and theory to others.

On the other hand, they claim to take seriously the contributions of historians to "the history of science, social change, and national purpose," while questioning the "relevance of scientific models to the search for historical truth or the role of history in shaping national identity." While this final statement of Appleby, Hunt, and Jacob suggests a pragmatic position, it holds out a place for history as advocacy and places them at some remove from the old objectivist attitude. Among historians in biblical studies, objectivity continues to be strenuously debated, with particular attention to personal "ideology."

Brian Fay begins a recent article with a quotation from Nancy Partner:

> it is my impression that the "linguistic turn" was a revolving door and that everyone went around and around and got out exactly where they got in. For all the sophistication of the theory-saturated part of the profession, scholars in all the relevant disciplines that contribute to or depend on historical information carry on in all essential ways as though nothing had changed since Ranke...[76]

Fay adds that with some interesting exceptions at the margins of the discipline, "historical practice is pretty much the same in 1997 as it was in 1967: historians seek to describe accurately and to explain cogently how and why a certain event or situation occurred, and they do so by means of meticulously detailed research and responsiveness to the evidence as it has best been ascertained by relevant historians working in the field. He concludes, "For all the talk of narrativism, presentism, postmodernism, and deconstruction, historians write pretty much the same way as they always have (even though what they write about may be quite new)."[77]

11. *Conclusion*

If historians continue to write as they did in the past, then what has changed in the decades since the war? Certainly the notion of what constitutes history has been forced into the consciousness of historians, who

---

75. Ibid., 8.

76. Nancy Partner, "History in the Age of Reality-Fictions," in *A New Philosophy of History* (ed. Frank Ankersmit and Hans Kellner; Chicago: University of Chicago Press, 1995), 21–39 (21–22).

77. Brian Fay, "Nothing but History?," *History and Theory* 37 (1998): 83–93 (83).

by and large prefer to write history rather than think about it. Methodology, after a shift to the statistical, has settled into a period of eclectic approaches, including those of geography, anthropology, demography, topography, biology, economics, psychology, and the traditional political and diplomatic. Criticism of narrowly focused approaches, such as those based on economic determinism or those following diplomatic developments, made it clear that research into a specific area by itself could not account for historical change. Too much was left aside. Failure to consider a broad range of factors resulted in inadequate explanations and in explanations that did not address contemporary concerns. As Brian Fay remarked, the topics investigated by historians have expanded considerably. These include the histories of ethnic groups, women, gays and lesbians, African Americans, immigrant and labor groups, native Americans, and regional and local histories. As historiography now includes a significantly greater range of methodologies than in the past, so the subjects investigated have proliferated.

Historians of past generations assumed that objectivity was important to the rigor of their research. This notion has suffered devastating criticism in the past several decades. Opposition is based first on the impossibility of the historian to achieve significant detachment, an argument that has been debated since the founding of the discipline. In recent discussion, the position of the researcher in regard to class, background, education, sex, and all other personal factors is held to compromise irremediably his or her objectivity. The second blow to the notion of objectivity comes from theories of language which hold that there is no reality unmediated by language and language as a construction of culture does not hold fixed meanings.

Important to the support of objectivity in the past has been the idea of universalism, a rejection of any sort of advocacy for a particular group, region, or cause. The means for enforcing this old standard of professionalism weakened as historians moved into the public sectors, but a corresponding threat came from the historians of particular groups whose histories they claimed as their own province. These historians, most notably women and African Americans, insisted that, as members of certain groups, only they had the authority to write history for their group. Maintaining a workable balance between the professional expectations of the discipline and their interest in promoting interest in their history proved difficult, but equally damaging to professional notions of objectivity as the testimony of public historians in the interest of their employing agencies. Conformity and orthodoxy as hallmarks of professionalism were weakened by histories advocating particular groups or causes, but the discipline maintained itself by the critical peer evaluations made within the profession in such important issues as tenure and promotion.

Whereas pre-professional historians understood themselves to be rhetoricians forging useful lessons for the present from the experiences of the past, the historian today is much more likely to be indicting the past for wrongs done to groups or classes of people. The historian's audience in the past consisted of a broad segment of the educated classes, those in positions of power, and those of similar tastes and beliefs who supported them. Today, a great part of history writing is produced to satisfy the requirements of the academic life and to support the claims of certain groups to greater recognition.

The change in the character of the audience for written history has left the field more varied in subject, as Fay suggested, but there are other changes as well. The shift in the status of science and the resulting proliferation of approaches to historical research, and the greater complexity in perceptions regarding the use of language have also produced more nuanced explanations for change, both social and technological, and a field more sophisticated with regard to issues concerning who is writing whose history and who is left out. Chapter 7 will investigate the field of Hebrew Bible studies for evidence of these elements in the study of Israel's history.

Chapter 7

WRITING ISRAEL'S HISTORY TODAY

> Every history, critical or uncritical, is constructed from a present point of
> view with a present purpose to serve.[1]

Over the past few decades, departments of history have struggled with
issues introduced by postmodern notions of language and the resulting
inaccessibility of an objective past, while biblical scholars have focused
attention on their own controversies framed in terms of method as it
applies to the interpretation of texts and artifacts. Historiography in biblical studies exhibits hints of the discussions regarding the non-referential
character of language and the impossibility of writing "true" history, but
these notions are used in support of particular positions dear to each
contending group, not as issues to be established independently.

The ongoing bitter disputation in biblical history remains mired in
attacks over individual bias or point of view and appropriate method.
Though scholars across the field make prefatory remarks about the subjectivity of the writer, the inescapable influence of background, religion,
and so forth, and often include nods to the notion that placing facts into
narrative makes history suspiciously like fiction, they quickly return to
problems of how best to handle the material at hand. Issues in Israel's
history are chiefly related to the reliability of the biblical text. In one way
or another the various interpretation of artifacts, the use of extra biblical
texts, the incorporation of other scientific and social science studies all
function to prove or disprove the Bible's story of Israel's past.

In the years since the publication of Thomas Thompson's *The Historicity of the Patriarchal Narratives* (1974), there has been a move to
disengage the history of Israel, or the area or entity supposed to have
constituted Israel and Judah, from biblical history. The designation
Syro-Palestinian history has been employed to indicate distance from

1. Ernst Axel Knauf, "From History to Interpretation," in *The Fabric of History:
Text, Artifact and Israel's Past* (ed. Diane Edelman; JSOTSup 127; Sheffield: JSOT
Press, 1991), 26–64 (50).

traditional biblical reconstructions and to include a larger contextual basis. Similarly, William Dever, who first popularized the term "Syro-Palestinian archaeology," has from time to time pleaded the case for an archaeological discipline distinct from "biblical archaeology." The advance of these projects and their points of contact with the larger field of academic history is the topic of this chapter.

The present debate between the so-called "minimalists" and "maximalists"[2] has some antecedents in the debate between Alt and Noth, and Albright and his followers, and in the earlier reaction to Wellhausen's work. The "minimalists" are a loose cohort of scholars represented chiefly by Thomas Thompson, Niels Peter Lemche, Philip Davies, and Keith Whitelam, sometimes supported in their arguments by the work of such scholars as Gösta Ahlström and Ernst Axel Knauf. Their opposition has two faces. The first is represented by William Dever, supported by Herschel Shanks, who, through his influential publication, *The Biblical Archaeological Review*, provides a forum for an unrelenting attack on the "minimalist" position. A second outspoken dissenter from the "minimalist" view is Iain Provan from the University of Edinburgh. These scholars represent quite different approaches and are driven by different motives.

In portraying the recent shifts in history writing in biblical studies against the background of the changes described in the last chapter, it is clear that the interest in historical examination of gender roles and relationships, the accomplishments of women, and the status of gays and lesbians is less a part of historical studies of ancient Israel than of other areas of history. Biblical studies, touched by the general disaffection with macrohistory and the *grand narrative*, and political and diplomatic histories, began in the 1980s to seek ways to make female biblical characters more visible and to turn attention to the everyday life of ancient times.[3] This is most visible in exegetical work on particular narratives

---

2. These expressions are vague and have no agreed-upon meaning. "Minimalist" is a general term used to describe those scholars who do not accept the biblical narrative as a historical account and demand external evidence in support of any claim for historicity. No discrimination is made among the many and varied positions that fall generally within this description. "Maximalist" is used to indicate those who make the case that the Bible contains historical material. These designations are most often employed polemically and, as will be shown below, are vigorously disputed by those so characterized.

3. See, for example, Phyllis Trible, *God and the Rhetoric of Sexuality* (Philadelphia: Fortress, 1978); idem, *Texts of Terror: Literary-Feminist Readings of Biblical Narratives* (Philadelphia: Fortress, 1984); Norman Gottwald, *The Hebrew Bible: A Socio-literary Introduction* (Philadelphia: Fortress, 1985); Peggy L. Day, ed., *Gender and Difference in Ancient Israel* (Minneapolis: Fortress, 1989); Lester Grabbe, *Priests, Prophets, Diviners, Sages: A Socio-historical Study of Religious Specialists*

and in theological interpretations based on reclaimed texts. To be fair, historians of ancient cultures are in an especially difficult position with regard to the real possibilities for writing history of everyday life. History writers who study the middle ages, the colonial period or the early republic, or the development of nineteenth-century industrialization, have many records available—demographic, economic, and religious. Land and property records, personal accounts, and clues from literature shed light on the cultures under investigation, but for the historian of ancient societies sources are unusually scarce and represent some periods well and some not at all, according to the vagaries of preservation and discovery. Everyday life in the ancient world may be approached through language and content analysis of the few existing texts and primarily through archaeology, often interpreted by means of models devised by economists, demographers, and sociologists.[4] Law codes exist, often incomplete, or in the case of the Bible compromised as historical sources by later editing or even retrojection into earlier contexts. Numbers given for tribes, families, or armies are notoriously inflated. The impossibilities of producing *thick descriptions* of an ancient culture, and the lack of material illustrating life in ancient times, limit the types of history that can be written for Israel.

For similar reasons, the roles of men and women in ancient times are not easy to reconstruct.[5] In some ancient cultures, records of law suits provide a glimpse into personal lives. Even from these it is not possible to draw general conclusions, for it cannot be known whether any given case is typical of a particular class and certainly not whether it is typical of the society as a whole. For ancient Israel the textual record is extremely

in *Ancient Israel* (Valley Forge, Pa.: Trinity, 1995); Karla Bohmbach, "Convention/ Contraventions: The Meanings of Public and Private for the Judges 19 Concubine," *JSOT* 83 (1999): 83–98.

4. For an example of reconstruction of ancient life based on archaeological research, see Philip J. King and Lawrence E. Stager, *Life in Biblical Israel* (Louisville, Ky.: Westminster John Knox, 2001); see also Paula M. McNutt, *Reconstructing the Society of Ancient Israel* (Louisville, Ky.: Westminster John Knox, 1999).

5. See Gerda Lerner, *The Creation of Patriarchy* (New York: Oxford University Press, 1986); several chapters of Carol Meyers' *Discovering Eve* (New York: Oxford University Press, 1988) offer historical treatment of everyday life and the status of women; Zafira Den-Barak, "The Status and Right of the Gebira," *JBL* 110 (1991): 23–34; Mary Shields, "Subverting a Man of God, Elevating a Woman: Role and Power Reversals in 2 Kings 4," *JSOT* 58 (1993): 59–69; Victor Matthews, Bernard Levinson, and Tikva Frymer-Kensky, eds., *Gender and Law in the Hebrew Bible and the Ancient Near East* (JSOTSup 262; Sheffield: Sheffield Academic Press, 1998); Deborah Sawyer, "Gender-Play and Sacred Text: A Scene from Jeremiah," *JSOT* 83 (1999): 99–111.

limited. No personal correspondence exists, no royal inscriptions, no legal or business records. The relevance of texts from related cultures in periods contemporaneous to some of the biblical narrative is sharply disputed. Convincing conclusions about historical details of everyday life, of sex roles and gender status in the times spoken of in the Bible cannot be made. For these practical reasons, the concern for gender issues and for the experience of minorities that has flourished in the broader culture has not been part of the historiographical debate in biblical studies.

1. *The Argument*

I will argue that the challenge to writing ancient history in terms of the available sources tends to keep discussion focused on questions of reliability and objectivity. While history writing in biblical studies has been affected by larger historiographic trends toward interdisciplinary methodologies, by discussions in the academic community insisting on the inevitable subjectivity of historians and, indeed, all writers, and by increasing sensitivity to the experiences of groups not dominant in their culture, biblical historians face particular issues that are outside of the considerations of other professional academic historians. Critical biblical studies, even before Wellhausen, confronted opposition from faith communities and those believers who fear that attacks on the historicity of the Hebrew Bible constitute attacks on belief in the efficacy of the sacred text. The history of ancient Israel is experiencing a major shift begun by Wellhausen, a shift from the province of the church to that of professional academic historians. Thomas Thompson notes that those associated with the shift in the "field's presuppositions understand themselves more as scholars than ministers."[6] The approaches followed by many of the new generation of historians of ancient Israel are commensurate with those of historians in academic departments of history, but the theoretical problems discussed in these departments have not attracted passionate partisans among historians of ancient Israel whose energies are absorbed in defending their view that the Bible is, or is not, a book of history. Thus, what Thompson wishes to call a "paradigm shift" is actually the application of critical method within the traditional "scientific" model.

I argue that history writing in biblical studies no longer is primarily an apologetical project addressed to an audience largely made up of interested, educated laypeople and church professionals. While apologetic

6. Thomas L. Thompson, "A Neo-Albrightean School in History and Biblical Scholarship," *JBL* 114 (1995): 683–98 (694).

issues continue to be a concern in biblical studies,[7] the historiographical project as practiced by some contemporary scholars has begun to acquire the character of history writing in academic departments of history. The efforts to move historical studies of Syria–Palestine into mainstream historiography have not included the theoretical discussions familiar in the broader field, but in practice the critical evaluation of evidence, use of models, and information from related fields, such as climatology, demography, and botany have provided a first step toward gaining a new audience for the history of the region.

This chapter will proceed in three steps. First, I will give a summary of the research of the past three decades which has provided the grounds of controversy. Second, I will establish the outline of the critical debate within biblical studies—the so-called "maximalists/minimalists" controversy—and discuss the issues of method, reliability of the Hebrew Bible for history writing and the implications for the audience for a critical history of Syria-Palestine. In the third step, I will relate this debate to the critical and theoretical controversies of the last quarter century in the larger field of academic history.

2. *Historiography of Ancient Israel*

The past quarter century has seen significant changes in the historiography of ancient Israel. In 1974, Thomas Thompson published *The Historicity of the Patriarchal Narratives* in which he challenged the usefulness of Genesis for historical research. Thompson's book was followed a year later by John Van Seters' *Abraham in History and Tradition* which independently offered similar conclusions. Their arguments pointed out that biblical studies had been devoted to discovering early contexts for the patriarchal narratives at the expense of attention to the final forms of the text. These books served as an introduction to a new round of discussion on particular theories of origins, settlement, religion, and statehood. Niels Peter Lemche produced a socio-anthropological study called *Early Israel* in 1985 and completed *Ancient Israel* in 1988. Thompson published *The Origin Tradition of Ancient Israel* in 1987, and, in 1988, Israel Finkelstein's book, *The Archaeology of the Israelite Settlement*, appeared.[8] These books offered a new possibility for writing history independent of the biblical materials. Thompson's book, *The*

---

7. See James Barr, *History and Ideology in the Old Testament* (Oxford: Oxford University Press, 2000), 1–15.

8. Israel Finkelstein, *The Archaeology of the Israelite Settlement* (Jerusalem: Israel Exploration Society, 1988).

Early History of the Israelite People, was published in 1992, the same year as Philip Davies' *In Search of "Ancient Israel"*. They were followed the next year by Gösta Ahlström's *The History of Ancient Palestine*. In these two decades, historical-critical methods of text analysis and practices of archaeology were examined and the assumptions about the historicity of the biblical texts gave way to caution regarding the historical usefulness of the traditional narratives.

3. The Challenge to Genesis

a. *Historicity of the Patriarchal Narratives*

Thompson presented his 1974 study of the patriarchal narratives as "an attempt to review the central arguments that are currently held by biblical scholars in favor of the historicity of the patriarchs in Genesis." He notes that at the time of his writing the premise was "generally accepted as proven, or at least as probable," with various exceptions and arguments over particular aspects, but "nearly all accept the general claim that the historicity of the biblical traditions about the patriarchs has been substantiated by the archaeological and historical research of the last half-century."[9] He goes on to point out that the assumption was so firmly established that the patriarchal narratives served as a basis for further interpretation using knowledge of the patriarchs' customs, and their relation to the land and to those around them.[10] Thompson insists instead that historians of the ancient Near East must distinguish among types of available material and that each must be independently examined: "Thus, archaeological materials should not be dated or evaluated on the basis of written texts which are independent of these materials; so also documents should not be interpreted on the basis of archaeological hypotheses." He notes especially the tendency to make the argument for the historicity of the biblical texts on the basis of analogy to the history of the second millennium rather than developing arguments for the reliability of the text itself.[11]

Thompson points out that Noth's opposition to acceptance of the historicity of many of the traditions was not a dismissal of archaeological research, but rather was based on the inadequacy of the evidence to support arguments of historicity. He further states that archaeological researchers such as Albright and Wright cannot claim objectivity in their historical interpretation, for their methodology

---

9. Thomas L. Thompson, *The Historicity of the Patriarchal Narratives* (Harrisburg, Pa.: Trinity, 2002), 1.

10. Ibid., 2 and n. 2.

11. Ibid., 3–4.

distorts its data by a selectivity which is hardly representative, which ignores the enormous lack of data for the history of the early second millennium, and which wilfully establishes hypotheses on the basis of unexamined biblical texts, to be proven by such (for this period) meaningless mathematical criteria as the "balance of probability," which itself is established by the extremely undependable principles of analogy and harmonization.[12]

Thompson's criticism goes beneath the well-known dispute between Albright and Noth, between archaeologists and those who work with texts. He argues that parallels between life described in the Bible and that found in the texts from Mari or Nuzi can be established only after the biblical texts are evaluated with regard to their relation to the time they purport to be about and their literary purpose.

In Thompson's view, questionable method undermines arguments for the historicity of the patriarchal narratives. He draws attention to Albright's attempts "to establish a sufficiently strong chain of circumstantial evidence" on which to plead his case for various claims. The strong presumption is that the traditions must represent original events, that they "grow out of real historical events of that early time."[13] He argues that the lack of understanding of the literary forms has allowed researchers to assume that the narratives have an historical intent that has not been proven. He sketches the procedure thus:

> if the patriarchs are to be seen as leaders of large tribal groups, then to show that tribal migrations of related linguistic people took place in a way reminiscent of the patriarchal movements demonstrates the historicity of these narrative and establishes for us the date of the patriarchal period.[14]

He suggests that here "historical probability" becomes the sum of "the various degrees of not knowing" and since the historical possibilities are infinite that surely this is illegitimate method. "Rather, we have either adequate or inadequate evidence for believing that something happened, and the probability that an event occurred does not increase with the accumulation of inadequate evidence." The burden of proof "always belongs to the one who attempts a synthetic interpretation of the historical data. The possibilities of interpretation are never limited to those that have been proposed."[15]

12. Ibid., 7.
13. Ibid., 52–53.
14. Ibid., 53.
15. Ibid., 54.

Albright, Wright, and Bright were convinced of a historical core in the patriarchal narratives. Their assumption was that the common themes, appearing as they do in separate documents, must derive from a single antecedent source and so must represent a legitimate picture of the past. Thompson shows that Albright and his followers, while speaking "of a basic historical tradition which has been passed on orally," at the same time ignored "the implications of the documentary hypothesis" which maintains that a text tells us about the time when it was written, not the time written about.[16] Thompson insists that to serve as a historical source for comparison with extra-biblical material, the biblical texts first must be shown to be historical themselves. To the contrary, he says, "The intentions of the biblical traditions about the patriarchs are not comparable to those of the modern historian. They are rather sociological, political, and religious."[17]

The biblical story of Abraham's journey is not an independent tradition, according to Thompson, but rather a historiographical reconstruction "based on several originally independent and conflicting traditions," and "not only must be understood as unhistorical, but any attempt to find movements analogous to Abraham's in the history of the Near East are essentially misdirected for the purposes of biblical interpretation." He concludes that "the biblical chronologies are not grounded on historical memory, but are rather based on a very late theological schema that presupposes a very unhistorical worldview."[18]

Genealogies and chronologies in Genesis are similar at numerous points to those of the classical world and to those of Babylon and Assyria. Thompson concludes, on the basis of what is known about the genres, that the function of these texts is to provide explanations of the names of tribes, peoples, and places, and to show connections to the past, between groups and places, and between Israel and surrounding lands. He argues against the early second millennium as a setting for the patriarchs on the grounds that the names of the patriarchs have no special connection to this period and, indeed, are found through all the periods for which there is evidence for West Semitic names. Thompson also disputes arguments that suppose Amorite migration from South Mesopotamia and the settlement of semi-nomads. He shows that the Middle Bronze I period was one of "extensive, albeit poor, agricultural settlement, with many major settlements."[19]

16. Ibid., 8.
17. Ibid., 315.
18. Ibid.
19. Ibid., 319–20.

Arguments for the fifteenth and fourteenth centuries BCE background for the patriarchs, based on parallels in custom and family law from Nuzi, fail on the ground that their uniqueness cannot be established. Thompson states, "Customs and contracts of this sort are found throughout the entire Near East, in Mesopotamian legal codes and contracts from the Old Babylonian Period to the Persian Period."[20] Thompson points out that while one close parallel may suggest a relationship, the discovery of "two or three parallels from different sources and different regions show us rather the distinctiveness and uniqueness of each."[21]

An alternative possibility for the historical background of the patriarchs is the Israelite period during the Iron Age. Those touches in the narratives, explained by other hypotheses as anachronisms, are, in fact, "those aspects of the traditions which specifically distinguish the narratives from the rest of Near Eastern folk-literature as Israelite and Palestinian...that some aspects of the stories can be dated to the Israelite period is the very basis for calling them anachronistic."[22] Thompson builds his case by pointing out the close connections between the patriarchs and the Arameans who were not in Transjordan before the end of the twelfth century BCE, those of North Mesopotamia dated after the twelfth century BCE, and those of South Mesopotamia who were not there before the beginning of the tenth century BCE. He further claims that many elements in the traditions presuppose knowledge of Israel "as a political and geographical entity." Support is added by archaeological research which shows that the cities of Palestine mentioned in the narratives are all only known and occupied during the Iron Age.[23] Thompson concludes his argument for Iron Age Israel/Palestine as the locus of the patriarchal traditions by remarking that

> To search beyond this source seems to carry us outside of the context in which the traditions had meaning and significance for Israel... For it is at the point that they are taken up and become a part of the traditions belonging to the Israelite people that they achieve a constitutive existence as traditions about Israel's ancestors.[24]

For those researchers for whom faith must be founded on history even to the exclusion of theology, Thompson contends, "it is not ultimately in the Bible that this 'biblical faith' is grounded, but in the events of history, and in the Bible only insofar as the Bible retells historical events." He

20. Ibid., 323.
21. Ibid., 324.
22. Ibid.
23. Ibid., 325.
24. Ibid., 326.

calls this a "positivistic historicism," by which he seems to mean the historicizing of the biblical narratives and failing to understand their function as meaningful traditions constitutive of the Israelite people.[25] Thompson offers instead the possibility of original literary study of the patriarchal narratives, especially in terms of their folkloric characteristics, free from the preconception that these stories were historiographical. It is particularly interesting that Thompson makes no appeal to newer strategies associated with postmodern literary study for understanding these stories. In presenting these arguments for procedure in biblical research and in his own conclusions regarding the patriarchal narratives, Thompson calls for the rigor in establishing Israel's history that is demanded in the broader field of history. Certainly within the scientific model of academic history, he insists on standards of detachment, objectivity in dealing with ancient sources, and logical argument.

b. *The Abraham Tradition*
Immediately following Thompson's investigation of the historicity of the biblical traditions in Genesis, John Van Seters completed his study of the Abraham narratives.[26] He notes in his Preface that he and Thompson come independently to "many of the same conclusions regarding the antiquity of the patriarchal traditions."[27] Van Seters takes up the admittedly short tradition of Abraham with the purpose of investigating a series of issues surrounding the evaluation of the narratives. To establish the antiquity of the tradition would have especial significance for validating the origins of Israel or proto-Israel.

Van Seters, like Thompson, refers to the firm consensus among biblical scholars of the previous generation regarding a patriarchal age in the second millennium BCE based on parallel customs and names found in the Mari and Nuzi documents. He notes that this scholarship produced what was considered a "hard-won gain against the older criticism such as that expressed by Wellhausen."[28] Opposing such scholarship, Van Seters points to the lack of precise dating within the second millennium and to comparisons drawn between the patriarchs and nomadic groups and also to sedentary communities. He argues that a conclusion must be reached regarding which parallels are appropriate. Finally, he, like Thompson, insists that the desire to support an early date for the patriarchs keeps

25. Ibid., 327.
26. John Van Seters, *Abraham in History and Tradition* (New Haven: Yale University Press, 1975).
27. John Van Seters, "Preface," in his *Abraham*, ix–x (x).
28. Van Seters, *Abraham*, 7.

researchers from investigating the persistence of customs of the second millennium into the first. Van Seters says, "The obvious prejudice for the second millennium, created largely by the mood in biblical studies, has resulted in very meager treatment of the first millennium materials." Such treatment by "scholars dealing with the patriarchal stories does not inspire confidence in existing studies and more closely resembles an apologetic than a scholarly investigation."[29] Van Seters organizes his study around the problems of the patriarchal age as a historical period represented more or less accurately in the text. He asks if it is instead an idealistic notion or even an ideological construct of a later time.[30]

Van Seters' argument against the second-millennium setting for the patriarchal period takes issue with the characteristics of nomadism ascribed to the patriarchs. The theme of land inheritance so prominent in the patriarchal stories "is utterly foreign to the nomadic way of life but a fundamental principle of the settled economy."[31] The variety of animals in Abraham's herds is not found in the second millennium, in particular "it was not until the eighth and seventh centuries that [the camel] became commonplace as a beast of burden within the region of arable land as well as the desert."[32] The household of the patriarchs portrayed in Genesis includes several levels of dependents and slaves. In contrast to nomads who maintained close ties with groups of kin, Abraham relied on his herdsmen for his fighting force. Van Seters notes, "Considering the basic characteristics of nomadism—transhumance, belligerence, and migrations—the stories, on the whole, reflect little of the nomadic way of life, and a distinction is made between the patriarchs and the full nomads of the desert or even the hunters." According to Van Seters, The emphasis on the inheritance of the land, the structure of the household, including slaves, suggest a settled life, and the mention of tents and camels places the stories firmly in the first millennium.[33]

Support for the second millennium as the setting for the patriarchal stories based on the similarity of biblical names to those found in the Mari texts, in Van Seters' view, is unfounded. That the names are eponyms of tribes can only prove that tribal entities may have originated in the second millennium, while "the stories about the eponymous ancestors may all be much later."[34] Van Seters finds the interpretation of biblical

29. Ibid., 10.
30. Ibid., 11.
31. Ibid., 16.
32. Ibid., 17.
33. Ibid., 38.
34. Ibid., 39.

social customs supposedly illuminated by the Nuzi texts flawed and thus of no value in arguing for the second-millennium date for the patriarchs.

Archaeological evidence for the early second millennium, in Middle Bronze I, as the patriarchal period, Van Seters argues, is insufficient. He notes the discontinuity of the period with those periods immediately before and after, both characterized by urban settlement, a sedentary way of life, and political forms more familiar to the patriarchal stories. A more attractive option is MB II, marked by a developing urban civilization in contrast to the semi-nomadic occupation of MB I. The continuity of MB II with Late Bronze, however, makes dating the patriarchs to either of these periods inconclusive. He says that the site of Beersheba raises questions about "the whole archaeological approach." The assumption that the patriarchal traditions were preserved at local sanctuaries and that "the emphasis on altars in the stories points to their use as means of legitimating the sanctity of these places" cannot be sustained, claims Van Seters. To the contrary, he suggests that "perhaps all these patriarchal allusions reflect only the sacredness of the place in Israelite times with no great antiquity to the stories."[35] Furthermore, "the strong association of the patriarchs with Beersheba, which did not become a significant site until the Judean monarchy, point again to a later date."

Finally, the political realities of the Neo-Babylonian period are more compatible with the features of the narratives referring to Ur of the Chaldeans and a route from the East, while at no time before the mid-eighth century could a story of "an invasion from the direction of Mesopotamia be written."[36]

The careful analysis that Van Seters gives each position offered in support of a second-millennium date for the patriarchs issues in the conclusion that "the tradition as it now stands reflects only a rather late date of composition and gives no hint by its content of any great antiquity, in terms of biblical history."[37] The substantial agreement between Thompson and Van Seters on the late dating of the patriarchal narratives opened debate on the assured results of the previous generation.

c. *The Use of Traditions*
Thirteen years after Thompson's initial criticisms of the historicity of the patriarchal narratives, he writes:

35. Ibid., 111–12.
36. Ibid., 119.
37. Ibid., 121–22.

> Theories and ideas which had then been dominant...are so much a part of
> the past history of research as to appear today quaint or reactionary... What
> had needed to be argued then...can now be taken for granted... Issues
> today at stake are no longer those of historicity at all. Much more they deal
> with the historiographical quality of traditional narrative on the one hand,
> and the foundations of the modern historiography of ancient Israel on the
> other.[38]

Rather than investigating how a tradition might have occurred, scholarship is now concerned to know if there might be any usefulness in the tradition for history writing. He reminds his readers that Alt and Noth, using historical-critical methods developed from the source and form criticism of Wellhausen and Gunkel, and Albright, employing the methods of archaeology, were all asking historical questions. The concern of all three was narrowly directed toward the goal of discovering the historical events which presumably lay behind the biblical text.

Beginning in the 1960s, as Biblical Theology lost favor, and with it "*Heilsgeschichte*," theological and historical interests diverged.[39] Whether a tradition has a background in a real event that might be reconstructed has ceased to be a problem for investigation. Instead, the pressing question is: "Are the traditions about early Israel useful to the historian at all?" Thompson specifically excludes "debates about the exactitude of history as a science."[40] The issue for the biblical scholar is rather what evidence, if any, the traditions offer for the history of early Israel. Thompson traces the collapse of the historical constructs of Wright, Albright, Noth, von Rad, and Roland de Vaux to the failure of the Biblical Theology movement. "It was beyond the ability of any critical scholarship to establish a link between tradition and originating event, and between uniqueness and divine causality."[41]

d. *The Origins of Ancient Israel*
Manfred Weippert's 1967 work on the Israelite settlement[42] evaluated Noth's theory of peaceful infiltration, Bright's view of a conquest, and George Mendenhall's peasant revolt. Though his intent was to support Noth's settlement theory, Weippert's thesis ultimately promoted a new discussion of Israel's origins. Thompson says that here "a generation of

---

38. Thomas L. Thompson, *The Origin Tradition of Ancient Israel* (JSOTSup 55; Sheffield: Sheffield Academic Press, 1987), 11.

39. Ibid., 12–13.

40. Ibid., 11.

41. Ibid., 15.

42. Manfred Weippert, *The Settlement of the Israelite Tribes in Palestine: A Critical Survey of Recent Scholarly Debate* (Naperville, Ill.: Allenson, 1971).

debate over the affirmation or denial of the historicity of conquest narratives" was brought to an end on the basis of evidence from destruction layers at major excavations.[43] The conquest/settlement issue was transformed "into an analysis about the *origins of the society* of the nation Israel."[44] Thompson's own contribution, *The Settlement of Palestine in the Bronze Age*, was published in 1979. He remarks that while there are few written sources for the period of MB to LB, the intense activity of explorers and archaeologists over the previous fifty years makes Palestine "one of the few regions of the world where a history of regional settlement and agricultural exploitation in this very early period is a possibility."[45] Through his survey of sites he concludes that at no time in this period did a system of city-states control the area. A pattern of larger settlements in the valleys and an absence of significant settlement in the hill country occurs in LB in contrast to the extensive settlement here during the Iron Age. He speculates that decreasing political stability may have caused declining settlement in LB, and he mentions advances in technology, cisterns, and terraces as factors favoring the Iron Age settlements in the highlands.[46]

In 1974, A. D. H. Mayes published his critique of Noth's amphictyony based on a rejection of the notion "all Israel."[47] He concludes that there is no biblical evidence for any central authority before the monarchy nor any communal activity involving all the "tribes of Israel." Thompson comments that "In the process of establishing his argument, Mayes was able to formulate a series of significant judgments that have subsequently undermined acceptance of the historicity of the narratives about judges in Old Testament scholarship."[48] Mayes' study was followed by C. H. J. De Geus' conclusions that the origins of Israel must be seen in an indigenous population, agricultural and sedentary. Furthermore, he holds that tribes were the product of the social structure of a settled, agrarian population, one comprised of extended families.[49] Thompson cites both of these studies as early contributions to "deconstructive" shift in Old Testament studies. The Hayes–Miller volume, *Israelite and Judean History*,

43. Thompson, *Origin*, 15.
44. Ibid., 20.
45. Thomas L. Thompson, *The Settlement of Palestine in the Bronze Age* (Wiesbaden: Reichert, 1979), 1.
46. Ibid., 63, 66.
47. A. D. H. Mayes, *Israel in the Period of the Judges* (SBT 2d series 29; Naperville, Ill.: Allenson, 1974).
48. Thomas L. Thompson, *Early History of the Israelite People from the Written and Archaeological Sources* (New York: Brill, 1992), 96.
49. Ibid., 101.

Thompson suggests, focuses the shift sharply. Over half of the contributions were concerned with traditions and periods leading up to the monarchy, and clearly "revealed the consensus that little to nothing was known about Israel's origins, that it was highly unlikely that extrabiblical materials would add greatly to our knowledge of Israel's prehistory, and that the biblical tradition is at best an inadequate source for historical knowledge." Among the contributors, however, many disagreements are evident, both in conclusions and in method, so that the consensus on origins cannot be seen as the view of a single school, Thompson says, but rather as "a movement already widely entertained in the field."[50]

4. *New Methodology*

Thompson remarks that it is not the new conclusions of historians of ancient Israel that mark a significant change in the field; it is instead the methodology that has made the difference. He distinguishes between exegesis and interpretation and history writing:

> The success of the movement challenging historicity represents the growing departure of mainstream Old Testament historical research from such earlier more conservative approaches... [A] major step forward has been taken in contemporary biblical historiography, in that a heretofore centrally used source for the early history of Israel can now be seen as both inappropriate and of limited use to the task of writing a history of Israel's origins.[51]

To write an independent history of Israel, one must consider three types of direct evidence: material from archaeological excavations and surveys, ancient written remains related to ancient Palestine, and biblical traditions. Thompson, however, restricts the use of biblical traditions to the reconstruction of the Israel portrayed in the text, its authors, and ideology.[52] The socio-political reality of Israel must be researched in the same way as the history of other states. He claims, "Historical reconstructions are based on research, not theoretical models. They must be related to established evidence if they are to be historically viable. History is Wissenschaft, not metaphysics."[53] Thompson's assessment of the changes in the direction of research, the use of sources, and the procedures, represents a case for "objective" evaluation of evidence, "scientific" history, and the establishment of Israel's history in the same manner as the history of other states is established.

50. Ibid., 102.
51. Ibid., 111.
52. Ibid., 127.
53. Ibid., 116.

5. *The New Archaeology*

It was not until the mid-1970s that the archaeology of Syria-Palestine was spoken of as an independent discipline. Prior to this, archaeology in this area was focused on the attempt to provide a Near Eastern context for the biblical traditions. William Dever writes in 1985 that the earlier approach is no longer possible, nor desirable. He cites new discoveries in southern Lebanon and Syria, Jordan, and Israel that are of such "bulk and complexity" that it is difficult to ascertain the larger significance of the new material. More important, he says, is the identity of Syro-Palestinian archaeology as a field separate from Near Eastern Studies and from biblical studies. He continues, "Syro-Palestinian archaeology's stature as a branch of general archaeology now requires us to analyze it as a field of inquiry in itself and to render an account of its progress, its current research objectives and strategies, and its prospects." Dever calls biblical archaeology "a unique chapter in American intellectual history."[54]

The "New Archaeology" developed from refinements in method and field techniques, in particular Kathleen Kenyon's innovations. Several American cultural trends aided in the development. First, excavations were increasingly staffed by student volunteers, both undergraduates and graduate students. The emphasis on teamwork and the use of students in the sorting and cataloging of the excavated material provided training for large numbers of excavators and promoted the spread of the new techniques. Second, the increasing costs of excavation made it impossible for theological seminaries to fund major projects. Consortia of large universities and other institutions took up projects in the region, bringing a secular orientation to the research. Government funding became available as the religious identification faded. The diverse background of the student volunteers added to the shift from a particular biblical point of view. A third factor, often emphasized by Dever, was the employment of "geologists, geographers, paleo-ethno-botanists and zoologists, climatologists, hydrologists, physical and cultural anthropologists, ethnographers, historians of technology, computer programmers" alongside "traditional statigraphers, architects, and ceramic typologists." In addition to refined method, broader institutional sponsorship, new funding sources, and student staffing, requirements for "sophisticated research design" in proposals for grants and other funds led "American archaeology in the Middle East [to begin] to develop and to articulate a *general theory*."[55]

---

54. William Dever, "Syro-Palestinian and Biblical Archaeology," in Knight and Tucker, eds., *The Hebrew Bible and Its Modern Interpreters*, 31–74 (31).

55. Ibid., 39–40.

By the end of the 1970s, Syro-Palestinian archaeology (Dever's terminology) was moving from a descriptive phase to an explanatory phase, based on "assumptions borrowed...from American anthropology and archaeology." These included attention to the environment, to ethnographic parallels, a systemic theory of culture, and a scientific approach using quantitative analysis and hypothesis testing.[56] Explanation of cultural change shifted from the customary reliance on information gleaned from art and religion to an emphasis on environmental and technological factors. Dever says that the

> influence of the explicitly scientific school is seen in the deliberate development of research design, in the emphasis on problem solving, and in the testing of hypotheses in general, which increasingly characterized the more sophisticated American projects of Syro-Palestinian archaeology in the late 1970s.[57]

The prevailing academic trend toward "scientific" investigation of the 1960s and 1970s is clearly visible in Dever's description of the "New Archaeology." He eagerly and optimistically promoted this new outlook and new methodology in several essays and articles written in the 1970s and 1980s.[58] He points to the independence of the discipline and supports his argument for its diminishing parochialism by noting that the younger generation of archaeologists participate in meetings of the broader discipline, the Archaeological Institute of America and the Society of American Archaeologists, and publish in the *Journal of Field Archaeology*, *American Antiquity*, and the *American Anthropologist*.[59]

Dever is insistent that biblical studies "can no longer dominate the burgeoning field of Syro-Palestinian archaeology or even provide its basic agenda,"[60] and has maintained that "archaeology...is obviously our only possible source of new factual data capable of elucidating the Bible, without which we are reduced to the endless manipulation of the received texts or the application of ingenious but frequently

---

56. Ibid., 49.
57. Ibid., 51.
58. See William Dever, *Archaeology and Biblical Studies: Retrospects and Prospects* (William C. Winslow Lectures; Evanston, Ill.: Seabury-Western Theological Seminary, 1974); idem, "Archaeology," *IDBSup*, 44–52; idem, "Palestine in the Second Millennium BCE: The Archaeology Picture," in *Israelite and Judean History* (ed. J. H. Hayes and J. M. Miller; Philadelphia: Westminster Press, 1977), 70–120; idem, "The Impact of the 'New Archaeology' on Syro-Palestinian Archaeology," *BASOR* 242 (1981): 15–29; "Archaeology," *IDB* 1:354–67.
59. Dever, "Syro-Palestinian," 52.
60. Ibid., 64.

inconclusive hypotheses."[61] In spite of his case for the independence of Syro-Palestinian archaeology, this statement carries traces of biblical archaeology's program to illuminate the Bible. Dever concludes that it is archaeology's role to provide a "general setting for biblical events," to show "daily life in biblical times," and to offer "an alternate perspective" or "corrective" to the biblical narratives and "corroborative detail for particular biblical texts…"[62] It is this view that leads Dever's opponents to argue that he, like Albright's students in the past, tends to support the biblical account, presuming its "essential historicity."

a. *The Present Situation*
Thompson initially argued, in 1974, that extra-biblical comparisons could not legitimately be made with the Genesis narratives until these texts had been evaluated for their historicity. He suggested that the patriarchal stories exhibited many characteristics of folktales and could profitably be studied as a literature whose function was more sociological rather than historical. In the Hayes–Miller volume, he says:

> More promising for a basic understanding of the Joseph and Moses narratives is the renewed interest given to the literary and theological questions involved in the analysis of the Pentateuchal composition, in contrast to the historical interests which have dominated critical scholarship on the Pentateuch from Meyer to Noth.[63]

He next pointed out that the search for the historical events behind the traditions should be abandoned in favor of the more significant consideration of the historical value of the traditions themselves. He called for the history of Israel's origins to be based on archaeological evidence, both textual and artifactual. He says:

> The biblical tradition…causes great difficulty in affirming the historicity of the Israel of tradition at all, and suggests rather that in dealing with this concept, the perspective of the tradition suggests we are involved with an entity that is both intellectually and literarily an entirely new creation beginning in the late Persian period's transforming revisions and collections of tradition.[64]

In another context, he reaffirms his position:

---

61. Ibid., 65.
62. Ibid., 64–65.
63. Thomas L. Thompson, "The Joseph and Moses Narratives," in Hayes and Miller, eds., *Israelite and Judean History*, 149–213 (178).
64. Thompson, *Early History*, 353.

Apart from biblical tradition, this Israel never existed as a historical reality open to independent historical research and judgment. It was in the
formation of tradition as such that…Israel of tradition, for the first time,
became a dominant reality in the history of ancient Palestine.[65]

Though he argues that the Israel of tradition is a "new creation,"
Thompson insists that this traditional Israel as it appears in the biblical
text has a very specific past and that past context is necessary to a
contemporary understanding; indeed, "the tradition itself created the
population of Palestine as Israel out of the ashes of the Assyrian and
Babylonian empires." Biblical tradition is related to Israel's history in the
sense that it is used to "understand Israel as the end result of a literary
trajectory." To use the tradition as a source for historical events, however, is to make the error Wellhausen warned against, to produce an
anachronistic reconstruction of Israel. Thompson insists that it is the
Israel of tradition that must be explained historically.[66] On the other
hand, Thompson offers a negative judgment of the possibilities for writing a history of the Israel of tradition. This creation of the exilic and
postexilic periods is embedded in the traditions of Chronicles, Ezra, and
Nehemiah, but these traditions were recorded "long after the exilic and
early postexilic periods" and thus cannot be assumed to be a reliable
source for history.[67]

b. *The Search for Ancient Israel*

Following Thompson's discussion of the Israel of tradition, Philip Davies
published *In Search of "Ancient Israel"* (1992) in which he describes the
emergence of "an alternative to 'ancient Israel' in the form of the historical society that really generated the literary Israel."[68] Davies' literary
Israel shows similarities to Thompson's "Israel of tradition." Davies
says, "From this point onwards, we are no longer looking for any kind of
Israel, but for a society which, in producing the literary Israel, is seeking
to create for itself an identity it does not yet have." He argues that a
literature produced by those with a worldview that understood all aspects
of life and reality to be controlled by divine powers, will inevitably have
a religious cast, though it will not necessarily be the expression of any
particular religious view. He adds, "the biblical literature almost certainly must have emerged as a political-cultural product of the Jerusalem

65. Thompson, "Text, Context and Referent," in Edelman, ed., *The Fabric of
History*, 65–92 (72).
66. Thompson, "Text," 71, 73.
67. Ibid., 92.
68. Philip R. Davies, *In Search of "Ancient Israel"* (JSOTSup 148; Sheffield:
Sheffield Academic Press, 1992), 18.

'establishment.'" This literature came over time to be associated with and to define a traditional culture. Though it was concerned with "deity or deities, cult practice, cosmogony, prophetic records and wisdom sayings, that does not immediately place it in the category of 'scripture,'" though over time this literature assumed the functions of scripture.[69]

Distinguishing among the "Israels" in current discussion, Davies offers a possibility for moving the historical project forward. Accordingly, he says, biblical Israel is the subject of the Bible, directly available to all readers. Though the representations of biblical Israel are often conflicting and incoherent, this is a problem only to the historian, not to the reader. The historical Israel "is the only Israel an archaeologist or historian…can encounter, and it existed in the northern and central Palestinian highlands between roughly the ninth and precisely the late eighth centuries BCE." This Israel has little resemblance to the biblical Israel. Finally, ancient Israel, holds Davies, is a "scholarly construct." This ancient Israel "lies between literature and history—or rather, it straddles the two."[70] Davies suggests that without the biblical literature, archaeologists finding Iron Age sites in the area would have no reason for calling them Israelite. They have evidence of a state called Judah, but have no archaeological reason to associate this state with "Israel" unless they assume it existed as part of the kingdom of Israel to the north, which is the "only 'Israel' which an archaeologist or historian, as opposed to biblical interpreter, can encounter."

Davies argues that "ancient Israel" is neither biblical nor historical, the result

> of taking a literary construct and making it the object of historical investigation. In seeking to impose what is *literary* upon a time and place that are *historical*, biblical scholarship and its own "ancient Israel" betray both literature and history, and vindicate the charge that "biblical history" is indeed neither biblical nor history.

He amplifies this conclusion by noting that a history of biblical Israel can be written (though he supposes that no paraphrase is likely to improve on the original text) and a history of the historical Israel, the entity which occupied the central highlands of Palestine for slightly more than two centuries, can be written, but "ancient Israel," a confusion of the two previous categories, is not a subject for historical investigation.[71]

69. Ibid., 20.
70. Ibid., 16.
71. Ibid., 17.

Two problems come to light through Davies' discussion. First, claims are made for the historicity of biblical figures who are attested in extrabiblical materials and, by extension, for the historicity of the Bible. Davies rejects these claims since the use of the characters by the biblical writers is not historical but ideological. Their intent is not to narrate events in ways that "accurately" describe them, but to demonstrate Yahweh's interest in Israel's fate. The second problem is that of the "history of a people whose real character has been obliterated by a literary construct." Davies argues that these are the people whose relics archaeologists discover whenever they dig for "ancient Israel."[72] This problem is met by researching the historical Israel. Both problems are related to the assumption that the "biblical Israel" is the "historical Israel."

Davies traces the "misconstrual of 'ancient Israel'" to the basic presupposition that the biblical writers lived in the time that the narratives recount.[73] This view holds that the biblical writers were knowledgeable about the past and concerned to portray it accurately and the numerous examples of biblical literature assigned to particular settings and reigns of various kings may be relied upon for their dates. Plausible connections to specific periods are established for other sections of the narrative on the basis of the details of the accounts. In the case of a redactor, though removed in time from the events retold, a strong presumption is made for the writer's reliance on sources or traditions close to the events.[74] Davies argues that through a process of circular reasoning, inferred sources are fixed to certain biblical settings and then "used to embellish the literary account itself." The biblical literature "becomes a *contemporary witness to its own construct*, reinforcing the initial assumption of a real historical construct and giving impetus to an entire pseudo-scholarly exercise in fitting the literature into a sequence of contexts which it has itself furnished." Independent verification of the historicity of the biblical literature or of its date of composition would bring an end to the circularity that has rendered the entire discipline invalid.[75] Davies has shown how the assumption that the biblical literature issues from the time it describes constrains both the investigation of the historical Israel and understanding of the text.

With the publication of *In Search of "Ancient Israel"* in 1992, the case was complete for a new approach to the study of the Hebrew Bible. It was demonstrated by Gunkel that the creation and flood stories are related

72. Ibid., 31.
73. Ibid., 36.
74. Ibid., 36–37.
75. Ibid., 38.

to cycles of Near Eastern myths. Alt presented, in 1925, the model for the peaceful settlement of Palestine.[76] By the mid-1970s, Thompson and Van Seters had offered sharp criticism of the notion of the patriarchal age that had been established in the years following World War II. After further discussion of the settlement and conquest, the historicity of the monarchy next came under assault. Thompson proposed that the period of the "united monarchy" has no historical basis and represents a literary "golden age." Lemche questioned the biblical portrayal of the exile. At the present moment, debate continues on points both specific, such as the authenticity of an inscription which, some argue, may refer to the House of David, and more general points concerning the reliability of the biblical text for reconstructing history. These problems will be discussed below. Having established an outline of the methodological problems for writing a history of Israel, I turn now to the debate between the "maximalists" and the "minimalists."

6. *"Maximalism" and "Minimalism"*

The tensions produced by the publication of the more recent works cited above and related articles, and the implications for Israel's history, have issued in the often acrimonious controversies in biblical studies. In order to understand the point of view of those often called "maximalists," it is useful to recall G. Ernest Wright's statement, made in 1952: "In biblical faith everything depends upon whether the events actually occurred."[77] Here one sees the stark contour of the debate. As to the designations "maximalist" and "minimalist," the attributes of each group are generally assigned by the opposition. Thus, Lemche characterizes the approach taken by those who defend the Bible as a source of history in this way: "Until the present, most scholars have offered in the guise of research efforts which are by no means independent scholarly interpretations of the history of Israel, but more or less rationalistic paraphrases of the biblical version of the history of Israel and its religions."[78] Philip Davies, responding to Iain Provan, argues that Provan's

> objections seem to stem from the view that the Bible is in some way a divine, or at least a specially privileged source, containing divine truth and not amenable to rationalist(ic) methods of investigation, least of all to

76. Albrecht Alt, *Essays on Old Testament History and Religion* (trans. R. A. Wilson; The Biblical Seminar; Sheffield: JSOT Press, 1989).

77. Wright, *The God who Acts*, 126.

78. Niels Peter Lemche, *Ancient Israel: A New History of Israelite Society* (The Biblical Seminar 5; Sheffield: JSOT Press, 1988), 7.

the principle that you do not call an unsupported statement a historical
fact until or unless you have sufficient evidence or argument to support
your claim.[79]

Thompson remarks in his Introduction to the first section of *The Mythic
Past*:

> Although biblical scholarship has roots in the critical historical work of
> the nineteenth century, the twentieth century has seen critical advances
> eroded by the growth in an understanding of the Bible that might best be
> described as a form of "naive realism." The Bible's own story of the past,
> centered on the rise and fall of old Israel, still dominates historical recon-
> structions within biblical studies.

The biblical stories "are seen only in their transformations as accounts of
events: they have become history."[80]

The "minimalists" in turn are castigated for treating the biblical text
with skepticism regarding both its intent to portray history and its
reliability in providing historical information. Provan finds it "difficult to
understand why the position which insists that biblical data be verified
before being accepted as historically valuable should be considered any
more acceptable than the position which insists that these data must be
historically valuable even when they are apparently falsified."[81] "Minimalists" are opposed because of their demands for external verification
as the requirement for assuming historicity. Archaeology is often their
source of validation for historical facts, but "minimalists" are criticized
for relying on the interpretation of artifacts, which, the "maximalists"
insist, is even more liable to "subjectivity" than the interpretation of texts.
Finally, "minimalists" are repudiated for suggesting that the Bible is a
collection of ideological, tendentious literature and further that "ancient
Israel" is a scholarly construct.

a. *The Debate*

The "maximalist/minimalist" controversy comprises three sets of issues.
The first often appears in charges of ideology, both postmodern and theological. The second concerns the historicity of the biblical text, and the
third takes up the particular evidence, textual and archaeological, for
biblical events and characters. The postmodern tag is used to discount

79. Philip R. Davies, "Method and Madness: Some Remarks on Doing History
with the Bible," *JBL* 114 (1995): 699–705 (700).

80. Thomas L. Thompson, *The Mythic Past* (London: Basic Books, 1999), 5.

81. Iain Provan, "Ideologies, Literary and Critical," *JBL* 114 (1995): 585–606
(603).

"minimalist" views by supposedly revealing their ideological bias. "Postmodern" is not defined for the purposes of this debate and has little or nothing to do with theories of the non-referential character of language or its consequences for the writing of history. It suggests, instead, a general challenge to cherished beliefs and obscures the lurking problem of who has the authority to write Israel's history. Postmodernism, it is claimed, fosters the skepticism of "minimalist" writers toward the historicity of the biblical narratives. It is not clear just how postmodernism is supposed to be related to this particular skepticism, but because of their ideology and their archaeological incompetence, such writers are not judged reliable sources for the history of Israel. A theological bias has been suggested as another prejudicial factor undermining scholarship, though Thompson often claims rather that "bad" scholarship is the issue.

The problem of the historicity of the biblical text has several facets. Whether or not the narratives were intended as history is a question with a long life in the debate. Scholars have argued both that the tales, the events, and the characters in the Bible are "fictionalized history" and "historicized fiction." If the stories are fictionalized history, then there must be a core of historical knowledge available from the text. This view was supported by both historical and theological work on the "themes" of the Pentateuch as the basis for the cultic identity of ancient Israel. On the other hand, if the stories are fiction, dressed up as history, another motive must be found for the production of the literature.[82] The elusive quest for the historical core, nonetheless, is the premise on which much biblical scholarship has been based, though in the past quarter century this premise has come under attack.

Working on the assumption that there is a historical background recorded in the text which can be traced, both textual scholars and archaeologists have offered reconstructions of Israel's history. These reconstructions are also significant points of contention. The arguments in the past between the American and German schools centered on the contributions of archaeology to historical reconstruction, but artifactual evidence was not itself the issue. A circular process involving the texts as the basis for archaeological research, followed by the appeal to the artifacts for validation of the narratives, proved to be the problem. Archaeologists accused text critics of rejecting the work of archaeologists, whereas, in fact, the archaeologists often went into the field with the unevaluated, uncriticized text in hand, hoping to match artifacts to

---

82. Thompson (*Historicity*, 188–89) refers to Milman Parry's work on Serbo-Croatian oral tradition demonstrating the indiscriminate use of historical characters, times, and places in popular lore.

narrative. Argument has persistently addressed the need for an historical evaluation of the biblical text before comparison is made with extra-biblical material. Specific points of contention through the years have been conquest and settlement models, the date for the patriarchal period, and the genre of the patriarchal narratives and their usefulness in providing historical information. More recently, disputes have centered on the identity of the highland settlers based on material culture remains, social patterns, and the understanding of pastoral modes of socio-economic organization, on the existence of the Davidic monarchy, and the reality or scope of the exile.

Much of the "maximalist/minimalist" controversy features the interpretation of very specific data, the physical evidence of settlement, the extent of settlement, or estimates of population that could be supported within a given set of conditions, including climate, technology, and social organization. Extra-biblical references to political situations, to Israel, to biblical monarchs, are all used by specialists to advance their particular case. The charges of ideological agenda provide a frame for the argument, but they are, in every case, vague and lacking in content. The theoretical presupposition that the Bible must be an historical account of Israel's past, frequently challenged by Thompson, Davies, and their colleagues, serves as a source for polemical accusations that history is "being erased." The debate continues, however, at the level of methodology, how to use the artifacts, how to use the text, what dates are more probable, which characters were real persons.

b. *The Development of the Debate*
In his 1977 essay in the Hayes–Miller volume, Dever describes biblical archaeology as "an interdisciplinary inquiry in which biblical scholars and archaeologists engage in a dialogue."[83] In practice, however, the dialogue is unbalanced, and often "hidden theological presuppositions determine the outcome of the inquiry."[84] Recalling the debate between Noth and Albright, he says, "the American position could be termed 'maximalist' and the German 'minimalist.'" Dever writes that "The chief justification for reviving the old debate on the contribution of archaeology to biblical studies is that the issues were never resolved."[85] The Germans continued in their critique of the positivist basis of American biblical archaeology, while many liberal American scholars "regarded biblical archaeology as an unfortunate accompaniment of neo-orthodoxy,

83. Dever, "Palestine in the Second Millennium BCE," 72.
84. Ibid., 73.
85. Ibid., 77.

a thinly-disguised fundamentalism appealing now to archaeology for external support."[86] He concludes that the recent works of Thompson (1974) and Van Seters (1975) "alone would justify resuming the old discussion on archaeology and biblical studies."[87] Nevertheless, in reviewing Thompson's and Van Seters' positions, Dever's chief concern remained more specific, whether MB I or MB IIA–B is the more appropriate setting for the patriarchs.

Thompson responds in a 1978 article, saying that Dever's recommendation for "a divorce between the disciplines of archaeology and biblical studies is more appropriate."[88] He continues in this mode of affirmation, "The independence of Palestinian archaeology, which he [Dever] advocates, is the more to be welcomed, however, because it is to archaeology, *rather than to biblical studies*, that the question of the origin of the people of Israel and Judah…is to be directed."[89] Thompson acknowledges Malcolm Clark's criticism, writing with Dever in the Hayes–Miller volume, of his own "failure to address the new 'ethnographic and anthropological' studies of the Early West Semites"[90] and failure to provide an alternative model of nomadism. He proceeds to outline his approach and to criticize the studies mentioned by Clark and then to give his evidence and conclusions in regard to Bronze Age settlement in Palestine. This is a painstaking response in the tradition of academic debate. It shows no rancor. At this point, though Dever had reintroduced the relationship of archaeology and biblical studies as a topic of discussion, and had offered the terms "maximalist" and "minimalist," both Thompson and Dever direct their interest toward the problems of the patriarchal period.

c. *Escalation of the Debate: The Inscription from Tel Dan*

At the meeting of the Society of Biblical Literature in Washington, in November, 1993, the discovery of the Tel Dan inscription was announced by Avraham Biran and Joseph Naveh. This announcement immediately elicited a cascade of responses. Problems with the location of the discovery surfaced, and epigraphic evidence suggested a rather late date for the inscription. Thompson catalogues a series of objections to the proposal that this inscription offers proof for the existence of David and his dynasty. The absence in Hebrew of a dot in *bytdwd* to separate the two

86. Ibid.
87. Ibid., 78.
88. Thomas L. Thompson, "The Background of the Patriarchs: A Reply to William Dever and Malcolm Clark," *JSOT* 9 (1978): 2–43 (3).
89. Ibid., 5.
90. Ibid., 6.

elements indicates that the word is a place name rather than a personal name. Thompson marshals evidence from the Bible and West Semitic nomenclature to support his case for the inscription's character as a place name. He parallels the term House of David to the House of Ahab, the House of Israel, and the House of the King. He argues that there is no sense of dynasty implied by these terms and proposes instead the meaning "'adherents to,' 'all that belong to,' the 'chiefdom of', or, even better, the 'patronage of...'"[91] Thompson relates the family terminology that permeates ancient Near Eastern society to the structures of the Mediterranean economy "oriented towards limited associations of the small village and a dominant small market town...where everything from partnerships to the sale of a concubine or an orchard function with the language of the family."[92] It is within this family structure that the term House of David can be understood to represent the eponymous founder. Thompson argues that the concept of patronage is reflected in the language in terms such as the house of the Lord, house of the king, and so forth, and concludes that *bytdwd* refers, "not to an historical David, but rather to the divine epithet *dwd*."[93]

In his article in the following issue of the *Scandinavian Journal of the Old Testament*, Thompson reviews the publication of two new fragments related to the *bytdwd* inscription. Again, he compliments the speed with which Biran and Naveh have published their finds, while noting that they have not responded to criticism of their first reconstruction. He notes several technical problems in alignment, size, and spacing of the letters and, in addition, dismisses the interpretation of the text based on the alleged juncture of the fragment, calling the reconstruction "cooked."[94] Thompson, commenting on his discomfort with the location of the finds, says, "I would be even more comfortable if one or two of these fragments had been found in Biran's dump."[95] He refers to the publications of Biran and Naveh as being prone to "particularly unwarranted and tendentious gap-filling and biblicistic interpretation."[96] To this point, the discussion is sharp, turning nasty, but still within the bounds of customary academic debate.

91. Thomas L. Thompson, "'House of David': An Eponymic Referent to Yahweh as Godfather," *SJOT* 9 (1995): 59–74 (66).

92. Ibid., 65.

93. Ibid., 72.

94. Thomas L. Thompson, "Dissonances and Disconnections: Notes on the *bytdwd* and *hmlk.hdd* Fragments from Tel Dan," *SJOT* 9 (1995): 236–40 (238).

95. Ibid., 237.

96. Ibid., 236.

d. *Charges of Ideology*

Iain Provan increased the tension between "maximalists" and "minimalists" with his article in the 1995 winter issue of the *Journal of Biblical Literature*, opening with a challenge to "those who care about the integrity of biblical narrative."[97] He identifies an "enthusiasm for 'the Bible as literature'" as a force promoting late dating, skepticism toward earlier sources, and a tendency to see the biblical narratives as historicized fiction.[98] The article cites quotations from several "minimalist" scholars that Provan arrays as a series of moves "against history." Thompson and Davies, Provan points out, have claimed that much biblical scholarship has been "ideological," motivated by religious and theological points of view. Provan claims that, where the "minimalists'" own work is concerned, the insights of professional academic historians regarding the impossibility of objective observation and the ideological nature of all historical texts, from the selection to presentation of material, are conveniently downplayed. They speak of "independent" research into the history of Palestine and "unprejudiced" archaeological investigation.

Provan pursues the issue of scholarly detachment, accusing Davies of separating biblical scholarship into two sorts, that of the "misty-eyed theologians, prevented by faith from engaging in 'real historical research,'" and those "hard-nosed historians, striving to exercise critical scholarship in a hostile environment."[99] He professes confusion, wondering if it is "part of a more deliberate authorial strategy—part of an elaborate deception whose purpose is to highlight the ideology of others while concealing one's own." He adds that, in fact, he believes Davies' approach is an ideology "no more free of unverifiable presuppositions, than those other approaches he so vehemently attacks."[100] He argues that "minimalist" scholars "have already embraced a particular philosophy, a particular worldview, which informs their thinking as historians." This he designates "positivism" based on "its dogmatic anti-narrativist stance, its inherent reductionism, and its secular, antitheological and antimetaphysical orientation…"[101] Provan claims at the close that his purpose is to expose the scholarly posture of the "minimalists" as driven as much by ideology as that of more traditional scholars and, indeed, the biblical writers themselves. Yet, the closest he comes to describing the "revisionists'" ideology is to accuse them of traditional positivist or empiricist tendencies.

97. Provan, "Ideologies," 585.
98. Ibid., 586.
99. Ibid., 599.
100. Ibid., 600.
101. Ibid., 601.

Thompson and Davies respond in the same issue. Davies charges that Provan confuses bias and method. Provan states that because the Bible is ideological, Davies believes it to be unreliable, whereas Davies argues that because the Bible is "historically unreliable it has to be understood as ideological." Further, "in the case of 'ancient Israel' a *certain set* of ideological notions is interfering with the application of a method which most scholars fundamentally accept."[102] Davies says:

> ancient historiography and modern historiography are different kinds of stories, because they operate with different conventions. Ancient historiography, for example, permits myth and legend to be mixed in and allows plagiarizing and deliberate invention. Modern historiography doesn't permit these...their hypotheses must conform to principles of probability, appeal to analogy, or use certain other widely understood kinds of argument.

Davies addresses the theoretical positions taken in modern departments of history, "Modern historiographers may allow (though many don't) that there is no 'objective history' out there, but the conventions of the genre, of the discipline, still operate as if there is an 'out there' about which we can make statements that are in principle true or false."[103]

Thompson addresses Provan's case for scholarly ideology by remarking that "we have at times quite pointedly argued that some scholars in the field have been motivated by reasons other than historical science, our objection has not been so much to ideology, nor even to religious and theological bias, as simply to bad scholarship."[104] Thompson is at pains to point out the misquotations Provan has included to shape his case. He suggests that Provan is disingenuous when he labels Thompson a "positivist," omitting Thompson's statement that "history belonged not to the 'natural or physical sciences' but rather to the social sciences and to *Geisteswissenschaft*. Thus, I describe history as both particular and non-predictive..." following the classical historicist rejection of the natural science model.[105] Thompson claims that "we do strive to be objective scholars" and that as a group the so-called "minimalists" have no binding ideology, that "we do not attack the text for the ideology contained in it... We rather attack wrong uses of the text and bad scholarship... What we do say about the text is that it cannot be used for a reconstruction of the South Levant's past in the Bronze and Iron ages."[106] Thompson

102. Davies, "Method and Madness," 702.
103. Ibid., 703.
104. Thompson, "A Neo-Albrightean School," 687.
105. Ibid., 689.
106. Ibid., 693.

concludes that the "school" that Provan attacks does not exist, but that all the "proponents of contemporary historical methods in our field" would comprise a list of "dozens of participants" in "the academic field called 'history.'" Not positivist, this branch of historical studies insists "on external evidence before assuming the historicity of biblical narrative, themes, and motifs" and on "independent evaluation of biblical and other data useful for historical description."[107]

This exchange, though introducing topics related to theoretical discussions in academic departments of history, actually continued the long-standing debate over the purpose and intent of the biblical texts and their proper use for historical reconstruction, matters of evaluation of texts, of evidence and argument, all features of historical method.

e. *"Maximalists" and "Minimalists" Face to Face*
In 1997, Herschel Shanks gathered Thompson, Dever, Lemche, and Kyle McCarter to talk about issues relating to "minimalist" and "maximalist" positions. Shanks states clearly at the outset that his readers are interested in history, that is the history of Israel as recounted in the Bible.[108] History from Shanks' and Dever's point of view, says Lemche, remains a matter of excavating the biblical text, seeking the earliest strata and its historical clues. Lemche argues that this approach increases the speculative quality of any reconstruction and that it is "much better to say, 'We have here a piece of literature, reflecting the time in which it was finished.'" The biblical writer had many historical recollections available, but did not know where to put them. "He was not really writing history. He was making it up. He didn't know the genre of history writing."[109] Thompson made the same point earlier saying that, "the compounding of 'if' clauses in the development of an interpretation makes a suggestion less likely rather than more probable, and that this diminishment of probability is geometrically cumulative."[110]

Concerning the history of Palestine in the period customarily ascribed to Saul, David, and Solomon, Thompson and Lemche hold that the picture is quite unlike the story in the Bible: "This is not because 'the Bible is wrong', but because the Bible is not history, and only very recently has anyone ever wanted it to be."[111] Dever agrees that the Exodus and the

107. Ibid., 697.
108. Hershel Shanks, "Biblical Minimalists Meet Their Challengers Face to Face," *BAR* 23 (1997): 26–42 (28).
109. Ibid., 29.
110. Niels Peter Lemche and Thomas L. Thompson, "Did Biran Kill David? The Bible in the Light of Archaeology," *JSOT* 64 (1994): 3–22 (3).
111. Ibid., 18.

conquest do not represent historical events and insists that he and Israeli archaeologists have given up looking for them. He also has "given up the patriarchs" and agrees on late dating of the documents, but he says, "the rise of the Israelite state is not a dead issue...we should look at the Book of Judges. That fits a lot better with the facts on the ground as we know them."[112] Lemche argues, to the contrary, that Judges "reflects what we call a heroic society, heroic in the Greek sense...we love those stories, but we don't believe them to be true."[113] Here the discussion turns to specific elements of the text. Thompson finds the king lists and a number of place names mentioned in the narratives to be old and "there is a lot of commentary about traditions that are understood to be old," but he rejects the notion put forward by Dever that these form an outline that can be filled in by archaeology.[114] Dever continues, "When you do have a convergence of the archaeological reconstruction that we come up with and a history behind the history that one can seem to see, what is the problem with saying so? That's not fundamentalism."[115] He argues that archaeology can provide an independent witness: "We can show that the text will fit in the tenth and ninth century, but it won't fit anywhere else."[116] Here again is the problem mentioned by Noth and presently by the "revisionists," that the text is taken at face value and "convergences" with extra-biblical evidence used to make the case for the text.

While disassociating himself from biblical archaeology, Dever's crusade for "new" archaeology was primarily an effort to establish professional field methodology, not to change traditional approaches to Israelite history. Maxwell Miller says:

> Dever, like Wright before him, is convinced that the Bible story of ancient Israel has an essentially accurate historical core; he attempts to get at this historical core, not by examining the literary stratigraphy and texture of the Bible, but by placing the Bible story "as is" alongside the archaeological evidence and adjusting the one and interpreting the other to achieve the best fit possible.[117]

Miller suggests that Dever is aware that the objections raised against the old approach of biblical archaeology still apply to his own work.

---

112. Shanks, "Biblical Minimalists," 29.
113. Ibid., 32.
114. Ibid.
115. Ibid., 42.
116. Ibid., 33.
117. J. Maxwell Miller, review of William Dever, *What Did the Biblical Writers Know and When Did They Know it? What Archaeology Can Tell Us About the Reality of Ancient Israel*, *BASOR* 329 (2003): 84–88. Online: http://proquest.umi.com.

Knowing that biblical scholars undermined the old version of Israelite history, Miller says, "Rather than confronting [the methodological objections], he prefers to dismiss biblical scholars and tell the story of the controversy in a fashion that gives credit to 'secular archaeologists' (particularly to himself) for the changes in thinking that have taken place," whereas biblical scholars, in fact, have produced the studies that have reshaped the understanding of Israelite history.[118]

f. *"Minimalism," Ideology, and Anti-Semitism*

The ongoing debate has been intense, with "sneering" epithets directed at each side, sarcastic evaluations of the opposition's position, and sharp claims of misunderstanding. Ideology continues to be an issue, though precisely what ideology and how it functions remains ill-defined. Charges of membership in certain "schools" are made and emphatically denied. The purpose and intent of the Bible and its authors and the place of archaeology in illuminating the Bible's meaning are long-standing features of the dispute, though in this round of polemics content is a decidedly secondary consideration.[119]

Thompson has repeatedly asked why he and certain other scholars are thought to be a "school" and are called by names chosen to be unflattering.[120] Davies notes that the term "minimalist" and other appellations, "revisionist," "nihilist," are used only by those who oppose the work of scholars such as Thompson, Davies, Whitelam, and Lemche, while "none of the 'minimalist' scholars is aware of being part of a school or group." The work of scholars targeted by the opposition is, according to Davies, "no more monolithic than any mainstream movement is, and there exist more differences among those assigned to it than there are between them all and many other scholars."

Davies argues that "the appraisal and use of ancient literary sources are technical matters; what counts is the method and the reasoning." He holds that there is such "concentration on the 'minimal' outcome that the issues of historical argumentation are usually lost or pushed into the background" and "other invented 'motives' are attributed" to the work of

118.   Ibid., 86.
119.   It is interesting to note that Richard Leakey, speaking about his experiences as a paleontologist, remarks, "I was very disappointed by the venality of the infighting and personalities who if they didn't like what you found, didn't discuss the fossils but discussed the personalities behind the fossils" (NPR, National Geographic Radio Expeditions, August 7, 2003).
120.   Philip R. Davies, "Minimalism, 'Ancient Israel,' and Anti-Semitism," n.p. [cited 2 October 2003]. Online: http://www.bibleinterp.com/articles/Minimalism.htm.

his colleagues. As the historicity of the Bible is acutely important for religious groups, Zionists, and biblical archaeologists, "one can readily understand not merely the coining of the term 'minimalism' but also the rage, the invective, the orchestrated assault, against a number of scholars who argue that it is not very reliable." Davies declares that "history is an agenda of many anti-'minimalists,' and it remains by and large the popular view of the Bible as well." To the contrary, for Davies, the Bible is best approached as "a monumental project" to create a society and its religion over several centuries, but "essentially after the period of independent statehood had disappeared."

In 2000, the *Biblical Archaeological Review* published together three articles addressing the topic "The Search for History in the Bible."[121] One is a selection from Thompson's *The Mythic Past* that Shanks places under the heading, "Can You Understand This?," a clue for readers of the *BAR* that Thompson's piece may be discounted. In the other two Davies and Dever offer comments. Davies argues that "not much" separates a "minimalist" from a "maximalist." He points to agreement on dates and procedure and similar interests in archaeology, evidence, and facts. He sums up thus, "we need a reliable history of Israelite and Judahite society and religion in order to explain biblical literature."[122]

Dever, in his article in the same issue, "Save Us from Postmodern Malarkey," makes a serious charge: "In my view most of the revisionists are no longer honest scholars."[123] He says:

> a postmodern theory of knowledge states that there is no real knowledge, not of the objective, external world perceived by the senses, no facts, only interpretation. Moral relativism and multi-culturalism must prevail. Issues all become those of politics: race, class, gender and power. I would argue that the typical postmodern approach to texts…has been adopted by the biblical revisionists…[124]

To Davies' perception that not much separates "minimalists" and "maximalists," Dever retorts in a later number of the *BAR*, "The issue between the two schools is absolutely fundamental."[125] Though it is difficult to relate Dever's account of the "revisionists" approach as one rejecting the

121.   See the following in *BAR* 26.2 (2000): Philip R. Davies, "What Separates a Minimalist from a Maximalist? Not Much," 24–27, 72–73; William Dever, "Save Us from Postmodern Malarkey," 28–35, 68–69; a selection from Thomas L. Thompson's *Mythic Past*, called by Shanks "Can You Understand This?," 26–37.

122.   Davies, "What Separates a Minimalist from a Maximalist?," 73.

123.   Dever, "Save Us from Postmodern Malarkey."

124.   Ibid., 30.

125.   Ibid.

very notion of knowledge to Davies' stated interest in evidence and facts, Dever insists that the "minimalists" are all, "practically speaking, nihilists" who contend that the Hebrew Bible is "nothing but a late Hellenistic phantasmagoria…simply political propaganda."[126]

The latest round in the dispute has taken a more vicious turn, with accusations of anti-Semitism, anti-Bible, anti-Judaism, anti-Zionism, and a bias against Israel. Attacks on the integrity and competence of scholarship have been traded. At stake is the existence of ancient Israel. Thompson, Davies, and Lemche have all published research on the historical states of Israel and Judah, all agree that the Israel of the Bible shows little correspondence to the historical evidence. Davies states, "Bringing the notion under critical scrutiny that Israel was the natural or rightful owner of this piece of land" is inflammatory and an element of biblical studies that has no present analog in departments of history. He continues, "Biblical scholarship inevitably focuses on the Israelite identity of a land that has actually been non-Jewish in terms of its indigenous population for the larger part of its recorded history."[127] In no other geographical area would the claims of history have such an effect. Davies goes on, "This state of affairs is due to the Bible and its influence in the West where our inherited Christian culture supports the notion that the territory west of the Jordan is and has always been somehow essentially 'the land of Israel.'" Keith Whitelam has pointed to the fact that a thousand years of Muslim occupation is disregarded in favor of recent settlement.[128] The authority of the very notion of "biblical" scholarship prejudices the issue in the direction of Jewish entitlement to the land. Davies argues that biblical scholarship promotes an attitude toward the land that "tends to regard modern Palestinians as trespassers or 'resident aliens' in someone else's territory."[129]

126. Ibid., 31.
127. Davies, "Minimalism, 'Ancient Israel,' and Anti-Semitism."
128. See Whitelam, *The Invention of Ancient Israel.*
129. Modern Palestinians cite propaganda circulated in the early to mid-twentieth century holding that Jewish immigration was encouraged through the slogan, "a people without a land for a land without people" (Online: http://www.palestineremembered.com/Acre/Famous-Zionist-Quotes/Story637.html): "Since the inception of Zionism in the late 19th century and until this date, the vast majority of the Zionist leaders insisted that the Palestinians do not exist as a people or a nation. Such blind attitude was concocted to facilitate the usurpation and suppression of Palestinian political, economic, and human rights. As it will be demonstrated from the quotes below, it was often argued by most Zionists that Palestine was empty & destitute place until Zionists 'redeemed' it from the desert; and the indigenous Palestinian people were backward, primitive, and mostly nomadic who are not worthy of any political rights whatsoever."

This leads to a feature of the "maximalist/minimalist" debate that cannot be ignored, though it falls outside of arguments about historicity and methodology—the charge of anti-Semitism. Thompson cites remarks on the internet and personal encounters in which "minimalism" has been associated with anti-Semitism.[130] Dever has claimed of Whitelam, "in my opinion his work borders on anti-Semitism... [His] book is certainly a potent manifestation, heavily pro-Palestinian."[131] Dever quotes Lemche to the effect that Jews "could not be objective" in writing Israel's history. Davies suggests that the misunderstood claim of "minimalists" that ancient Israel never existed provides a basis for attacks of anti-Semitism. He defends the "revisionist" position: "the point at issue is not whether an Israel ever existed, but rather whether the historical ancient Israel was like the portrait in the Bible."[132] That the "minimalist/maximalist" debate has been characterized by personal hostility, vitriolic offenses, and nasty counter-attacks is well known. The charges of anti-Zionism, anti-Bible, anti-Israel, and anti-Semitism are more extreme examples of the *ad hominem* exchanges that have occurred over many years.

7. Academic Historiography

a. *Scientific History*

In her preface to *The Fabric of History* in 1991, Diana Edelman provides a telling outline of historiography in biblical studies. Edelman's sources are significant. She quotes from G. R. Elton's famous guide, *The Practice of History* (1967), from Marc Bloch's *The Historian's Craft* (1953), and other historiographical sources, none later than 1971. Her "boundaries of historical investigation" set out clear parameters for the collection and interpretation of historical evidence based entirely on traditional assumptions.[133] She states at the outset that historical studies "are accomplished through standard multistep process," beginning with immersion in all materials that could inform the researcher on the given investigation. Once intimately acquainted with the culture, era, habits, and so forth, the historian "uses instinctive understanding and imagination" to devise an interpretive construct and provide inductive verification.[134] She

130. Thomas L. Thompson, "The View from Copenhagen," n.p. [cited 3 October 2003]. Online: http://www. bibleinterp.com/articles/Minimalism.htm.
131. William Dever, "Contra Davies," n.p. [cited 3 October 2003]. Online: http://www.bibleinterp.com/articles/Minimalism.htm.
132. Davies, "Minimalism."
133. Diana Edelman, "Preface," in Edelman, ed., *The Fabric of History*, 7–9 (8).
134. Edelman, "Doing History in Biblical Studies," in Edelman, ed., *The Fabric of History*, 13–25 (15–16).

distinguishes history from social science by recalling that history "particularizes," while social science works to "establish general laws or models."[135] She concludes by relating the procedure explicitly to biblical studies, calling on the historian of ancient Israel to collect and evaluate all relevant textual materials by means of the available critical methods, to critically judge the archaeological findings, and then proceed through the steps outlined for proper practice.

Edelman has given a clear summary of a traditional "scientific" model of history writing, indeed, a model promoting German historicism's "understanding and imagination" for historical interpretation. Writing in the early 1990s, she makes no reference to Lawrence Stone, Hayden White, Dominick La Capra, J. E. Toews, or Lynn Hunt, whose criticisms of history writing were novel in the previous decade and before. She shows no awareness of either the prominence of statistical history or the shift to cultural history that characterized academic history in the 1960s and 1970s, nor the disputes of the 1980s surrounding the problems of language and postmodern critiques of history. Her interest centers on the possibilities for combining archaeological and textual research, a clear continuation of the focus of biblical studies since Alt and Albright.

Dever assessed the state of archaeology in biblical studies in his article in the *Anchor Bible Dictionary* published the same year as Edelman's piece.[136] He says:

> Biblical and Syro-Palestinian archaeology, however, have always been deficient in awareness of the importance of theory and method, being practically inclined instead—in surprising contrast to the voluminous and lively literature in Americanist archaeology. This lack may be explained by the rather parochial and backward nature of our discipline until recently.

While Edelman supports the traditional approaches taken in biblical studies, Dever advocates a sharper sense of theory and method. He argues that the questions chosen for inquiry "shape the manner of inquiry," and in biblical archaeology, he says, "questions were drawn from issues in biblical history and theology" such that "evidence was gathered selectively, conclusions drawn and debated, and interpretations advanced" all on the basis of an appeal to history.[137]

The most obvious controversy in biblical historiography has been, for many years now, the debate between the "revisionist" historians and those who hold a more traditional position in regard to the historical

135. Ibid., 17.
136. Dever, "Syro-Palestinian and Biblical Archaeology" (*ABD*).
137. Ibid., 1:362.

possibilities of the Hebrew Bible. As this chapter has shown, these discussions clearly fall within the boundaries of scientific history. For example, as mentioned above, Thompson wishes to separate exegesis and "independent" historiography: "Historical reconstructions are based on research... They must be related to established evidence... History is Wissenschaft, not metaphysics."[138] He argues that even the Israel of tradition must be explained historically, by which he means that the biblical Israel must be accounted for as the product of a certain set of writers. Davies adds that the historical Israel, known from extra-biblical material, must be investigated archaeologically, epigraphically, and by whatever scientific means are available, while knowledge of those who wrote the story of "ancient Israel" must also be established historically.

"Revisionists" have been labeled "positivist," a term that James Barr notes has been used traditionally in a pejorative sense in theology and biblical studies, in particular against more "critical or radical" views.[139] Indeed, here it indicates a skepticism that demands material evidence or "proof" for the specific details of biblical history. In this line, Thompson and several "revisionists" have called for a historiography more firmly grounded in archaeology. Lester Grabbe argues that "our goal as historians is to find out 'what actually happened.'" Information may be too scanty to reach certain conclusions and "our reconstructions may be tentative at best; our actual work will be relativistic (though we would not be doing reconstructions in the first place if we did not have a positivistic goal)."[140]

Grabbe claims that "Ranke's 'wie es eigentlich gewesen ist' still continues to be a desirable goal..."[141] He argues that for most historians doing history is about trying to reconstruct a particular past entity or event. He adds that skepticism of texts "has been a basic presupposition of critical historical study at least since the Enlightenment."[142]

b. *Dissent from the Scientific Model*
Hans Barstad believes that he sees "the beginning of the end of a history project which over the years has become more and more problematic." He claims that

138. Thompson, *Early History*, 116.
139. Barr, *History and Ideology*, 69.
140. Lester Grabbe, "Introduction," in Grabbe, ed., *Can a "History of Israel" Be Written?*, 11–18 (14).
141. Lester Grabbe, "Are Historians of Ancient Palestine Fellow Creatures—or Different Animals?," in Grabbe, ed., *Can a "History of Israel" Be Written*, 19–36 (20).
142. Ibid., 21 n. 6.

> What, above all, characterizes the present "state of the art" is that the old models of historical science, which have dominated historical scholarship from the nineteenth, and at least through the first half of the twentieth century, and which were, basically, determined by the culmination of the critical historiography of Renaissance humanism in Germany from the end of the eighteenth century, by most theoreticians today are regarded as inadequate.[143]

Barstad argues that "the intellectual climate of the last thirty years or so appears not to have caught up on biblical studies at all."[144] Indeed, "much of biblical studies in general, has been, and still is, more firmly embedded in historicist methods and truth values than many other academic disciplines today."[145] For example, he says, "Lemche and Thompson, apparently unaware of the fact that what we may call a conventional concept of history today is *highly* problematic, still work within the parameters of historical critical research, assuming that history is a science and that one must work with 'hard' facts."[146] As a corrective, Barstad advocates a greater awareness of epistemological and ontological questions and suggests "a healthy relativism with a multimethodological approach to history."[147] In particular, he suggests a "renewed interest in *narrative history*," which he connects to postmodernist developments.[148] Barstad pulls back here, saying, "we cannot, and should not, let history go completely in our dealings with the Hebrew Bible, we must allow it less space as well as less importance."[149] He argues that as novels provide historical details or offer readers *insight* into life in other times and places, so "the relationship between narrative and reality in the Hebrew Bible is comparable."[150]

Grabbe, taking the Homeric poems as an example, argues to the contrary, "Historical elements within the text have been demonstrated, but much of the elucidation has not come from a study of the text itself but from archaeology and other sources."[151] This must be taken as a defense of empirical research, evidence, and "scientific" method. Grabbe may be seen as close to the "revisionists" on the issue of methodology, and,

143. Barstad, "History," 39.
144. Ibid., 46.
145. Ibid., 45. By "historicist methods," Barstad apparently has in mind "scientific" approaches to historiography.
146. Ibid., 51.
147. Ibid., 44.
148. Ibid., 52.
149. Ibid., 61.
150. Ibid., 62.
151. Grabbe, "Fellow Creatures," 23.

indeed, as noted above, Dever and the "revisionists" are not far from one another on the issue of evidence.

8. *Biblical History and History*

The most strident positions in biblical historiography are used here for purposes of comparison with practice in academic departments of history. The poles of argument are assumed to encompass the range of debate. Barr notes that many current conclusions are "shared by circles of revisionist historical scholarship and by circles that continue the basic values and methods of the older criticism."[152] Indeed, all parties to the controversies in this area have an abiding interest in history. For some whose audience includes interested, educated laypeople and church professionals, history is the essential matter of faith. Davies quotes Frank Cross: "To suggest that many things in the Bible are not historical is not too serious. But to lose biblical history altogether is to lose our tradition."[153] For others whose audience is comprised primarily of scholars, history is the story of people coming to terms with their environment and creating a social world, a culture, throughout some designated period of time. In both cases, their interest in history sets them apart from those whose theoretical dispositions deny any possibility for writing history.

"Revisionist" historians in biblical studies have been called both positivists and postmodernists. Certainly, these scholars have made numerous arguments for critical use of the biblical texts. Davies describes the conventions of "critical historiography":

> to contain nothing that the data contradict, never to promote the improbable over the probable (without specific argumentation), to evaluate all sources of information critically, and to exclude obvious bias from description. Generic features include footnotes, bibliographies, discussion of alternative interpretations, and priority of primary over secondary sources.[154]

"Revisionists" have specifically asked for a more rigorous standard for verifying names, dates, and places. They have insisted that plausibility is insufficient and historical claims may not be made absent evidence. Biblical narratives may not be assumed true until proven false, but must

---

152. Barr, *History and Ideology*, 20.

153. Davies, "Biblical Histories, Ancient and Modern," in Grabbe, ed., *Can a "History of Israel" Be Written?*, 104–22 (114). Barr (*History and Ideology*, 9–10) makes the related point that most people find the question, "Did it happen or not?" an important, obvious, and appropriate one.

154. Davies, "Biblical Histories," 119.

first be substantiated on the basis of extra-biblical material. This emphasis on evidence, reliability, and validity has led to the charges of positivism, though the "revisionists" have made it clear that they reject the natural science model for history writing, stating clearly that history is particular and unrepeatable and does not provide grounds for prediction.

The charges of postmodern commitments, made by Dever, Barr, and Provan, identify the "revisionists'" interest in the history of those whose story has not been told and their heightened consciousness of ideology. Thus, Palestinian history becomes the most sensitive issue, because of the implications for Israel's modern day claims to the land. It is unquestionable that Keith Whitlam's work participates in the postmodern agenda of concern for the history of the marginalized, silenced, or forgotten. Thompson and Davies are interested, on the other hand, in writing the histories of both the socio-political entity Israel of the ninth-century highlands and the group whose work produced the Hebrew Bible.

Barr criticizes the "revisionists" for their extreme skepticism of the historical value of the biblical text, for their demands for extra-biblical evidence, and for "the excessive weight placed upon the concept of ideology."[155] On the other hand, he notes the "revisionists" maintain an interest in history in contrast to those whose focus is on narrative. Barr cites a number of trends in the present, "one in the retirement of historical criticism into the background, the second in its vigorous reassertion, and the third in the changed perspective of revisionist historians." These trends "have in common at least one thing, a concern with history in some shape or form. A fourth major trend, on the other hand, looks in a non-historical direction... I am thinking now of the vastly increased influence of modern literary criticism."[156]

Modern literary criticism has promoted new strategies for reading, interest in questions of knowing, of objective reality, and the possibilities of meaning. These discussions have been reflected in academic departments of history as they have tried to come to terms with the function of narrative. Several "revisionist" historians have spoken of the Bible as literature. Thompson particularly has shown the existence of folk genres in the Bible by comparative examples from extra-biblical traditions, and with Davies has called for reading the Bible as literature. At the same time, Provan calls Thompson and Davies "anti-narrative," suggesting that he, too, has an interest in narrative approaches. Barstad bids readers to take up narrative strategies. Narrative strategies in postmodern thought are claimed to be especially useful in displacing historical criticism and

155. Barr, *History and Ideology*, 82. See Chapter 4, "The History of Israel."
156. Ibid., 20–21.

its attempts to establish "correct" or "monolithic" meaning. Barr notes
that the opposite complaint was often made of historical critics in the
past, that they made no attempt to determine meaning.[157] He cautions that
rejecting historical approaches puts interpretation at risk of losing all
meaning.

9. *Conclusion*

Barstad's call for narrative history has not moved debate from questions
of the historicity of the biblical text to questions of the inadequacy of old
models of historical science. Even the "revisionists," skeptical though
they are of the Bible as a source for history, do not abandon the historical
quest. While Barstad hopes to gain a sense of the past, an insight into
ancient times, from a narrative approach, Thompson and Davies, by
contrast, remain inclined toward critical history and, while pressing the
notion of the Bible as literature, seek in the various genres an historical
understanding of the past. Thompson echoes Barr in his remonstrance to
the effect that "Ancient texts are very hard to read unless we know something about the world they are written in and for."[158]

Historiography in biblical studies continues to be grounded in traditional historical method, concerned with issues of validity, reliability,
and objectivity. Criticisms traded among scholars tend to take the form
of accusations of ideology or bias and charges of inappropriate skepticism or credulity. There are significant strains between scholars regarding
their audiences. While most "revisionist" scholars address an audience
almost entirely made up of other academics within biblical studies, some
less radical scholars and some in other areas of biblical studies who practice postmodern criticism find their audience among educated laypeople,
both Christian and Jewish, and church professionals. Historiography in
biblical studies has moved closer to historical practices in academic
departments of history, while remaining almost completely separate in
regard to current theoretical discussion. In the face of the postmodern
credo that there is no objective truth, that all knowledge is a human
construction, and history and science are inevitably ideological, even the
"revisionists," like many professional academic historians, continue to
write history. "We pride ourselves that we argue and deduce what happened in the past from evidence and by method...that is how the genre of
critical historiography works," declares Davies.[159]

157. Ibid., 37.
158. Thompson, *The Mythic Past*, 4.
159. Davies, "Biblical Histories," 118.

Chapter 8

CONCLUSION

The real discussion has only begun, and now is the time to have a thorough and proper debate. I think there is far too much time and energy spent on fixed positions, defending them by clever rhetoric, by the use of partial data, by publication by like-minded editors and media, and—not to put too fine a point on it—by what amounts to little more than name calling. We need to push past the *ad hominem* stances and grapple with the real issues in an atmosphere of seeking to understand other positions even if in the end we dispute or reject them.[1]

Was the Bible written by historians or writers with historical motives? If not, is there history to be found within its pages? Did the authors intend a collection of writings that would guide, instruct, entertain, or inspire? Or were they writing to define an identity for a particular society or community? These questions are closely related to the more basic one: What is it that we want from the Bible? The often unstated conflict between commitment to empirical or "scientific" research and commitment to the theological enterprise remains unresolved. This dilemma has driven controversy in scholarly biblical studies since the nineteenth century and separated historiographic research in biblical studies from that in academic departments of history. Scholars approach these questions from two different angles. The first insists on the importance of history for the integrity of the Bible. The second takes sufficient interest in the process of the Bible's construction to relinquish its claims to history. The struggle between demands for proof of the Bible's historicity and the quest for an understanding of the Bible on its own terms have shaped the course of biblical studies and, of particular interest for this study, the work of historians of ancient Israel.

The suggestion is frequently heard that the Bible be read or studied as "literature." This notion is the source of some confusion. While one surely can read the Bible as an instance of classic literature for edification or enjoyment, reading as "literature" often means to read the

1. Lester Grabbe, "Hat die Bibel doch Recht?," *SJOT* 14 (2000): 117–40 (139).

narratives without a historical frame for their meaning in the present. Reading as literature in this sense is thus the opposite of reading the Bible as history. Studying the Bible as literature unquestionably means, for historical scholars, to investigate the text for clues to the various genres and their purposes, for references to historical data known from other sources, for signs that may be used to date the composition. Historians trying to "prove" the Bible's historical value and those who are interested in the identity and motives of the writers both study the literary features of the text. While not always true in the past, present-day historians in biblical studies support their work with the results of research in many other areas, demographics, climatology, sociology, for example, and especially archaeology. Though the elements of methodology are generally agreed upon, bitter disputes develop over the application of these approaches and most especially their results. Ideology is now a frequent charge, casting doubt on the reliability of scholarship.

The most significant circumstance that sets historical research in biblical studies apart from the broader discipline of historiography is the focus on a single text held sacred by certain religious communities. The broader field is concerned with limitless topics for investigation and few, if any, have quite the potential for causing distress and conflict as study of the Bible. This is illustrated beginning a hundred and twenty-five years ago by the reaction to Wellhausen's work. The publication of the *Prolegomena* generated fierce opposition, ecclesiastical trials, and the conviction that Wellhausen had distorted for all time the direction of biblical studies. For more than fifty years following Wellhausen, scholars worked to salvage history in the Bible. Only in the 1970s, did historiography in biblical studies begin to reclaim a position comparable in rigor to professional academic historiography.

The second circumstance that separates historiography in biblical studies and that in academic departments of history is audience. Professional academic historians have over the past two centuries written confidently for an audience both educated and interested in the past. In both Germany and the United States, historians through World War I believed they had an obligation to elevate their audiences, to interpret their own national characteristics and the historical processes that molded them, and to promote understanding of their own country's particular vision of national destiny. More recently, many historians have focused attention on the scholarly audience, knowing that professional advancement depends exclusively on this group.

In biblical studies, the audience for historical scholarship has, in the same way, embraced an educated, thoughtful laity. There is a crucial distinction, however, for while this audience is engaged by new information, it resists negative results regarding the historical claims of the Bible. Furthermore, the audience for history in biblical studies also includes professional clergy, who constitute an unquantifiable, but still real, constraint, because they are trained within the academy. These two elements of audience offer resistance to independent scholarship done in the manner of scholarship in academic departments of history. Indeed, it may be recalled that Wellhausen left Old Testament studies because the direction of his scholarship was not compatible with the preparation of clergy.

Recently, there has been a suggestion of a third audience. Restricted primarily to the scholarly world, an audience for "independent" or "secular" histories appears to be coalescing. Thompson lists dozens of scholars who fall into this category. Occasionally, an article outlining recent developments in the field appears in a publication read outside biblical studies, but without fear of contradiction, it can be claimed that little notice is taken in the broader public. The *Biblical Archaeology Review* continues to report controversies, but the general tone of the *BAR* is avid interest in new discoveries of items and locations related to the Bible's historical view.

1. *Wellhausen*

Wellhausen's approach to the biblical text was "scientific" in keeping with the standards of the German historicism of his day. Following Ranke, he understood that recounting deeds and events was not enough. A paraphrase of the text does not constitute history; rather the historian must critically investigate available textual material, become fully acquainted with the world of the text, and through an intuitive process achieve an empathic understanding of the historical moment. German historicism argues that culture is comprised of all its expressions—art, politics, law, religion—and that social change influences each of its aspects. By means of this perception, Wellhausen was able to evaluate the collections of law and place the composition of the Pentateuch long after the time it sought to describe.

Standing firmly within the German historiographical tradition, Wellhausen's "scientific" treatment of the text specifically excluded any procedure of the natural sciences that sought for laws or generalizations derived from history. The rigorous, "objective" approach he applied, like other German historians, discovered "facts" which were allowed to "speak for themselves." Without bias, then, the historian was to divine the essential meaning of these facts. This process of interpretation must be seen in the context of German thought. As Rogerson explained, in the

German tradition knowledge is found within.[2] This is in striking contrast to the objectivity so prized by American historians based on the empirical traditions of Locke, where knowledge exists outside the observer and must be perceived by the senses. The German historian is able to achieve understanding on the basis of the bond that exists between humans. One can understand what other humans have made or thought or done in a way that is never possible in the natural world. This world can only be known, never understood.

Wellhausen's assumptions included the notion that history is comprised of particular, unique, and unrepeatable events. History may be best understood as the unfolding of individual potential. This unfolding or development of an individuality is the expression of its spirit. Wellhausen, with Humboldt, knew that this development was not inevitable, as he showed in his views of the decline of Israelite religion. His distaste for institutional influence or hierarchy, in part a legacy of German Protestantism, colored his views of late biblical religion. Idealism and Romanticism are clear influences on Wellhausen, both in his conception of the *Geist*, or spirit, and in his preference for the fresh, immediate expression of the early Israelite folk. German historians, Wellhausen included, were committed to presuppositionless inquiry, but finally failed to show awareness that their conception of the development of individualities, or the *Geist*, influenced their interpretation of history.

Wellhausen's scholarship was the culmination of the critical work on the Bible done by previous generations of scholars and entirely appropriate to German historical practice, but ultimately raised difficulties within biblical studies. Serious opposition to his work appeared in Germany, but most especially in the English-speaking world. He was called negative and over-critical. His work was seen as destructive to belief. These are criticisms that appear again and again in the course of biblical scholarship over the succeeding century. Thus, while Wellhausen himself participated in the contemporary practice of historians, the discipline as a whole built up resistance to his conclusions and thus retreated from the methods of the professional academic historian.

2. *Mid-Century*

Discoveries of the texts of ancient myths and evidence indicating the great antiquity of humans advanced new perspectives in biblical studies and the research most often associated with Hermann Gunkel. The early traditions of Israel assumed new significance against the views of

2. See above, pp. 55–56.

Wellhausen. It appeared that the myths and traditions of the Bible derived from oral material passed on with remarkable fidelity and that these traditions then provided access to original historical memories. Archaeology exerted a real influence on research through the variety of discoveries which supported the faithfulness and accuracy of the traditions.

As historians working during and after World War II, both Bright and Noth claimed to value archaeological investigation, but they debated the use of extra-biblical materials and their relation to the biblical text. The enduring difference between the two is found, however, in their respective historiographical traditions. The attention to the organic nature of nations or societies in German historiography provides the background for Noth's interest in the biblical traditions and their particular stages and developments. It is most certainly from his position within the German tradition that Noth understood the history of Israel as the "idea" of the people as it comes to full consciousness in the land. That the identity and expression of the people, for Noth, is tied to and ultimately dependent on their historical awareness and self-understanding may be recognized as an aspect of historicism. Through immersion in the cultural world of ancient Israel, as prescribed by German historians since Ranke, Noth discovered the *real* or *essential* meaning of Israel's history.

Bright, in the American tradition, sought meaning through objective facts. Meaning in history, it is assumed, emerges from the objective presentation of historical facts, and, moreover, the meaning of the Bible is directly dependent on its reliability as an accurate account of history. Bright made a confident effort to eliminate personal bias and to give an account of Israel that, while illuminated by information from extra-biblical sources, remained close to the events of the biblical record. The American historical tradition's emphasis on the usefulness of history for the present guides Bright's search for enduring theological meaning relevant for contemporary life. For Noth, the historical inquiry centered on ancient Israel's search for meaning; for Bright, the issue was the meaning of Israel for today.

While Bright and Noth exhibit characteristics of their respective traditions, they are also part of the attempt in biblical studies to recover the historicity of the text in reaction to Wellhausen's negative critique of the historical reliability of the Pentateuchal narratives. In this sense, they abandon the critical scrutiny of texts called for in both their respective traditions, assuming from the outset that the Bible is a source of history. They depart further from historical convention in their treatment of divine influence. The German tradition had earlier relied on a divine or providential principle for ultimate harmony in history, but never based historical conclusions on supernatural intervention. All reference to metaphysical principles had been abandoned by World War I. Certainly, the assumption that the United States had a destiny determined by providence was often seen in American history, but again Progressive History had capitulated to relativism by the post-war period. Both Noth and Bright, on the other hand, explicitly point to God's work in Israel's history. The presuppositions that God is actively involved in historical events and that the Bible is a source of history separate Bright and Noth from critical practice in academic departments of history.

3. *History in the Present*

The perplexing nature of history resists the categories of science, philosophy, and art. Hayden White insists that to be science, history would have to have a technical language and derive theories from data. Neither science nor philosophy, however, can accommodate the infinite variety of historical actions and events. Both offer deterministic models or systems for human behavior. To allow for agency and moral will as well as irrational motives in the activity of human beings, descriptive efforts cannot be constrained by these models. Ranke said history was an art because it recreates and portrays past events; at the same time, he also demanded a "scientific" approach to the data of history. By this, of course, he meant critical and unbiased. In the intervening years, it has become clear that, even in the limited sense called for by Ranke, objectivity is a strict impossibility. The Prussian historians felt a duty to propagate Prussia's historic mission of unification. Historians on all fronts during the wars lost every pretense to objectivity in their efforts to further their national agendas. Aside from political bias, historians have clearly represented particular notions of development and progress, alongside their commitments to certain methodological preferences. In biblical studies these commitments are complicated by religious convictions.

The artistic aspects of history writing have been highlighted in recent years as it was argued that writing history is no different from writing fiction. All writers have points of view, they cannot know every detail nor see from every perspective, and thus they inevitably produce an account generated in their imagination, a fictional account. Rhetoric, too, has figured in the recent discussions. As with the conviction that writers have ideologies, it is understood that all writing takes a rhetorical position. Whereas in the past, historians strove to achieve felicitous portrayals of the past through fine rhetorical figures, present writers have recovered an understanding of the persuasive nature of historical presentation. Historians speaking for certain segments of society offer a case for the inclusion of the particular history of the group among other histories. Cultural history, too, has ceased speaking of a common humanity. Searching cultural practices for the "myths" that order society, cultural history assumes that differences are merely repressed by these "master fictions." The old objectivity has been rejected and replaced by history with the purpose of bringing attention to a particular group, history with an ideological agenda to expose power and subversive resistance, history that seeks knowledge of the past in sources far removed from public verbal forms, in very private notations, signs, and rhetorical symbols.

4. *The History of Ancient Israel*

Since the mid-1970s, historiography in biblical studies has returned to critical questions regarding biblical history. Many insights of the previous half century are compatible with the current research, but many of the "assured results" of earlier study are seen now as products of tendentious scholarship. Attention given to the second millennium as a background for the patriarchal stories appears to have been at the expense of the first. Names, customs, and places used to anchor the patriarchs in the earlier period have been found to be as or more appropriate in the later times. New information on the form and functions of folk tales and genealogies have reshaped interpretations of the historical content of the Bible. Claims for the faithful transmission of traditions have been sharply modified by comparative study of the folk genres of other cultures. The erosion of the consensus of the 1950s and 1960s has left the field with two very visible camps in historical research.

Several issues from the past are nurtured in the "maximalist/minimalist" dispute. First, the claim continues to be made that the Bible should be seen as an accurate record of history unless or until it is proven wrong. In the past, this has led to paraphrases of the text purporting to be history. Presently, it is argued that many specific texts are reasonably assumed true and others should not be dismissed as possibly truthful. Most scholars appear to agree that much of the Bible was not written as history, but strong disagreement occurs over other possible intentions. The second issue from the past that continues to be disputed is the place of archaeology in biblical studies. There is agreement on the significance of archaeology, but no consensus on how it is to be applied. "Maximalist" assumptions hold that the Bible contains history and that archaeology can confirm it. "Minimalists" assume that the Bible does not record history, that the stories, statements, and people are literary creations.

Archaeology, they believe, can illuminate history unconstrained by the Bible. Israel Finkelstein has produced an independent picture of settlement in the highlands of Judah. Because the population numbers and the life implied do not closely match the biblical narratives, there is sharp reaction to his findings. Dever, representing an opposing view, finds connections with the text, though he claims not to seek them. These two issues, in the present as well as several decades ago, involve the application of method, text criticism, and archaeology, but both fall within the larger model of "scientific research" seen as determining and evaluating facts. The project is to ascertain the existence and reliability of history in the Bible.

The more difficult controversies involve ideology and accusations of ideology. Those who promote the Bible as a reliable historical source mount their objections to those whom they call "minimalists" on grounds that their intent is to erase history, that they are ideologically driven in their "nihilism." Whitlam and Lemche write about Palestinian and Canaanite history and thus have become the objects of fierce attacks regarding their ideology. Thompson and others in the "minimalist" camp depend on archaeology for much of their evidence and receive the label "positivist" and criticism for a reliance on "facts." At the same time, "minimalists" are accused of postmodern tendencies and ideology, meaning, at the least, that they have no confidence in history.

Thompson and Davies have stated that the Bible is not the history of any actual society and that the Bible has been gravely misinterpreted by efforts to see it as history. They agree that a small state called Israel existed in the eighth and ninth centuries BCE, but it can only be known on the basis of archaeological material. "Minimalists," certainly Davies, continue to have a historical interest in the biblical text. They find clues to the constitution of the society of the authors in the implicit ideology of the texts. Droysen's principle that history is the foundation for cultural identity is warrant for their interpretation. The Bible story is of interest for reconstructing the society that produced the work and is the progenitor of Judaism and Christianity. Remarkably, this is the very reason for earlier historical study of the text, but the outline of the society sought by researchers has changed radically.

5. *The Scope of This Study and Future Research*

This study has compared history writing in Hebrew Bible studies to history writing in academic departments of history in three periods. The relation of history to the fields of natural science, literature, and philosophy constitutes one set of questions. The position of the writer/scholar and the worldview he or she has developed affects the question of objectivity, important throughout all three periods. The purpose of the writer/scholar is closely related to worldview and ideology and to the intended audience. The effects of these elements on history writing have guided this study. I have demonstrated the influence of professional academic historiography on the practice of history writing in biblical studies. I have shown that for Wellhausen critical historiography was important and yielded a set of results that was compatible with academic scholarship in the broader field. Progress in this direction was halted by strong reaction to the perceived loss of historical reliability of the Bible. Bright and Noth, while affected by their respective historiographic traditions, worked to recover a historical approach to the interpretation of the Bible. In the third period considered, critical historiography again has been employed with the result that many of the conclusions of the past two generations have been discarded and controversy has increased. Presently, the debates in biblical studies have little to do with the discussions in academic departments of history. There, debates concern the symbolic aspects of culture, especially as they resemble linguistic systems, the role of economic and social factors as they constitute relationships within cultural systems, and history as it arises from the discourse of intellectual communities. The importance of symbolic gestures, images, and rhetoric for professional, academic history is not mirrored in historiography in Hebrew Bible. Ideological criticism is one area of academic history that may be seen in the more radical scholarship in Hebrew Bible. It was by observing the ideological position of the biblical texts that Thompson, Whitelam, Davies, and Lemche became convinced of the unreliability of the historical content of the Bible and through analysis of ideology that they posited the identity of the authors.

I have not attempted to evaluate the claims and counter-claims of experts in text criticism, epigraphy, demography, or archaeology. I have endeavored rather to identify the historiographic assumptions of biblical scholars and to relate them to those held in the broader field. I have argued that writing the history of ancient Israel has been and continues to be constrained by theological interests, the audience of believers, scholarly, lay, and clergy. That the discipline inevitably suffers from the conflict of historical and religious interests is clearly apparent. Historical studies in Hebrew Bible are intensely centered on the single text and what supporting disciplines can offer to understanding the text. Whether or not one accepts the conclusions of more radical scholarship, it must be clear that reconstruction of the history of the region, state, and people, as such histories are compiled in the broader discipline, has not occurred. Such a reconstruction would have to be made without reference to the

Bible. It would have to be based on studies of artifactual remains, inscriptions, and documents other than the Bible, just as histories of other ancient civilizations are written. Should such a history be written, it would have significant implications for the study of the Hebrew Bible. At that point, conclusions about the history of the Bible could be drawn with some certainty. Thus, history will continue to be important to biblical studies for understanding ancient texts in any approach requiring knowledge of their historical setting and production.

Returning to the observation made at the beginning of this study that no biblical scholar is included in standard lists of historians, I suggest that future research could fruitfully address that exclusion. First, as histories of ancient Israel are written independent of the Bible, their authors will take their places among historians of other ancient cultures. Second, while scholars devoting their energies to understanding sacred texts will, no doubt, continue to be seen as apologists rather than impartial investigators, their studies in light of new historical insights will illuminate the purpose and character of the Bible. In the meanwhile, greater understanding of the history of biblical studies, in particular of Hebrew Bible studies, would be invaluable. Robert Oden maintains that "surprisingly revealing and broadly applicable conclusions…can result from the study of individual traditions of learning." He continues, "[in] classics and ancient history, the task of the scholar has long been understood to include not just the investigation of the ancient past but also the examination of influential students of antiquity."[3] Few biographies exist of the great biblical scholars of the past and fewer critical studies of the corpus of their work. This lack should be addressed in future research with favorable results for the field.

---

3. Robert Oden, *The Bible Without Theology: The Theological Tradition and Alternatives to It* (San Francisco: Harper & Row, 1987), 1–3.

BIBLIOGRAPHY

Adams, Herbert Baxter. "New Methods of Study in History." *Johns Hopkins University Studies in Historical and Political Science* 2d series, nos. I–II (1988): 101–31.

Albright, William Foxwell. "The Israelite Conquest of Canaan in the Light of Archaeology," *Bulletin of the American Schools of Oriental Research* 74 (April, 1939): 11–23.

Alt, Albrecht. "Die Landnahme der Israeliten in Palästina" (1925). Reprinted in pages 193–202 of *Kleine Schriften zur Geschichte des Volkes Israel*, vol. 1 (Munich: Beck, 1953).

—*Essays on Old Testament History and Religion*. Translated by R. A. Wilson. The Biblical Seminar. Sheffield: JSOT Press, 1989. Translation of *Kleine Schriften zur Geschichte des Volkes Israel*. 3 vols. Munich: Beck, 1953–59.

Anderson, Bernhard W. Introduction to *A History of Pentateuchal Traditions*, by Martin Noth. Atlanta: Scholars Press, 1981.

Antoni, Carlo. *From History to Sociology*. Translated by Hayden White. Detroit: Wayne State University Press, 1959.

Appleby, Joyce, Lynn Hunt, and Margaret Jacobs. *Telling the Truth About History*. New York: Norton & Co., 1994.

Barr, James. "Allegory and Historicism." *Journal for the Study of the Old Testament* 69 (1996): 105–20.

—"Biblical Theology." *Interpreter's Dictionary of the Bible*, supplementary vol., 104–11. Nashville: Abingdon, 1976.

—*History and Ideology in the Old Testament*. Oxford: Oxford University Press, 2000.

—*The Semantics of Biblical Literature*. London: Oxford University Press, 1961.

Barstad, Hans. "History and the Hebrew Bible." Pages 37–64 in Grabbe, ed., *Can a "History of Israel" Be Written?*

Barton, John. "Wellhausen's Prolegomena." Pages 316–29 in *Text and Experience*. Edited by Daniel Smith-Christopher. The Biblical Seminar 35. Sheffield: Sheffield Academic Press, 1995.

Beard, Charles. "That Noble Dream." *American Historical Review* 41 (1935): 74–87.

—"Written History as an Act of Faith." *American Historical Review* 39 (1934): 219–31.

Becker, Carl. "Everyman His Own Historian." *American Historical Review* 37 (1932): 221–36.

—"Some Aspects of the Influence of Social Problems and Ideas upon the Study and Writing of History." *American Journal of Sociology* 18 (1913): 641–75.

Begg, Christopher T. "Martin Noth: Notes on his Life and Work." Pages 18–30 in *The History of Israel's Traditions: The Heritage of Martin Noth*. Edited by Steven L. McKenzie and M. Patrick Graham. Journal for the Study of the Old Testament: Supplement Series 182. Sheffield: Sheffield Academic Press, 1994.

236   *Writing the History of Israel*

Berlin, Isaiah. Foreword to *Historism*, by Friedrich Meinecke. London: Routledge & Kegan Paul, 1972.
—*Vico and Herder: Two Studies in the History of Ideas*. New York: Viking, 1976.
—*The Roots of Romanticism*. Edited by Henry Hardy. Princeton, N.J.: Princeton University Press, 1999.
Blanke, Horst Walter, Dirk Fleischer, and Jörn Rüsen. "Theory of History in Historical Lectures: The German Tradition of Historik, 1750–1900." *History and Theory* 23 (1984): 331–36.
Bohmbach, Karla. "Convention/Contraventions: The Meanings of Public and Private for the Judges 19 Concubine." *Journal for the Study of the Old Testament* 83 (1999): 83–98.
Bright, John. *Early Israel in Recent History Writing: A Study in Method*. Studies in Biblical Theology 19. London: SCM Press, 1956.
—*A History of Israel*. 3d ed. Philadelphia: Westminster, 1981. Originally published 1959.
—"The School of Alt and Noth: A Critical Evaluation." Pages 157–93 in *Old Testament Issues*. Edited by Samuel Sandmel. London: SCM Press, 1969.
Buckle, H. T. *History of Civilization in England*. 2 vols. 2d ed. New York: Appleton & Co., 1892. Repr. of vol. 1, 1858; vol. 2, 1861. First edition 1857.
Butterfield, Herbert. *The Origins of History*. Edited by Adam Watson; New York: Basic Books, 1981.
Chickering, Roger. "Young Lamprecht: An Essay in Biography and Historiography." *History and Theory* 28 (1989): 198–214.
Clements, Ronald E. "The Study of the Old Testament." Pages 109–41 in vol. 3 of *Nineteenth Century Religious Thought in the West*. Edited by Ninian Smart, John Clayton, Steven Katz, and Patrick Sherry. Cambridge: Cambridge University Press, 1985.
Dahl, Nils. "Wellhausen on the New Testament." *Semeia* 25 (1983): 89–110.
Davies, Philip R. "Biblical Histories, Ancient and Modern." Pages 104–22 in Grabbe, ed., *Can a "History of Israel" Be Written?*
—*In Search of "Ancient Israel"*. Journal for the Study of the Old Testament: Supplement Series 148. Sheffield: Sheffield Academic Press, 1992.
—"Method and Madness: Some Remarks on Doing History with the Bible." *Journal of Biblical Literature* 114 (1995): 699–705.
—"Minimalism, 'Ancient Israel,' and Anti-Semitism." No pages. Cited 2 October 2003. Online: http://www.bibleinterp.com/articles/Minimalism.htm.
—"What Separates a Minimalist from a Maximalist? Not Much." *Biblical Archaeology Review* 26, no. 2 (2000): 24–27, 72–73.
Day, Peggy L., ed. *Gender and Difference in Ancient Israel*. Minneapolis: Fortress, 1989.
Deegan, Joseph Albert. "Noth, Bright and Mendenhall on Early Israel: A Critique of Historical Explanation." Ph.D. diss., Claremont Graduate University, 1978.
Demandt, Alexander. Introduction to *A History of Rome under the Emperors*, by Theodor Mommsen.
Den-Barak, Zafira. "The Status and Right of the Gebira." *Journal of Biblical Literature* 110 (1991): 23–34.
Dever, William. "Archaeology." Pages 354–67 in vol. 1 of *Interpreter's Dictionary of the Bible*. Edited by G. A. Buttrick. 4 vols. Nashville: Abingdon, 1962.
—*Archaeology and Biblical Studies: Retrospects and Prospects*. William C. Winslow Lectures. Evanston, Ill.: Seabury-Western Theological Seminary, 1974.

—"Contra Davies." No pages. Cited 2 October 2003. Online: http://www.bibleinterp.com/ articles/Minimalism.htm.

—"The Impact of the 'New Archaeology' on Syro-Palestinian Archaeology." *Bulletin of the American Schools of Oriental Research* 242 (1981): 15–29.

—"Palestine in the Second Millennium BCE: The Archaeological Picture." Pages 70–120 in Hayes and Miller, eds., *Israelite and Judean History.*

—"Save Us from Postmodern Malarkey." *Biblical Archaeology Review* 26, no. 2 (2000): 28–35, 68–69.

—"Syro-Palestinian and Biblical Archaeology." Pages 354–67 in vol. 1 of *Anchor Bible Dictionary.* Edited by David Noel Freedman. New York: Doubleday, 1992.

—"Syro-Palestinian and Biblical Archaeology." Pages 31–74 in Knight and Tucker, eds., *The Hebrew Bible and Its Modern Interpreters.*

Dewey, John. *Logic: The Theory of Inquiry.* New York: Henry Holt, 1938.

Dilthey, Wilhelm. "Allgemeine Sätze über den Zusammenhang der Geisteswissenschaften." Pages 120–88 in *Gesammelte Schriften,* 7. Leipzig: Teubner, 1922–36. Repr. 1957.

—"Rede Zum 70. Geburtstag." Pages 7–9 in *Gesammelte Schriften,* 5. Leipzig: Teubner, 1924.

Droysen, Johann Gustav. "The Elevation of History to the Rank of a Science. Being a Review of the History of Civilization in England, by H. T. Buckle. Pages 61–89 in his *Outline.*

—"Nature and History." Pages 90–105 in his *Outline.*

—*Outline of the Principles of History.* Translated by Benjamin Andrews. Boston: Ginn & Co., 1893. Translation of *Grundriss der Historik.* Berlin, 1857–58.

Edelman, Diana V. "Preface." Pages 7–9 in Edelman, ed., *The Fabric of History.*

—"Doing History in Biblical Studies." Pages 13–25 in Edelman, ed., *The Fabric of History.*

—ed. *The Fabric of History.* Journal for the Study of the Old Testament: Supplement Series 127. Sheffield: Sheffield Academic Press, 1991.

Emerton, Ephraim. "The Practical Method in Higher Historical Instruction." Pages 31–60 in *Methods of Teaching and Studying History.* 2d ed. Boston: Heath & Co., 1885.

Encyclopaedia Britannica. 3 vols. Edinburgh, 1771.

Encyclopaedia Britannica. 29 vols. 11th ed. Cambridge, 1910.

Ewald, Heinrich. *The History of Israel.* Translated by Russell Martineau. London: Longmans, Green & Co., 1871–76.

Fay, Brian. "Nothing but History?" *History and Theory* 37 (1998): 83–93.

Finkelstein, Israel. *The Archaeology of the Israelite Settlement.* Jerusalem: Israel Exploration Society, 1988.

Finley, M. I. *The Use and Abuse of History.* New York: Viking, 1975.

Gerth, H. H., and C. Wright Mills. Introduction to Weber, *Essays.*

Gottwald, Norman. *The Hebrew Bible: A Socio-literary Introduction.* Philadelphia: Fortress, 1985.

Grabbe, Lester L. "Are Historians of Ancient Palestine Fellow Creatures—or Different Animals?" Pages 19–36 in Grabbe, ed., *Can a "History of Israel" Be Written.*

—"Hat die Bibel doch Recht?" *Scandinavian Journal of the Old Testament* 14 (2000): 117–40.

—"Introduction." Pages 11–18 in Grabbe, ed., *Can a "History of Israel" Be Written?*

238 *Writing the History of Israel*

54

—*Priests, Prophets, Diviners, Sages: A Socio-historical Study of Religious Specialists in Ancient Israel.* Valley Forge, Pa.: Trinity, 1995.

—ed. *Can a "History of Israel" Be Written.* Journal for the Study of the Old Testament: Supplement Series 245. Sheffield: Sheffield Academic Press, 1997.

Guilland, Antoine. *Modern Germany and Her Historians.* Westport, Conn.: Greenwood, 1970. Repr. of 1915 ed.

Gunkel, Hermann. *Das Märchen im Alten Testament.* Religionsgeschichtliche Volksbücher 2. Tübingen: Mohr, 1921.

Hayes, J. H., and J. M. Miller, eds. *Israelite and Judean History.* Philadelphia: Westminster, 1977.

Herder, Johann Gottfried. *Outlines of a Philosophy of the History of Man.* Translated by T. Churchill. New York: Bergman, 1966. Translation of *Ideen zur Philosophie der Geschichte der Menschenheit*, 1784–91.

Higginson, Thomas Wentworth. "A Plea for Culture." *Atlantic Monthly* 19 (1867): 29–37; *Nation* 4 (February 21, 1867): 151–52.

Higham, John. *History.* Englewood Cliffs, N.J.: Prentice–Hall, 1965.

—*Writing American History: Essays on Modern Scholarship.* Bloomington: Indiana University Press, 1970.

Hoff-Wilson, Joan. "Is the Historical Professional an 'Endangered Species'?" *The Public Historian* 2 (1980): 4–21.

Holborn, Hajo. "The History of Ideas." *American Historical Review* 73, no. 3 (1968): 683–95.

Howe, M. A. DeWolfe. *The Life and Letters of George Bancroft.* 2 vols. New York, 1908.

Huizinga, Jan. "A Definition of the Concept of History." Pages 1–10 in *Philosophy and History: Essays Presented to Ernst Cassirer.* Edited by R. Klibansky and H. J. Paton. New York: Harper Torchbooks, 1963.

Humboldt, Willhelm von. "Denkschrift über die deutsche Verfassung," December, 1813. Pages 95–112 in vol. 11 of *Gesammelte Schriften.* 18 vols. Berlin, 1903–36.

—"On the Historian's Task." Pages 5–23 in von Ranke, *The Theory and Practice of History.*

—*The Sphere and Duties of Government.* Translated by Joseph Coulthard. Bristol: Thoemmes Press, 1996. Originally published 1791.

Iggers, Georg G. *The German Conception of History.* Middletown, Conn.: Wesleyan University Press, 1968.

—"Historicism." *Journal of the History of Ideas* 56, no. 1 (1995): 129–52.

—*Historiography in the Twentieth Century: From Scientific Objectivity to the Postmodern Challenge.* Hanover, N.H.: Wesleyan University Press, 1997.

Iggers, Georg G., and Konrad von Moltke. Introduction to Ranke, *The Theory and Practice of History.*

Iggers, Georg G., and James M. Powell, eds. *Leopold von Ranke and the Shaping of the Historical Discipline.* Syracuse: Syracuse University Press, 1990.

Jameson, John Franklin. "The American Acta Sanctorum." *American Historical Review* 13 (1908): 286–302.

—*The History of Historical Writing in America.* New York: Antiquarian Press, 1961. Originally published 1891.

—"The Influence of Universities upon Historical Writing." *University of Chicago Record* 6 (1902): 293–300.

Jepsen, Alfred. "Wellhausen in Greifswald." Pages 254–70 in *Der Herr ist Gott: Aufsätze zur Wissenschaft vom alten Testament.* Berlin: Evangelische Verlaganstalt, 1978.

Jolles, André. *Einfache Formen: Legende, Sage, Mythe, Rätsel, Spruch, Kasus, Memorabile, Märchen, Witz.* Halle: Niemeyer, 1956.

Kegel, Martin. *Away from Wellhausen.* The Aftermath Series. Edited by Horace M. Du Bose. Nashville: Publishing House of the M. E. Church, South, 1924. Translation of *Los von Wellhausen!* Gütersloh, 1923.

Kelley, Donald R. "Mythhistory in the Age of Ranke." Pages 3–20 in Iggers and Powell, eds., *Leopold von Ranke and the Shaping of the Historical Discipline.*

King, Philip J., and Lawrence E. Stager, *Life in Biblical Israel.* Louisville, Ky.: Westminster John Knox, 2001.

Kluback, William. *Wilhelm Dilthey's Philosophy of History.* New York: Columbia University Press, 1956.

Knauf, Ernst Axel. "From History to Interpretation." Pages 26–64 in Edelman, ed., *The Fabric of History.*

Knight, Douglas A. Foreword to Wellhausen, *Prolegomena.*

—*Rediscovering the Traditions of Israel.* Chico, Calif.: Scholars Press, 1975.

—"Wellhausen and the Interpretation of Israel's Literature." *Semeia* 25 (1983): 21–33.

Knight, Douglas A., and Gene M. Tucker, eds. *The Hebrew Bible and Its Modern Interpreters.* Chico, Calif.: Scholars Press, 1985.

LaCapra, Dominick. "Rhetoric and History." Pages 15–44 in his *History and Criticism.* Ithaca, N.Y.: Cornell University Press, 1985.

Ladurie, Emmanuel Le Roy. *The Territory of the Historian.* Translated by B. Reynolds and S. Reynolds. Chicago: University of Chicago Press, 1979.

Lamprecht, Karl. *Deutsche Geschichte.* 12 vols. Berlin: Gärtners, 1891–1909.

Langenscheidts Enzyklopädisches Wörterbuch, Deutsch–English. 1 Band A–K. Berlin: Langenscheidt, 1996.

Langlois, Charles Victor, and Charles Seignobos. *Introduction to the Study of History.* Translated by G. G. Berry. New York: Henry Holt. 1898. Translation of *Introduction aux études historiques.* Paris, 1898.

Lemche, Niels Peter. *Ancient Israel: A New History of Israelite Society.* The Biblical Seminar 5. Sheffield: Sheffield Academic Press, 1988.

Lemche, Niels Peter, and Thomas L. Thompson. "Did Biran Kill David? The Bible in the Light of Archaeology." *Journal for the Study of the Old Testament* 64 (1994): 3–22.

Lerner, Gerda. *The Creation of Patriarchy.* New York: Oxford University Press, 1986.

Liebel, Helen P. "Philosophical Idealism in the *Historische Zeitschrift*, 1859–1914." *History and Theory* 3 (1964): 316–30.

Loader, Colin T. "German Historicism and Its Crisis." *Journal of Modern History* 48 (1976): 85–119.

Long, Burke O. *Planting and Reaping Albright: Politics, Ideology, and Interpreting the Bible.* University Park, Pa.: Pennsylvania State University Press, 1997.

Lovejoy, Arthur O. "Present Standpoints and Past History." *Journal of Philosophy* 36 (1939): 477–89.

Maclean, Michael J. "German Historians and the Two Cultures." *Journal of the History of Ideas* 49 (1988): 473–94.

—"Johann Gustav Droysen and the Development of Historical Hermeneutics." *History and Theory* 21, no. 3 (1982): 347–65.

Mannheim, Karl. "Historicism." Pages 84–133 in *Essays in the Sociology of Knowledge*. Edited by Paul Kecskemeti. New York: Oxford University Press, 1952.

Matthews, Victor, Bernard Levinson, and Tikva Frymer-Kensky, eds. *Gender and Law in the Hebrew Bible and the Ancient Near East*. Journal for the Study of the Old Testament: Supplement Series 262; Sheffield: Sheffield Academic Press, 1998.

Mayes, A. D. H. *Israel in the Period of the Judges*. Studies in Biblical Theology 2d series 29. Naperville, Ill.: Allenson, 1974.

McNutt, Paula M. *Reconstructing the Society of Ancient Israel*. Louisville, Ky.: Westminster John Knox, 1999.

Meinecke, Friedrich. *Die Entstehung des Historismus*. Munich: Oldenbourg, 1959.

—"Ernst Troeltsch und das Problem des Historismus." No pages. In his *Werke*, vol. 4. Stuttgart: Koehler, 1965.

—*Historism: The Rise of a New Historical Outlook*. Translated by J. E. Anderson, translation revised by H. D. Schmidt. London: Routledge & Kegan Paul, 1972.

—*Idee der Staatsräson in der neuren Geschichte*. Munich: Oldenbourg, 1924. ET *Machiavellism: The Doctrine of raison d'état and its Place in Modern History*. Translated by Douglas Scott. London: Routledge & Kegan Paul, 1957.

Meyerhoff, Hans. "Introduction." Pages 1–25 in Meyerhoff, ed., *The Philosophy of History in Our Time*.

—ed. *The Philosophy of History in Our Time*. Garden City, N.Y.: Doubleday, 1959.

Meyers, Carol. *Discovering Eve*. New York: Oxford University Press, 1988.

Miller, J. Maxwell. "Israelite History." Pages 1–30 in Knight and Tucker, eds., *The Hebrew Bible and Its Modern Interpreters*.

—Review of *What Did the Biblical Writers Know and When Did They Know it? What Archaeology Can Tell Us About the Reality of Ancient Israel*, by William Dever. *Bulletin of the American Schools of Oriental Research* 329 (2003): 84–88. Online: http://www.proquest.com.

Miller, J. Maxwell, and John H. Hayes. *A History of Ancient Israel and Judah*. Philadelphia: Westminster, 1986.

Miller, P. D. "Wellhausen and Israel's Religion." *Semeia* 25 (1983): 63.

Mommsen, Theodor. "Erklärung vom 15. November 1901 betreffend Universitatsunterricht und Konfession." Pages 432–36 in *Reden und Aufsätze*. Berlin: Weidmann, 1905.

—*A History of Rome under the Emperors*. Based on the lecture notes of Sebastian and Paul Hensel, 1882–86. Edited by Thomas Wiedemann. Translated by Clare Krojzl. New York: Routledge, 1996. German edition by Barbara and Alexander Demandt.

Mommsen, Wolfgang. "Ranke and the Neo-Rankean School in Imperial Germany." Pages 124–40 in Iggers and Powell, eds., *Leopold von Ranke and the Shaping of the Historical Discipline*.

Noth, Martin. *The Chronicler's History*. Translated by H. G. M. Williamson. Journal for the Study of the Old Testament: Supplement Series 50. Sheffield: Sheffield Academic Press, 1987. Translation of pages 29–106 of *Überlieferungsgeschichtliche Studien*. 2d ed. Tübingen: Max Niemeyer, 1957. Originally published 1943.

—*The Deuteronomistic History*. Journal for the Study of the Old Testament: Supplement Series 15; Sheffield: JSOT Press, 1991. Translation of pages 1–110 of *Überlieferungsgeschichtliche Studien*. 2d ed. Tübingen: Max Niemeyer, 1957. Originally published 1943.

—*The History of Israel*. Revised translation by P. R. Ackroyd of the 2d ed. New York: Harper & Row, 1960. Originally published 1954.

—*A History of Pentateuchal Traditions*. Translated and with an Introduction by Bernhard W. Anderson; Atlanta: Scholars Press, 1981.

—*Das System der zwölf Stämme Israels*. Darmstadt: Wissenschaftliche Buchgesellschaft, 1966. Originally published 1930.

Novick, Peter. *That Noble Dream: The Objectivity Question and the American Historical Profession*. Cambridge: Cambridge University Press, 1988.

Oakes, Guy. "The Verstehen Thesis and the Foundation of Max Weber's Methodology." *History and Theory* 16 (1977): 11–29.

Oden, Robert. *The Bible without Theology*. San Francisco: Harper & Row, 1987.

—"Hermeneutics and Historiography: Germany and America." Pages 135–57 in the *SBL Seminar Papers, 1980*. Edited by Paul Achtemeier. Society of Biblical Literature Seminar Papers 19. Atlanta: Scholars Press, 1980.

—"Intellectual History and the Study of the Bible." Pages 1–18 in *The Future of Biblical Studies, The Hebrew Scriptures*. Edited by Richard Elliott Friedman and H. G. M. Williamson. Atlanta: Scholars Press, 1987.

Oxford English Dictionary Online. 2d ed. Oxford University Press, 2000.

Partner, Nancy. "History in the Age of Reality-Fictions." Pages 21–39 in *A New Philosophy of History*. Edited by Frank Ankersmit and Hans Kellner. Chicago: University of Chicago Press, 1995.

Perlitt, Lothar. *Vatke and Wellhausen: Geschichtsphilosophische Voraussetzungen und historiographische Motive für die Darstellung der Religion und Geschichte Israels durch Wilhelm Vatke und Julius Wellhausen*. Beihefte zür die alttestamentliche Wissenschaft 94. Berlin: Töpelmann, 1965.

Perry, Bliss. *And Gladly Teach: Reminiscences*. Boston: Mifflin, 1935.

Pompa, Leon. Introduction to Vico, *Vico, Selected Writings*.

Popper, Karl R. *The Poverty of Historicism*. New York: Harper & Row, 1964. Repr., London: Routledge & Kegan Paul, 1957.

Provan, Iain. "Ideologies, Literary and Critical, Reflections on Recent Writing on the History of Israel." *Journal of Biblical Literature* 114 (1995): 585–606.

Rand, Calvin G. "Two Meanings of Historicism in the Writings of Dilthey, Troeltsch, and Meinecke." *Journal of the History of Ideas* 25 (1964): 503–18.

Ranke, Leopold von. "A Dialogue on Politics." Pages 102–30 in *The Theory and Practice of History*.

—"The Great Powers." Pages 65–101 in *The Theory and Practice of History*.

—*History of the Latin and Teutonic Nations, 1494–1514*. Translated by P. A. Ashworth. London, 1887.

—"On the Character of Historical Science." Pages 33–46 in *The Theory and Practice of History*.

—"The Pitfalls of a Philosophy of History." Pages 47–50 in *The Theory and Practice of History*.

—"On Progress in History." Pages 51–56 in *The Theory and Practice of History*.

—*The Theory and Practice of History*. Edited by Georg G. Iggers and Konrad von Moltke. New York: Bobbs–Merrill, 1973.

Ringer, Fritz. *The Decline of the German Mandarins: The German Academic Community, 1890–1933*. Cambridge, Mass.: Harvard University Press, 1969.

Robinson, James Harvey. *The New History: Essays Illustrating the Modern Historical Outlook.* New York: Free Press, 1965. Originally published 1912.

Rogerson, John. *Old Testament Criticism in the Nineteenth Century.* London: SPCK, 1984.

—"Philosophy and the Rise of Biblical Criticism: England and Germany." Pages 63–79 in *England and Germany: Studies in Theological Diplomacy.* Edited by S. W. Sykes. Frankfurt: Peter Lang, 1982.

—"W. R. Smith's Old Testament in the Jewish Church." Pages 132–47 in *William Robertson Smith: Essays in Reassessment.* Edited by William Johnstone. Journal for the Study of the Old Testament: Supplement Series 189. Sheffield: Sheffield Academic Press, 1995.

Ross, Dorothy. "On the Misunderstanding of Ranke and the Origins of the Historical Profession in America." Pages 154–70 in Iggers and Powell, eds., *Leopold von Ranke and the Shaping of the Historical Discipline.*

Rudolph, Kurt. "Wellhausen as an Arabist." *Semeia* 25 (1983): 111–55.

Sasson, Jack. "On Choosing Models for Recreating Israelite Pre–Monarchic History." *Journal for the Study of the Old Testament* 21 (1981): 3–24.

Sawyer, Deborah. "Gender-Play and Sacred Text: A Scene from Jeremiah." *Journal for the Study of the Old Testament* 83 (1999): 99–111.

Schecter, Solomon. "Higher Criticism—Higher Anti-Semitism." Pages 35–39 in his *Seminary Addresses and other Papers.* Cincinnati: Ark, 1915.

Shanks, Hershel. "Biblical Minimalists Meet Their Challengers Face to Face." *Biblical Archaeology Review* 23 (1997): 26–42.

—"The Search for History in the Bible." *Biblical Archaeology Review* 26 (2000): 22–23.

Shields, Mary. "Subverting a Man of God, Elevating a Woman: Role and Power Reversals in 2 Kings 4." *Journal for the Study of the Old Testament* 58 (1993): 59–69.

Silberman, Lou. "Wellhausen and Judaism." *Semeia* 25 (1983): 75–82.

Smend, Rudolf. "Nachruf auf Martin Noth." Pages 137–65 in *Gesammelte Studien zum Alten Testament Martin Noth II.* Theologische Bücherei Altes Testament 39. Munich: Kaiser, 1969.

—"Tradition and History: A Complex Relation." Pages 49–68 in *Tradition and Theology in the Old Testament.* Edited by Douglas A. Knight. Philadelphia: Fortress, 1977.

—"Wellhausen and *Prolegomena to the History of Israel.*" *Semeia* 25 (1983): 1–20.

Smith, Theodore Clarke. "The Writing of American History, 1884–1934." *American Historical Review* 40 (1935): 439–49.

Smith, W. R. "Wellhausen and his Position." *The Christian Church* 2 (1882): 366–69.

Soggin, Alberto. "Ancient Biblical Traditions and Modern Archaeological Discoveries." *Biblical Archaeologist* 23 (1960): 95–100.

Stahlmann, Ines. "Theodor Mommsen." Pages 299–301 in *Great Historians of the Modern Age.* Edited by Lucian Boia. New York: Greenwood, 1991.

Stendahl, Krister. "Biblical Theology, Contemporary." Pages 418–32 in vol. 1 of *Interpreter's Dictionary of the Bible.* Edited by G. A. Buttrick. 4 vols. Nashville: Abingdon, 1962.

Stone, Lawrence. "The Revival of Narrative: Reflections of a New Old History." *Past and Present* 85 (1979): 3–24.

Stone, Lawrence, and Gabrielle M. Spiegel. "History and Post-Modernism." *Past and Present* 135 (1992): 189–208.

Thompson, Thomas L. "The Background of the Patriarchs: A Reply to William Dever and Malcolm Clark." *Journal for the Study of the Old Testament* 9 (1978): 2–43.

—"Dissonance and Disconnections: Notes on the *bytdwd* and *hmlk.hdd:* Fragments from Tel Dan." *Scandinavian Journal of the Old Testament* 9 (1995): 236–40.

—*Early History of the Israelite People: From the Written and Archaeological Sources.* Leiden: Brill, 1992.

—*The Historicity of the Patriarchal Narratives: The Quest for the Historical Abraham.* Harrisburg, Pa.: Trinity, 2002. Originally published New York: de Gruyter, 1974.

—"'House of David': An Eponymic Referent to Yahweh as Godfather." *Scandinavian Journal of the Old Testament* 9 (1995): 59–74.

—"The Joseph and Moses Narratives." Pages 149–213 in Hayes and Miller, eds., *Israelite and Judean History.*

—*The Mythic Past.* London: Basic Books, 1999.

—"A Neo-Albrightean School in History and Biblical Scholarship." *Journal of Biblical Literature* 114 (1995): 683–98.

—"Offing the Establishment." *Biblische Notizen* 79 (1995): 71–87.

—*The Origin Tradition of Ancient Israel.* Journal for the Study of the Old Testament: Supplement Series 55. Sheffield: Sheffield Academic Press, 1987.

—*The Settlement of Palestine in the Bronze Age.* Wiesbaden: Reichert Verlag, 1979.

—"Text, Context and Referent." Pages 65–92 in Edelman, ed., *The Fabric of History.*

—"The View from Copenhagen." No pages. Cited 2 October 2003. Online: http://www.bibleinterp.com/articles/Minimalism.htm.

Toynbee, Arnold J. "The Unit of Historical Study." Pages 101–14 in Meyerhoff, ed., *The Philosophy of History in Our Time.*

Trible, Phyllis. *God and the Rhetoric of Sexuality.* Philadelphia: Fortress, 1978.

—*Texts of Terror: Literary-Feminist Readings of Biblical Narratives.* Philadelphia: Fortress, 1984.

Troeltsch, Ernst. *The Absoluteness of Christianity and the History of Religions.* Translated by David Reid. London: SCM Press, 1972. Translation of *Die Absolutheit des Christentums und die Religionsgeschichte.* Tübingen: Mohr, 1902–12.

—*Gesammelte Schriften,* 3. Tübingen: Mohr, 1912–25.

—*Historism and Its Problems.* First book of *The Logical Problems of the Philosophy of History.* Microfilm, post-1922.

—*Der Historismus und seine Probleme.* Tübingen: Mohr, 1922.

—"The Ideas of Natural Law and Humanity." Pages 201–22 in vol. 1 of *Natural Law and the Theory of Society, 1500 to 1800.* Edited by Otto Gierke. Translated by Ernest Barker. Cambridge: Cambridge University Press, 1934.

—"Die Krisis des Historismus." *Die neue Rundschau* 33 (1922): 572–90.

—*The Social Teachings of the Christian Churches.* Translated by Olive Wyon. New York: Macmillan, 1931.

Turner, Frederick Jackson. *The Early Writings of Frederick Jackson Turner.* Madison: University of Wisconsin Press, 1938.

Van Seters, John. *Abraham in History and Tradition.* New Haven: Yale University Press, 1975.

—"Preface." Pages ix–x in his *Abraham.*

Vico, Giambattista. *New Science.* Revised translation by Goddard Bergin and Max Harris Fisch of the 3d ed. Ithaca, N.Y.: Cornell University Press, 1968 (1744).

—"On Method in Contemporary fields of Study." Pages 37–45 in *Vico, Selected Writings.*

—*Vico, Selected Writings*. Edited and translated by Leon Pompa. Cambridge: Cambridge University Press, 1982.

Vierhaus, Rudolf. "Historiography between Science and Art." Pages 61–69 in Iggers and Powell, eds., *Leopold von Ranke and the Shaping of the Historical Discipline*.

Walsh, W. H. *Philosophy of History: An Introduction*. Rev. ed. New York: Harper & Row, 1967.

Webb, Walter P. "The Historical Seminar: Its Outer Shell and Its Inner Spirit." *Mississippi Valley Historical Review* 42 (1955–56): 3–23.

Weber, Max. *From Max Weber: Essays in Sociology*. Edited and translated by H. H. Gerth and C. Wright Mills. London: Routledge, 1993.

—"'Objectivity' in Social Science and Social Policy." Pages 49–112 in *The Methodology of the Social Sciences*. Translated and edited by Edward A. Shils and Henry A. Finch. New York: Free Press, 1949.

—*The Theory of Social and Economic Organization*. Edited and translated by A. M. Henderson and Talcott Parsons. New York: Macmillan, 1964.

—"Science as a Vocation." Pages 129–56 in his *Essays*.

Weippert, Manfred. *The Settlement of the Israelite Tribes in Palestine: A Critical Survey of Recent Scholarly Debate*. Naperville, Ill.: Allenson, 1971. Translation of *Die Landnahme der israelitischen Stämme in der neueren wissenschaftlichen Diskussion*. Göttingen: Vandenhoeck & Ruprecht, 1967.

Wellhausen, Julius. "Die Composition des Hexateuchs." *Jahrbuch für deutsche Theologie* 21 (1876): 392–450, 531–602; 22 (1877): 407–79.

—*Die Composition des Hexateuch und der historischen Bücher des Alten Testaments*. 3d ed. Berlin: Georg Reimer, 1899.

—"Introduction." In his *Prolegomena to the History of Israel*.

—"Israel." Pages 396–431 in *Encyclopedia Britannica*, vol. 13. 9th ed. 1881.

—"Pentateuch and Joshua." Pages in 505–14 in vol. 18 of *Encyclopedia Britannica*. 9th ed. New York: Charles Scribner's Sons, 1885.

—*Die Pharisäer und die Sadducäer: Eine Untersuchung zur inneren jüdischen Geschichte*. Greifswald: Bamberg, 1874.

—*Prolegomena to the History of Israel*. Atlanta: Scholars Press, 1994. Reprint of *Prolegomena to the History of Israel*. Translated by J. Sutherland Black and Allan Enzies, with preface by W. Robertson Smith and foreword by Douglas A. Knight. Edinburgh: A. & C. Black, 1885. Translation of *Prolegomena zur Geschichte Israels*. 2d ed. Berlin: G. Reimer, 1883.

—Review of H. Reckendorf, *Die syntaktischen Verhaltnisse des Arabischen*, *Göttingische Gelehrte Anzeigen* 158 (1895): 773–78.

—*Der Text der Bücher Samuelis untersucht*. Göttingen: Vandenhoeck & Ruprecht, 1871.

White, Hayden. *Metahistory: The Historical Imagination in Nineteenth-Century Europe*. Baltimore: The Johns Hopkins University Press, 1973.

—"The Politics of Historical Interpretation: Discipline and De-Sublimation." Pages 58–82 in his *The Content of the Form: Narrative Discourse and Historical Representation*. Baltimore: The Johns Hopkins University Press, 1987.

—Review of Peter Leyh's 1977 edition of Droysen's *Historik*. *History and Theory* 19 (1980): 73–93.

—Translator's Introduction to *From History to Sociology*, by Carlo Antoni. Detroit: Wayne State University Press, 1959.

Whitelam, Keith. *The Invention of Ancient Israel: The Silencing of Palestinian History.* London: Routledge, 1995.

Wiedemann, Thomas. "Mommsen, Rome and the *Kaiserreich.*" In *A History of Rome Under the Emperors*, by Theodor Mommsen.

—"Mommsen's Roman History." No pages. Cited 27 February 2001. Online: www.dur.ac.uk/Classics/histos/1997/wiedemann.html.

Woolley, Leonard. *Digging Up the Past.* London: Penguin, 1930.

Wright, George Ernest. "Modern Issues in Biblical Studies." *The Expository Times* 71 (1959): 292–96.

—*The God who Acts: Biblical Theology as Recital.* Studies in Biblical Theology 8. London: SCM Press, 1952.

INDEX OF AUTHORS

Adams, H. B. 94
Albright, W. F. 153
Alt, A. 134, 205
Anderson, B. W. 133, 134, 139, 140
Antoni, C. 66, 81, 82, 85, 87
Appleby, J. 13, 180, 181
Barr, J. 3, 70, 148, 188, 220, 222–24

Barstad, H. 5, 221
Barton, J. 51, 58, 60, 62, 68
Beard, C. 112, 113
Becker, C. 106, 110–12
Begg, C. T. 122, 123
Derlin, I. 18, 22, 24–27
Blanke, H. W. 44, 80
Bohmbach, K. 186
Bright, J. 144–47, 149–54
Buckle, H. T. 41, 78
Butterfield, H. 1

Chickering, R. 78, 79
Clements, R. E. 52, 54, 57, 58

Dahl, N. 54
Davies, P. R. 202–204, 206, 212,
    215–18, 222, 224
Day, P. L. 185
Deegan, J. A. 150
Demandt, A. 45, 46
Den–Barak, Z. 186
Dever, W. 148, 199–201, 208, 209,
    216–19
Dewey, J. 12, 106
Dilthey, W. 81
Droysen, J. G. 41, 43, 44, 84, 118

Edelman, D. 218, 219

Emerton, E. 94
Ewald, H. 53, 62

Fay, B. 181
Finkelstein, I. 188
Finley, M. I. 56
Fleischer, D. 44, 80
Frymer–Kensky, T. 186

Gerth, H. H. 82
Gottwald, N. 185
Grabbe, L. 185, 220, 221, 225
Guilland, A. 45
Gunkel, H. 138

Hayes, J. H. 120, 121
Herder, J. G. 26, 27
Higginson, T. W. 98
Higham, J. 97–99, 102, 104, 105, 107,
    109, 113–15, 164–66
Hoff–Wilson, J. 174
Holborn, H. 36, 40, 81, 94
Howe, M. A. D. 93
Huizinga, J. 12
Humboldt, W. von 27–30
Hunt, L. 13, 180, 181

Iggers, G. G. 17, 19–21, 28–32, 35,
    36, 38, 39, 44, 79–81, 83–85,
    87, 88, 90, 94, 158, 160, 162–
    64, 166, 168, 169, 174–77

Jacobs, M. 13, 180, 181
Jameson, J. F. 97, 103
Jepsen, A. 53, 70
Jolles, A. 138

Kegel, M. 60
Kelley, D. R. 30
King, P. J. 186
Kluback, W. 11
Knauf, E. A. 184
Knight, D. A. 52, 64, 130, 132–34, 141, 153

LaCapra, D. 177
Ladurie, E. Le Roy 163
Lamprecht, K. 78
Langlois, C. V. 95, 96
Lemche, N. P. 205, 213
Lerner, G. 186
Levinson, B. 186
Liebel, H. P. 79
Loader, C. T. 84, 87–89
Lovejoy, A. O. 12

Maclean, M. J. 40–43
Mannheim, K. 89
Matthews, V. 186
Mayes, A. D. H. 197
McNutt, P. M. 186
Meinecke, F. 10, 17, 19, 25, 26, 31, 35, 37, 77, 89
Meyerhoff, H. 10, 11, 14
Meyers, C. 186
Miller, J. M. 120, 121, 155, 214, 215
Miller, P. D. 62
Mills, C. W. 82
Moltke, K. von 32, 94
Mommsen, T. 45, 47, 68
Mommsen, W. 38

Noth, M. 124–32, 135–41, 143
Novick, P. 92, 93, 95–98, 100–102, 107, 108, 110, 113, 171–73, 179, 180
Oakes, G. 86
Oden, R. 56, 57, 63, 234

Partner, N. 181
Perlitt, L. 60
Perry, B. 91

Pompa, L. 23
Popper, K. R. 10, 17
Provan, I. 206, 211

Rand, C. G. 78
Ranke, L. von 20, 31, 33–37
Ringer, F. 89, 92
Robinson, J. H. 105–107
Rogerson, J. 52, 54–56, 61
Ross, D. 93
Rüsen, J. 44, 80
Rudolph, K. 54, 69, 72, 73

Sasson, J. 5
Sawyer, D. 186
Schechter, S. 64
Seignobos, C. 95, 96
Shanks, H. 213, 214, 216
Shields, M. 186
Silberman, L. 64, 65
Smend, R. 3, 52, 53, 58, 61, 62, 66, 70, 123
Smith, T. C. 103
Smith, W. R. 62
Soggin, A. 149, 154, 155
Spiegel, G. M. 177–79
Stager, L. E. 186
Stahlmann, I. 46
Stendahl, K. 144
Stone, L. 161, 162, 164, 167, 170, 175–79

Thompson, T. L. 6, 187, 189–93, 196–98, 201, 202, 206, 207, 209, 210, 212, 213, 218, 220, 224
Toynbee, A. J. 9, 147
Trible, P. 185
Troeltsch, E. 17, 84–87
Turner, F. J. 106

Van Seters, J. 193–95
Vico, G. 21–24
Vierhaus, R. 34, 38

Walsh, W. H. 8, 9
Webb, W. P. 94
Weber, M. 82, 83, 88
Weippert, M. 196
Wellhausen, J. 2, 53, 58–60, 63, 65–
    72

White, H. 42, 80, 176, 177, 179
Whitelam, K. 5
Wiedemann, T. 39, 46, 47, 116
Woolley, L. 118
Wright, G. E. 149, 156, 205